At-Risk Students:

Reaching and Teaching Them

Second Edition

Richard Sagor
Jonas Cox

EYE ON EDUCATION

EYE ON EDUCATION

6 DEPOT WAY WEST, SUITE 106

LARCHMONT, NY 10538

(914) 833–0551

(914) 833–0761 fax

www.eyeoneducation.com

Library of Congress Cataloging-in-Publication Data

Sagor, Richard

Ar-risk students : reaching and teaching them / Richard Sagor, Jonas Cox.--2nd ed.

p. cm.4504

Includes bibliographical references.

ISBN 1-930556-71-3

1. Children with social disabilities--Education--United States. 2. Problem children--Education--United States. 3. Motivation in education--United States. 4. Students--United States--Psychology. 5. Behavior modification--United States. 6. School management and organization--United States. I. Cox, Jonas, 1960- II. Title.

LC4091.S24 2004

371.93--dc22

2003064339

10 9 8 7 6 5 4 3 2 1

Editorial and production services provided by
Richard H. Adin Freelance Editorial Services
52 Oakwood Blvd., Poughkeepsie, NY 12603-4112
(845.471.3566)

Also Available from Eye On Education

Dropout Prevention Tools
Franklin P. Schargel

Helping Students Graduate:
A Strategic Approach to Dropout Prevention
Jay Smink and Franklin P. Schargel

Strategies to Help Solve Our School Dropout Problem
Franklin P. Schargel and Jay Smink

Achievement Now!
How to Assure No Child is Left Behind
Dr. Donald J. Fielder

Student Transitions from Middle to High School:
Improving Achievement and Creating a Safer Environment
J. Allen Queen

The Directory of Programs for Students at Risk
Thomas Williams

Constructivist Strategies:
Meeting Standards and Engaging Adolescent Minds
Foote, Vermette, and Battaglia

Beyond Vocational Education: Career Majors, Tech Prep,
Schools Within Schools, Magnet Schools, and Academies
David Pucel

Dealing with Difficult Parents
(And with Parents in Difficult Situations)
Whitaker and Fiore

101 "Answers" for New Teachers and Their Mentors:
Effective Teaching Tips for Daily Classroom Use
Annette Breaux

Motivating and Inspiring Teachers:
The Educational Leader's Guide for Building Staff Morale
Todd Whitaker, Beth Whitaker, and Dale Lumpa

Dedicated with deep gratitude
to our father and friend
Dealous Cox
Whose didication to education
has improved the lives of countless children.

TABLE OF CONTENTS

ABOUT
THE AUTHORS

Richard Sagor consults with schools and educational organizations internationally on local school improvement initiatives. Dick's 17 years of public school experience includes teaching literacy and social studies to students ranging from the gifted to those with severe learning challenges. He has been a head teacher at an alternative school, a High School Principal, a director of curriculum and instruction, and an Assistant Superintendent. Before founding the Institute for the Study of Inquiry in Education, Dick was a Professor of Educational Leadership at Washington State University. He has written extensively on student motivation, leadership and collaborative school improvement.

Jonas Cox is on the faculty in the School of Education at Gonzaga University in Spokane, Washington. Jonas's fifteen years in education include teaching elementary and middle school along with his work in higher education. He is a Piagetian Scholar and actively researches the development of logical thought in children. When he is not teaching, researching, or grant writing, he can be found on his small farm fixing his 1954 John Deere G tractor. He lives there with his wife Charlene, his son Aaron, his daughter Rachel, two dogs, five cats, and thirteen chickens.

PREFACE

Schools, Schooling, and Learning: Working our way through the minefields of purpose and function.

In all likelihood what brought you to this book was its title. Your interest and concern regarding reaching out to and teaching at-risk students creates a special bond between you the reader and us, the authors. We have organized this book to facilitate our working together, authors and reader, to improve the prognosis for our most vulnerable children.

Of course, what might have attracted your attention was the picture of the skateboarder on the cover. Frequently the very young people who are most disengaged at school are the same kids who willingly take risks and persevere for hours trying to master difficult skills outside of school. Intrigued by the motivation that kids willingly invest in skating, as well as being truly amazed at the tricks they could do, Dick began asking street kids to explain to him what it took to become good at their sport and why they stuck with it.[1] He learned that it did not matter how difficult the challenge, or what was the nature of their past experiences. In the right environment these "at-risk" young people could and would prevail at anything.

The ideas that we will be presenting throughout this book apply the very lessons on motivation we learnied from these kids to the acquisition of academic content and skills for life-long learning.

The preface that follows and part one of the text will be devoted to getting us on the same page regarding the context of school reform. Later in parts two and three of the text, we will explore a number of "how to's" for school improvement. The focus of part two is strategies that have demonstrated success in lifting the achievement of all students when faithfully implemented in heterogeneous classrooms. Later, in part three we will shift our focus to schoolwide initiatives that have succeeded in public schools serving diverse student populations.

---

1   See "Lessons from Skateboarders," Richard Sagor, *Educational Leadership*, September 2002: (60)1.

As we sat down to work our way through the writing of this book, the second edition of *At-Risk Students: Reaching and Teaching Them*, the very first thing we did was revisit the dreams we held for the kids we have had the pleasure of teaching. We believed then and we still believe today that this is where all discussions regarding school improvement should begin.

In Chapter 10, where our focus becomes evaluating our at-risk prevention efforts, we will explore in some detail the importance of beginning school improvement work with "dreams." We decided this concept should be introduced at the outset, because "dreaming" was critical for us in the writing of this book. We found that basing our work upon this common denominator (our hopes and dreams for our students) enabled us to turn differences in professional perspective into productive dialogue.

As parents we find the process of dreaming about children's futures to be quite natural and pleasurable. Among the nicer aspects of dwelling on our own children's "hoped-for" futures, is the way it provided us with a momentary reprieve from those pesky realities that often seem to overwhelm us. More importantly, dreaming about a "rosy future" is a reminder of why one went into the parenting business in the first place. However, the best part about looking down the road is the opportunity it affords a parent to get back in touch with our deepest and most profound emotions. This is because the sweet dreams we hold for our children were born of the purest of all sentiments, unconditional parental love.

For the two of us the task of building a single shared dream for the students we've had in class was quickly accomplished. This was because it required so little additional work. The dream we hold for every child we've ever had in class, is the same glorious dream that we hold for our own children. No doubt this explains why we chose education for our careers. Not only do we share a single dream for the future of every child we've worked with, but, we believe that there is no better place for a non-parent to contribute to the development of youth and help them negotiate their transition to adulthood, then in schools and classrooms.

Once an educator has dreamed-up a "destination" (the purpose of dreaming) then the next step is preparing an itinerary (a set of milestones) that must be successfully passed along the way. If the resulting list is truly comprehensive, then the achievement of these milestones should lead to arrival at the Promised Land. As authors we found reaching agreement on a set of "essential milestones" was easy.

The essential milestones/goals that emerged became the outline for this book. Specifically, we deeply believe that every student needs to develop personal mastery of a set of essential academic skills and a deep understanding of the context in which they are to be used. We will not attempt to dictate to you, the reader, what those academic skills"should be. We feel this would be presumptuous and redundant, as nearly every state and province has its own list of essential skills that form the backbone of our new standards-based education system.

Therefore, this book will focus on academic goals that cut across all the traditional disciplines. We believe success with these goals results directly from the methods we utilize when teaching academic material. The generic goals we will address concern the development of attributes and attitudes that allow students to derive authentic feelings of

- competence,
- belonging,
- usefulness,
- potency and
- optimism.

Furthermore, it is our view that students must be in possession of irrefutable concrete evidence of their success if they are to be convinced that these emotive feelings (competence, belonging, usefulness, potency, and optimism) will ultimately empower them as adults in the key life-long domains of

- work,
- leisure,
- family,
- community affairs, and
- personal relationships.[2]

Few would argue with the above as worthy goals for education. However, our knowledge of social science reminds us that the stated purposes and ultimate social function of social institutions are often two very different things. Nowhere is this more true than with schools.

Social function refers to the actual role an "organizational practice" furthers for a society.

Ever since America hatched the idea of universal free public education, commentators have had a field day discussing the social functions of the 13 years of compulsory schooling. These include everything from fueling the economy, to protecting the jobs of adults (by keeping kids out of the sweat shops), to preparation for democratic citizenship. Occasionally our understanding of the social functions of schools were drawn from an objective review

2   These goals were adapted from the work of Arthur Pearl, Professor at Washington State University, Vancouver.

of reality, but, not infrequently, such statements are a reflection of the biases of the commentator. This was particularly true when a national commission told us that our public schools were placing the "Nation at Risk" through the promotion of "a rising tide of mediocrity." Such a statement implied that a key social function of the public school was preparation of young people for the world of work. Otherwise, it would be illogical to blame the schools for the low level of worker productivity that prevailed at the time. (When the economy is booming, many of us wish those same critics would give the schools credit for the nations's economic strength.) On the other end of the spectrum, we've all heard radical commentators argue that the real social function of public schooling has been sorting out kids, and preparing them to fit neatly and proportionately into an inequitable class structure.

It is not our purpose here to resolve these conflicts nor to argue that our schools should or should not carry out any specified list of social functions. However, our many years attending school, working in schools, and conducting research with schools has made us certain about one thing: the very act of spending 13 years in full-time attendance at a public institution, along with your age-mates, plays a key role in defining who you are, where you are going, and how you see yourself in relationship to the rest of society.

Whatever one's biases, it is clear that those students who experience academic and social success in school are more likely to feel good about their emerging relationship with society, while other kids, specifically those whose school experiences are filled with failure and rejection, will draw very different conclusions.

This brings us to our overriding purpose in writing this book...our desire to provide you, the reader, with a potpourri of helpful suggestions to consider as you attempt to make each student's 13 years of public school a journey rich with success and filled with authentic feelings of competence, belonging, usefulness, potency, and optimism.

Wistfully one could argue that it would be nice if teachers could be completely free to construct all the mechanisms necessary to realize this dream. But, alas, that is not an option. Today's public school teachers work in local systems, which are part of larger state, and provincial systems, which themselves are responsible for carrying out national education policies. Consequently, external requirements (some we agree with and others we have concerns about) are placed both on educators and on the students they are working with. The current educational landscape in North America now demands that students be educated in accordance with an agreed upon government curriculum, that student performance be measured by mandated objective tests, and that performance must meet or exceed a set of predetermined, unambiguous standards.

Severe high stakes consequences are already beginning to impact those students and schools that are not measuring up. Schools are losing their local control as well as state and national funding (and a commensurate loss of respect from their patrons) while students are facing retention when standards are not met. Worse yet, when students fail to keep up with their peers on these mandated measures, they often become frustrated, lose self-esteem and emotionally (if not physically) drop out.

Without question, the current wave of standards based reform will create winners and losers. There is no getting around this conclusion. Therefore, the issue before us has become (regardless of how we feel about these policies), how can we re-invent our schools and classrooms so that everyone is likely to emerge a winner?

As educators we may differ on what is the best theory of learning. For example, Jonas finds himself attracted to what Dick sometimes calls the "unstructured and nebulous" perspective of constructivism. Meanwhile Dick often finds himself arguing for positivist behavioral pedagogy. Sometimes listening to the two of us debate could move a student of Shakespeare to paraphrase the Bard, "Me thinks they do protest too much!"

Throughout this book we will try to be lighthearted about our differences and the problems we've encountered in reconciling these often caricatured and competing ways of knowing. However, there is a method to our madness. Primarily we see teachers as professional decision makers. Folks who, on a daily basis must pick and use strategies to best achieve their goals—in this case promoting success for all of their students. Furthermore, we recognize that often circumstances specify criteria by which school success will be determined. Frequently these criteria are established by folks other than educators. Because today's teachers find themselves standing on ever shifting sand we thought that the best thing we could offer to you, the professional educators in the trenches, are options not prescriptions.

Our plan is to offer different strategies in each chapter. Each program or technique included is one with strong potential and proven track record of helping young people achieve educational success. But, that is all we can provide. You, the reader must then take a hard look at your students, examine your context and make your own professional decision on which strategy appears to hold the most potential for your classroom.

We have decided to use an abbreviated shorthand to refer to the two primary approaches or *theories of learning* used in this book:

Model 1   Classical Positivism

Instructed Skills➜   Success➜ Application➜ Meaning

Model 2   Developmental Constructivism

Meaning➜ Constructed Understanding➜ Application ➜ Success

In Model 1 skills are mastered (oftentimes without regard to the whether or not they were chosen by or hold meaning for the learner). Then, once the learners have mastered the directly taught skills, they are encouraged to discover and explore real world applications. Ultimately, they are encouraged to pull all the learning together and create a project that is personally meaningful.

In Model 2 the learner is first engaged in finding meaning in an area of study. This process begins with allowing the child's natural curiosity to set the stage for their own learning. Once the learner's curiosity has been aroused the child will develop an internal need to know. Then, based upon this need, the child can construct the critical knowledge and skills and apply them to the construction of further knowledge. Ultimately this process leads to the development of feelings of success.

In both models the process concludes with the learner in possession of valued knowledge and skills. However, each approach takes the learner on a significantly different route to that end. Which model is best and which is more in keeping with the way humans learn? We don't intend to answer that question. The present text neither provides us with the space nor will our publication schedule allow us to resolve this issue (we will, however, at the end of each chapter endeavor to direct the reader through references to material which should prove helpful when pursuing answers to those questions). However we will endeavor to provide readers with guidance and criteria to use when making their own individual teaching decisions.

The Idea of Triage

Our colleagues in the medical profession have developed a concept that we find a helpful analogy to classroom and program decision making. The *triage* process is the way medical people prioritize their energy and focus when they face competing demands for their finite time and energy. Of course, with medicine the greatest priority is always clear, saving lives. This is followed by the desire to relieve pain and end suffering.

When visiting an emergency room on a busy night you may have noticed the work of a triage nurse. The nurse's job is to make a quick determination regarding the severity of each patient's condition and then arrange to have the patients seen in an order and manner that provides needed critical services as efficiently as possible. Patients with potential life threatening conditions are hurried directly into the examining room, meanwhile people suffering from non-critical, yet, emergency situations (for example a bad laceration, or a broken bone) are given immediate help to stop the bleeding or a sling to support the limb; however, they might have to wait to have the wound sutured or bone set. Meanwhile, other patients, those seeking help for non-emergency issues, will have to wait until everyone requiring critical care is served.

In the best of all possible worlds we both agree that Model 2 (that permits a slow approach and begins with the learner's innate curiosity) is the superior approach. Such an approach not only makes motivation less of an issue (as learners pursue knowledge in areas where they are already intrinsically motivated), but, more importantly there are volumes of evidence that retention of information is best achieved, when and if, the learners have an interest in the subject and have developed some scaffolding onto which they can attach their new learning. These are the reasons that the majority of national subject matter organizations such at National Council of Teachers of Mathematics and the American Associaiton for the Advancement of Science and recommend this method. Finally, when given the luxury of evaluating learning we see that when learning follows this natural organic model, not only is it generally retained longer, but it more frequently leads to more prolific learning and creativity. This goes a long way to explaining why this approach has enjoyed such popularity with educators serving advantaged populations and gifted students. Frequently when educators and parents are confident of a child's basic skills and ability to learn, they become less stressed about the quantity of content covered and become more invested in the development of deep connections between the learner and the learning.

Conversely, it isn't hard to understand the stress experienced by the educators and parents who see their children growing older and older and lacking those basic skills that we know are prerequisite to life long learning and future academic success. It is understandable that these educators often choose to use extrinsic reinforcement to encourage, cajole, or bribe children to quickly acquire the basic skills that are crucial for future school success, promotion, or self-esteem.

Throughout this book you will be challenged to apply the concept of triage to the strategies presented. These are the questions you will need to ask yourself as you reflect upon the ideas in this text:

- Is the knowledge/skill/attitude that you wish learners to acquire necessary for their survival in the school's academic system?

- Is the knowledge/skill/attitude that you wish learners to acquire necessary for their success in the school/community's social structure?

- Is the knowledge/skill/attitude that you wish learners to acquire necessary for students' intellectual and creative development?

Because of the devastating consequences of school failure, alienation, and dropping out for a young person's long-term success in our credentialed society, we will argue that whenever your answer to the first question is a *yes*, you would be well served to pursue immediate student success (the educational equivalent of "stopping the bleeding") by "whatever means necessary!" Often this will mean finding ways, which we will suggest throughout the text, to get the student to succeed as quickly as possible. This usually involves the use of Model 1 (classical positivism).

For example, in Chapter 3 you will be introduced to the mastery learning model that we see is an efficient and proven way to accomplish this. This choice is similar to a faculty decision to implement a direct instruction model for the children who are falling behind.

If you answered yes to the second question you might also find yourself reluctant to invest in a set of strategies where achievement results won't likely be apparent for a significant period of time. It is in those cases where educators would be wise to employ a combination of strategies. First, use a bandage to stop the bleeding or use a sling to stop the pain. For example, if we see a child associating with a group and/or making judgments about himself that are self-destructive, we ought to be aggressive in our effort to turn these trends around quickly and stop the child's slide down the slippery slope of alienation. However, at the same time we will want to provide the child with good reasons for making a long-term investment in the development of the habits of life-long learning. There is no better way to do this then by finding ways to encourage meaning–making by the learner. Model 2 (developmental constructivism) is very helpful here.

Finally, if we find ourselves and our children in situations free from immediate crisis, we may want to emphasize providing these students with opportunities to create personal justification for investing in their current and future educational endeavors. When we want to arm students with the antibodies of resiliency, providing them with rich educational environments, ones that both honor their curiosity and then make use of it to lead them into challenging, and perhaps, uncharted intellectual waters, Model 2 is a wise approach.

Many of you will recognize that you already engage in triage with your own work. Engaging in different strategies to meet different agendas in different aspects of our personal and professional lives has become standard operating procedure for most of us.

We know of many teachers who feel that Model 1, with its classical view that complex learning moves from the mastery of parts to an understanding of the whole, is the best for students. But, we have seen those same teachers succeeding beautifully when they were required to teach from a conceptual text with a constructivist curriculum.

Likewise, we know of many constructivist teachers who adamantly oppose the standards emphasis and are working diligently in the political arena to have these programs repealed. Nevertheless, many of these same teachers are absolute superstars in preparing kids for objective state proficiency exams. While they may argue in faculty meetings for broad conceptually based curricula, they willingly commit themselves to having their students succeed with whatever program is ultimately adopted. Are these teachers hypocrites? We would argue absolutely not! As we see it, they, like the emergency room physician, have concluded that lifesaving is priority number one. And, like us, they have concluded that school failure, especially for those children from communities that have been historically excluded from opportunity, is the equivalent to what Jonathan Kozol once labeled "death at an early age."

Be warned, if you opened this book expecting to see the contrasting views of learning theory fully explored, debated and resolved, you will probably be disappointed. If, however, you are using this book to actively engage yourself (and your colleagues) in lively discussions on alternative ways to help every single child leave school resilient and feeling competent, belonging, useful, potent, and optimistic, then you have come to the right place.

In keeping with the essential, philosophical basis of the standards movement, we are results oriented. If our book helps you and your colleagues reduce the rates of at-riskness for your students and enables you to develop practices that will make it more likely for them to live long fulfilling lives as workers, family members, and citizens then we will have met our goal.

As for resolving the learning-theory conflict, we have decided to leave that for another time. But, in the interim, let us know what is working for you. Perhaps the data from your classroom experiences will be what will ultimately help the rest of us more fully understand what it takes to make powerful learning occur for all kids all the time.

Richard Sagor
Institute for the Study of
Inquiry in Education,
Vancouver, WA

Jonas Cox
Gonzaga University, Spokane, WA

1

INTRODUCTION

Who Are These Kids
and Why Do They Behave the Way They Do?

The term "at risk" entered the educational vernacular with a vengeance. However, it seems that whenever this term was invoked it referred to a different subcategory of students.

Some experts on the at-risk problem speak only of the needs of children from abusive homes, others focus on the unique needs of the handicapped, while still others are concerned that we aren't doing enough to assist the gifted to adequately develop their talents. While it isn't correct to say that any of those definitions are inappropriate, having multiple definitions for any phenomenon makes maintaining focus and deepening understanding problematic. This book is being written for the classroom teacher and administrator; therefore, it seeks to concentrate on those students who present the greatest problems and cause the greatest consternation for educators in most public schools. For this reason, our focus will be on the child who might not be succeeding in your classroom but should be, the child who may be disrupting the learning of others as well as his own, and the child who alternatively pushes you to consider quitting teaching and/or reminds you of why you chose this profession in the first place. In order to accomplish this, we will use a succinct definition for the "at-risk student." It is a definition that captures both the academic and lifestyle consequences that will likely flow from their "at-riskness" if it is not arrested. The definition of at-risk that we are using is:

Any child who is unlikely to graduate, on schedule, with both the skills and self-esteem necessary to exercise meaningful options in the areas of work, leisure, culture, civic affairs, and inter/intra personal relationships.

This definition was adapted from the work of Professor Arthur Pearl (1972). In our opinion, Pearl's definition encompasses the issues that most reasonable people consider necessary for leading a fulfilling life. More importantly, the students who fit that definition are the same students who present the most pressing instructional and behavioral problems for today's teachers.

Needless to say, there are problems other than "academic skills" and "self-esteem" that make us fear for the future facing particular children. Many children come to school and are perceived as at-risk because they are burdened with a host of extreme hardships. Among these are the terrible consequences of poverty, abuse, physical handicaps, and personal or family chemical dependency.

However, in order to assist the practicing teacher with the children who are presenting the most persistent instructional problems, we have decided to focus this book on the one category of at-risk youth that currently receives the least attention, while accounting for, what some observers estimate, is 80 percent of the at-risk population in our classrooms. These are the students that teacher and educational consultant Jerry Conrath calls "defeated and discouraged learners."

One way we can understand the needs of at-risk students is by contrasting their school experience with that of their more successful counterparts: the "highly motivated students."

When teachers pause to consider the children they work with, the ones who seem on a clear trajectory for success as well as those who seem predestined for failure, they can often identify patterns of behavior that can be observed early and that foreshadow long-term negative outcomes.

The Think and Do exercise below, Identifying Characteristics of Successful and At-Risk Students, is designed to help you focus on the characteristics of at-riskness that students manifest in your school or classroom.

Think and Do Exercise—
Identifying Characteristics of Successful and At-Risk Students

Think of two youths that you recently worked with

One who was clearly headed for success, and

Another who seemed destined for failure.

Now recall the "observable behaviors" that led to your prediction and write them on the chart below (Figure 1.1).

In many ways the twin phenomena, motivation and alienation appear to many teachers as representing two opposite sides of the same coin. The basic needs that are being met for the motivated student, the child who is on a clear trajectory for success are often the very same emotional needs that have been left unfulfilled for the alienated student, our defeated and discouraged learner.

Figure 1.1. Characteristics Worksheet

Student Characteristics	
Student Headed for Success	**Student Headed for Failure**
1.	1.
2.	2.
3.	3.
4.	4.
5.	5.
6.	6.
7.	7.
8.	8.
9.	9.
10.	10.

The daunting task before us as teachers is to try and construct schools and classrooms that will provide the same quantity and quality of need fulfillment for the defeated/discouraged learner that are currently being provided for the successful student. While that may seem like a tall order, *it clearly is possible*.

Numerous schools have demonstrated that they can, in fact, succeed with *all* of their students. An entire body of "effective schooling" literature shows us it can be done. In the words of the father of the effective schools movement, Ron Edmonds:

> We can, whenever and wherever we choose, successfully teach all children whose schooling is of interest to us; we already know more than we need to do that; and whether or not we do must finally depend on how we feel about the fact that we haven't so far.
> (Ronald Edmonds, Educational Leadership October 1979).

However, having confidence that schools can be effective for all students does not mean that it will be easy to construct effective schools and classrooms. If it were, our passion to help these children would have long ago enabled us to eliminate their at-riskness.

To understand why the road ahead will be so difficult, it is worth contemplating a finding from a Phi Delta Kappa (PDK) study on the education of at-risk youth in America. The PDK study was the largest longitudinal study of this population ever conducted. In a summary of their work, the PDK researchers reported:

> In an attempt to determine what schools were doing for students who were at risk, teachers were asked who was responsible for various areas of learning. They responded in traditional ways. Teachers accepted responsibility for helping students learn in the areas of reading, writing, mathematics, and higher order thinking skills. But, they thought that parents and students were responsible for students' daily attendance, listening, attitude towards schools, completion of homework, general behavior in school, and attention in class. (Frymier and Gansneder, Phi Delta Kappan, 1989).

The reason these findings should be of concern for us is that the very patterns of behavior that can place a child into at-riskness: *poor attendance, inattentiveness, negative attitudes, and classroom misbehavior* were perceived by the teachers in these two studies as outside their span of control. Obviously and unfortunately, only when we acknowledge our influence over those factors and assert our preparedness to take control of them will we be able to remake our schools in a fashion that works for the defeated and discouraged learner. Parts 1 and 2 of this book focus on strategies that you can use and that other teachers have employed to change student performance in each of those critical areas. The success of these teachers gives convincing testimony to the fact that all of us *can* prevail.

In Chapter 8 we discuss behavior management, sharing detailed descriptions on how to implement the procedures these teachers used for improving classroom academic performance, improving behavior, and eradicating disciplinary problems. Then in Chapters 9–11, schoolwide improvement strategies will be explored. However, before we move to "strategies" it is important to reflect on the psychological makeup of our alienated young people.

Basic Psychological Needs of At-Risk Youth

There are certain psychological factors that, while applicable to people of all ages and stations, must be understood and internalized by educators before they can respond effectively to the problems faced by the at-risk student.

The first of these psychological factors is the innate need for satisfaction of our basic human psychological needs. When one examines the body of research on essential human emotional needs, from the work of Abraham Maslow to the work of William Glasser, five central feelings emerge as crucial to an individual's emotional well-being: these are the need to feel competent, the need to feel that they belong, the need to feel useful, the need to feel potent, and the need to feel optimistic.

These five feelings (competence, belonging, usefulness, potency, and optimism) will be discussed individually throughout this text. We will refer to them collectively by the acronym CBUPO. It is important to keep in mind while reading this text that CBUPO is an abbreviation. The feelings it incorporates are not a single unitary commodity.

The Essential Feelings

Competence

Stop for a moment to consider how you, as an adult, would respond to these circumstances. How likely would you be to arrive at work every day, thoroughly prepared and enthusiastic about your teaching if you viewed yourself as an *incompetent* teacher? If, in the private recesses of your heart, you believed that your students were better served in your absence when they were taught by a substitute, would you be inclined to continue to invest as much emotional energy in your teaching?

Consider now the fact that the "work" of school-age children is encompassed in their role as learners. It is in this role that they are asked to focus their attention and energy for six or seven hours per day while at school and with homework each night. When viewed from that perspective, it shouldn't seem surprising that students who constantly receive feedback on their academic incompetence will later decide to withdraw, both literally and psychologically, from the classroom.

Belonging

How likely would any of us be to continue to show up at our work place if we had reason to suspect that our co-workers and/or our associates disdained our company? As much as we adults need acceptance, youth are even more dependent in this area. It is not an overstatement to contend that every student, from the first day of kindergarten through their senior prom, is aware of and frequently consumed by thoughts of "in" groups and "out" groups and assessing which of their friends is and is not "popular" at any given moment.

A peculiar trauma of adolescence is the near universal belief that an "in group" does exist, and more importantly, that "I don't belong to it." We have long suspected that this phenomenon explains the continued popularity of class reunions. Specifically, our need as adults to return to our hometowns to show those members of the "in group" that we finally made it. If being denied a feeling of belonging is so significant for adults that we still carry the hurt twenty years later, its power must be incredibly intense. That being so, we ask you to imagine the emotions of a student who may not only feel incompetent but also feels out of place in his or her own school.

Usefulness

As teachers we all want to believe that we make a real difference in the lives of the young people we teach. This feeling of usefulness may be the reinforcement most responsible for our decision to stick with a career that frequently requires rising before dawn and working late into the night with little support and only meager compensation. A teacher's feelings of usefulness are so powerful that they can explain why our bodies rarely break down during the school year (a time when we're most needed). Apparently as teachers we save up our illnesses so that they can occur just in time to ruin our weekends or vacations.

But what is it that provides students with comparable and equally powerful feelings of usefulness? Some students derive this sense from their work as teacher helpers, student council representatives, or as athletes. But many youth suspect, way down deep, that they and their daily lives provide no meaningful service to anyone or anything outside themselves. Consider how you would feel if you believed that the world would not be affected one iota by your passing? Unfortunately, that is the perspective carried by many of our youth. Now stop and think how much worse it must be for those young people who, in addition to feeling insignificant, also see themselves as unwanted and/or incompetent?

Potency

Attribution theory posits that people can be placed along a continuum of causal attribution, often called *locus of control*. On the one hand we find those who believe that merit and hard work provide adequate explanation for their successes and/or failure. At the other extreme are those who attribute their victories and/or shortcomings to luck. This dichotomy produces two very different types of people, "internalizers" and "externalizers." In other words, some people see themselves as "actors" while others view themselves as "victims."

Overwhelmingly we find our at-risk youth on the externalizer end of the continuum. When they find themselves in trouble, they explain it away as someone else's fault; the mean teacher, or the unfair principal. Later as adults, these same individuals may assign blame for their personal misfortunes on the economy, the criminal justice system, or perhaps their inadequate upbringing and schooling. While we are not suggesting that one should understate the impact that these and many other very real social problems create for youth, we must recognize that in contemporary society successful individuals grow up believing that it is *their* behavior and the choices *they* make that are responsible for the good as well as the bad things that ultimately happen to them. In the long run, we find that the "internalizer" adults are people who felt empowered as youth and conversely the "externalizers" are people who grow up feeling powerless.

Now, again, we ask you to imagine yourself as a child. Imagine you feel inadequate as a student, unwanted by friends, unneeded by society, and powerless over your life. If you were in that situation what would motivate you to behave positively and continue to persevere at school?

Optimism

Students who have continuously received feedback on their competence, belonging, usefulness and potency have good reason to be optimistic. They intuitively know that there is no greater predictor of the future than the past. For this reason these children will be inclined to respond, as many of us did, to the suggestion that they defer immediate gratification for long-term rewards. They believe that if they simply do what is expected: complete school, attend college, and stay away from trouble, their future will be bright.

Likewise, those students who have repeatedly been told that they are failures, that they don't fit in, and that they aren't in control of their lives, will likely develop a pessimistic view of their future. They will conclude, "If the future looks so bleak, why defer gratification." Those youth are not behaving irrationally when they adopt the nihilistic motto, "Eat drink and be merry, for tomorrow we die."

We are all familiar with the story of "the little engine that could." Using that metaphor, we suggest you consider two types of children at school. One group continuously plays a mental tape recording saying, "I feel successful here, I feel like I belong here, people like me here, I feel needed here, I have the power to make things happen here, and I expect to be a success in the future." What would you predict regarding the eventual school success of that child?

Now, imagine another youngster, one whose mental tape recorder plays a very different tune, one that says, "At school I feel like a failure, I feel like an outsider, and no one seems to need me here or miss me when I'm absent. Furthermore, there is nothing I feel I can do about it, and I have no reason to believe it will get any better in the future." Would you expect that child to attend regularly, work hard, and act in a socially appropriate fashion? We suspect not. Under those same circumstances, most of us, even as adults, would probably retreat or rebel.

Those two categories of students help us understand the power of having or lacking the emotional well being that comes from feelings of CBUPO. It also helps us understand why some youth who do not feel CBUPO at school seek out those feelings through membership in gangs or other non-mainstream subcultures.

In an important study on a set of schools that demonstrated unusual success with at-risk youth, Gary Wehlage and his colleagues (1989) concluded that school success was due to 3 things:

- ♦ the level of *engagement* with school activities,
- ♦ the degree of *commitment* demonstrated by the students, and
- ♦ the degree to which they felt *membership* at their schools.

Those three key factors *membership, engagement,* and *commitment* only occur when, where, and if the students regularly feel CBUPO. Understanding the emotional needs of our students is a starting point, but it is also necessary for us to examine certain behaviors which are characteristic of alienated youth.

Characteristics of the Discouraged Learner

While there is some disagreement regarding the precise process for identifying students who are at risk, there are certain behaviors that generally characterize the defeated and discouraged learner. In his excellent handbook for teachers, *Our Other Youth,* Jerry Conrath (1986) describes the most common characteristics of these kids:

1. They are low in self-confidence and have a deeply held sense of personal impotency, helplessness, and lack of self-worth.

2. They are avoiders. They avoid school because it is demanding and/or threatening, or because it is confusing and unresponsive to their needs. They avoid contact and confrontation with other students and adults, for they are not confident of themselves. They avoid classes because they are "behind" and because there is often a more satisfying short-run payoff to skipping school than going to class and trying to figure out what is going on. Avoidance of adults and school begins in the very early grades.

3. They are distrustful of adults and adult institutions. Adults in their life have been unfair, unresponsive, or even abusive—mentally, intellectually, and/or physically. Gaining trust that you are not merely a continuation of a long line of ill-mannered adults is your primary task, but be patient; it will come only through your demonstration of good faith, good intentions, good deeds, and your skill in helping them learn.

4. They have a limited notion of the future. They are very responsive to short-run, measurable goals with demonstrations of success and competence. However, discouraged learners do not see the future as either bright or positive.

   Their life is usually grim and they have no cause to see the future any other way. Therefore, long-range class projects are deadening as are complicated career planning schemes. Even more than other youth, their life imitates a series of dreary, unimaginative TV dramas interrupted only by silly commercials of items not good for them. Teachers and other involved adults must be willing to compete for their attention and interrupt that tempo, rhythm, and pace. Or lose them.

5. At least by mid-school or junior high school, discouraged learners have good reason to be discouraged: they are behind others in academic skills. They usually lack adequate reading, writing, and math skills and have come to see themselves often as "dumb" rather than unskilled. Many adults see them that way too. Dumbness, goes the reasoning, cannot be cured so adults give up on them and the kids give up on themselves. School is often "nice" to them and stops taking them seriously as learners and only puts patty-cake worksheets in front of them that make no intellectual demands and offer no challenge. The students think that is "nice" but boring and continue to avoid. They are not convinced that skills not yet learned can be learned. They are poisoned by a sense of intellectual incompetence.

6. In fragile homes, their parents often suffer similar characteristics: low skilled, low self-confidence, distrustful of institutions, avoidance, suspicious of the future. Indeed, some of these kids come from homes with parents eager to help, but more often, parent response is to be grateful that an adult finally is helping their child. Some of these fragile parents don't care, treat sons and daughters with hostility, and even engage in serious physical and sexual abuse. That reality in the life of the discouraged learner, when it is reality, must be endured. Some come from homes of well-educated parents who are bewildered by their child's discouragement and lack of academic interest and success; these parents often feel great frustration, and the profile of their child is difficult, and sometimes impossible to pin down. Few of the youngsters under consideration here fit this category, but a few do and represent perhaps the most confusing child to deal with. Too often parents are of little help for they too are discouraged, feel impotent, sense helplessness in their lives. And far too many come from homes of poverty.

7. Discouraged learners often have, by textbook definition, adequate peer relationships. Some are powerfully lonely; others have friends that meet many emotional needs; caring, fun to be with, similar interests, supportive. Adults usually do not approve of the peer relationships, but the kids do and are unresponsive to school's attempts to get them to join into the social life as a strategy for combating discouragement.

This doesn't work, often to the surprise and sometimes disgust of the adult who thought the idea so "neat." For discouraged learners, self-confidence will begin to grow with success in learning and skill development; not through critiquing their friends.

8. They are impatient with routine, long-time sitting and listening, and classrooms with little variety; more so than kids who feel good about themselves as learners and have a better developed political sense of how to get along in adult institutions. Because of this, and their low skills, discouraged learners are often seen as disruptive when they demonstrate their impatience, or when they ask the intelligent question, "Why do we have to do this?" Once the disruptive label is attached, there is a predictable chain to difficult, dumb, delinquent, dropout.

9. Discouraged learners often come from the category of learning preference identified as "practical." With this, they are good at working out applications of what is being taught if that is allowed and encouraged. They learn well through their own private experience and can talk about that better than write about it. They remember very little of what is delivered in linguistic style to a physically passive, note-taking audience.

10. Most significantly, discouraged learners do not see a relationship between effort and achievement, but instead, see success as a matter of luck or ease of the task. They are "externalizers"—people who see the world as happening to them and one over which they have little control of events, especially failures and successes. When they do poorly, it is the result of an impossible task, bad luck, a bad day, or an adult who refuses to help them. And, of course, they attribute results to the "fact" that they are dumb, a situation of which they have no control and, therefore, can take no responsibility. It is the same when they do well: good luck, easy assignment, wonderful teacher. They will not take personal responsibility because they do not see the relationship; not, as adults often accuse, because they stubbornly refuse to. Because of this, conversations over how much effort they put into a task fall on deaf ears. To an externalizer, effort has little to do with it. Because of this phenomenon, these kids do not learn from their mistakes, and they do not learn from their successes. They think mistakes and success just happen and they cannot explain why or how. They are "crap shooters." They roll the dice each day and see what happens. To ask them "why" they did something prompts an impotent response, "I don't know. It just happened." They are a severe challenge for an internalizer adult who

understands internal responsibility but does not understand the impotent world of the externalizer youngster. If you do not think your actions cause your effects, you take no pride in effort, and no personal responsibility for your actions. It makes no sense to.

The behavioral characteristics delineated by Conrath help us describe these youth, but they don't explain why they are so difficult to help, especially when they are being taught by caring adults such as us. Although schools are chronically under funded, in recent years billions of dollars have been spent to improve the academic performance of disadvantaged youth. The sad reality is that very little success can be traced to most categorical programs and pilot projects designed to remediate educational disadvantages.

It is through the application of a major precept of behavioral psychology, cognitive dissonance theory, that we can begin to see why it has been so difficult to get these young people to shake their at-risk status, no matter how committed and dedicated we, their teachers, may appear to be. Cognitive dissonance theory, more than anything else, demonstrates why defeated and discouraged learners tend to remain stuck outside of the mainstream. Through our understanding of this concept we can begin to construct program interventions with much greater promise for success.

Cognitive Dissonance Theory

Cognitive dissonance theory (Festinger, 1954) is based upon the finding that whenever our attitude and behavior are in conflict we experience heightened levels of anxiety and stress.

For example if a chain smoker has internalized the Surgeon General's warning on cigarette smoking, then the very act of lighting up and inhaling will place that smoker in a state of increased anxiety and stress. This is because with each breath the smoker is reminded that this behavior choice will lead to life threatening consequences. This phenomenon is expressed by the following equation:

Attitude and Behavior in Conflict (dissonant) = Stress

However, when our attitudes and behavior are in agreement (consonant) stress is reduced. It is for this reason that we often will hear chain smokers expressing the attitude, "What the Surgeon General says may be true, "for most people," but it simply doesn't apply to me." This state (of cognitive congruence) is expressed with another equation:

Attitude and Behavior Congruent = Reduced Stress

Let's now apply this to the classroom.

Psychologists have traditionally seen dissonance as the relationship between two factors, *attitude* and *behavior*. However, when we apply this phenomenon to the social reality of the classroom, we find it important to add the dimension of *role*. This is because for many students school is largely a social experience. That isn't unreasonable when we consider that school is the primary place where young people are able to "hang out" with their friends and peers.

Figure 1.2 illustrates the way this phenomenon gets played out in our classrooms.

Figure 1.2. Cognitive Dissonance Cycle

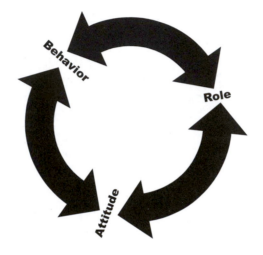

When adults talk of the awesome power of peer pressure we are usually speaking of the need and desire that most youth feel to live up to the expectations of their peers. If, for example, a child has earned the reputation as the "class clown," the "class brain," or the "class disrupter" that role will tend to be reinforced through both the *behavior* and the *attitude* of the student. If any one of these three factors (role, attitude, or behavior) change independently of the others, it will place the entire cognitive dissonance equation out of balance and thereby put the child into a heightened state of stress. Conversely, when left unchanged each of the three factors (attitude, belief, and role) will continue to reinforce each other, thereby both modulating the stress and deepening the behavioral habit.

To put this phenomenon in perspective it would be useful to consider the experience of two hypothetical third-grade math students. Student one is the classic "motivated" child, the one who is always prepared for math, has his books and materials ready and out, and attends faithfully to his teacher's every direction. Clearly, this pattern of behavior is supportive of success in math. One would expect such a youngster to hold a positive attitude toward math and perhaps, by extension, to his entire school experience. He might state that, "Math is fun, valuable and will be very important to my future." Finally, this student is likely perceived by his classmates as both a serious and committed math student.

Contrast this with student two, a defeated and discouraged learner. This is the child who seems to never have the proper materials at math time, can be counted on to be out of his seat and off task, and seems blissfully unaware of his teacher's expectations. When the teacher is ready to teach, this student is generally ready to disrupt the lesson with an irrelevant question perhaps concerning something trivial such as the scheduling of recess. On days when the teacher is absent this is the student who is both destined and ordained to make the substitute miserable. It is unlikely that this student's view of third-grade math will be as positive as that of his successful counterpart. In fact, we suspect this boy would describe his math class as "boring, stupid, or dumb." However, when we analyze his experience through the lens of cognitive dissonance we see that although his attitude is disappointing, it is quite logical and rational. It works for this child primarily because it is consonant with his behavior and, therefore, reduces his psychological stress.

These examples would just be an interesting sidelight were it not for the traditional way educators approach problems such as the ones presented by student two. The typical response is to send this student to the office for an "attitude adjustment." The hope being that the principal or counselor will be able to "scare" or better yet, "persuade" him to change his outlook and behavior. Unfortunately, and predictably, this rarely happens.

Why Don't Attitude Adjustments Work?

Every misbehaving child knows that when they return from the office they will face two choices. Because the classmates know why they were sent to the office, they will be watching to see the consequences of the "attitude adjustment" the student just experienced. While the student might choose to return announcing that "I have seen the light and will henceforth do everything in my power to become a super citizen as well as a math whiz," it is far more likely that the child will elect to wink at his buds, announcing that he had successfully avoided any real adjustment in attitude, and proceed to go right on conducting (or disrupting) business as usual.

Although the second option may not provide the happy ending sought by the teacher (or the principal for that matter), and while it may not be productive for the student's education, it will, nevertheless, avoid producing the stress, which flows from *role-attitude-behavior dissonance*.

Unfortunately, this predictable cycle encourages the defeated and discouraged student to hold onto their previously developed negative attitudes toward school. It is simply too hard to resist the powerful psychological and social forces that are pressuring the child to maintain them. For this student demonstrating a reformed attitude is tantamount to declaring his old pattern of behavior as wrong and consequently to repudiate his status in the classroom social structure. Nowhere do we find this pressure played out in a more profound or self-destructive manner than with the experience of many low income African American males. Referring to African Americans as an "involuntary minority," John Ogbu (1989), the eminent University of California anthropologist explains the phenomenon this way:

> Those (involuntary minorities) who adopt attitudes and behavior conducive to school success are accused by their peers of "acting white" or, in the case of black students, of being "Uncle Toms." They are accused of being disloyal to the cause of their group and risk being isolated from their peers. Consequently, involuntary minority students who want to succeed academically have to adopt strategies that shield them from peer criticisms and ostracism (page 196).

A decision to step out of one's social role places a child in a social "no man's" land. It is regrettable, but, cognitive dissonance theory goes a long way toward explaining the "rich get richer" and the "poor get poorer" phenomena with school success.

Fortunately, acknowledging the existence of the dissonance phenomenon does not require us to resign ourselves to seeing our at-risk students, like student two, serving life sentences of dysfunctionality. Old habits need not be reinforced. This is because if we get the at-risk student to "choose" to engage in positive behaviors, ones that are so compelling that they are worth engaging in despite the predictable and uncomfortable conflict with a prevailing negative attitude, then "attitude change" can and *will* occur.

The task before us is to create opportunities for our at-risk students to engage in "compelling" CBUPO rich behavior. Can our schools provide truly compelling CBUPO rich opportunities for all youth? The evidence suggests that they can.

Dissonance Managed

There are numerous creative ways in which teachers in grades K–12 can manage the dissonance phenomenon. One method, often used successfully with middle and secondary school students, is a form of community service called *cross-age tutoring*. Specifically, this involves inviting at-risk middle or high school students to serve as tutors for remedial elementary students. Several years ago Dick had the pleasure of directing such a program. The Chapter I high school students who served as tutors in his program were reading (on the average) four years below grade level. With such reading disabilities one can only imagine the level of their academic self-esteem!

The cross-age tutoring program was held during Dick's reading class, and it required three twenty-minute tutoring sessions each week. The tutoring sessions along with the bus ride to the elementary school (on the other side of town), left just two class periods (per week) for their chapter 1 "remedial reading" curriculum.

Even with this 60 percent reduction in class time, the tutors didn't feel shortchanged. This was primarily because the three weekly trips to the elementary school left the tutors feeling like veritable gods. The second grade tutees (Dick had to go to the primary grades to find children who might benefit from instruction from these "low performing" high school students, some of whom read at fourth grade level) looked upon their high school tutors as important people worthy of admiration. The elementary youngsters were blissfully unaware that these same high school students occupied the bottom rung of the social ladder at the high school. The second graders showered their tutors with original artwork, hugs, and other expressions of esteem. In exchange, the high school students taught their hearts out! At the conclusion of each tutoring session tutor and tutee were required to jointly fill in histograms which charted fluency, decoding proficiency, and spelling accuracy. As one might have predicted, the impact of each direct instruction tutoring session led to measurable growth. The recognition of that growth produced significant pride in accomplishment for both tutor and tutee.

These tri-weekly experiences became so compelling and so ego fulfilling for the high school students that they couldn't deny their enjoyment of this part of their "school" program. Yet, the very liking of tutoring produced dissonance. How could they square their love for third period (tutoring) with their otherwise negative view of school? Clearly they couldn't.

Figure 1.3 reflects the psychological state being forced on the tutors.

Figure 1.3. Deliberate Creation of Dissonance

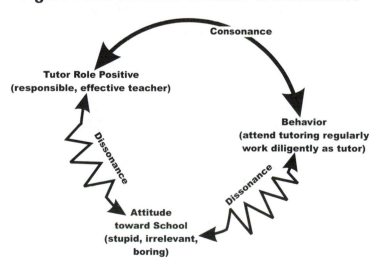

As a result of this dissonance the students were left with three choices.

1. They could drop tutoring,

2. Their attitudes toward school could change, or

3. They could maintain their attitudes and stay in a state of stress.

For this group of tutors choice two was the best and only reasonable choice. School became, "okay," (even if it was only because of third period). But, consider this; even that small change in attitude opened a crack in their negative view toward school. This was all that was needed to thwart the enticements from their peers to "ditch" school and miss their cherished tutoring class. Best of all, each of the tutors involved in the program showed dramatic improvement in their own reading skills (this finding is consistent with what has been found in similar "cross-age" programs (Cohen, Kulik, Kulik, 1982).

Dick and his colleagues soon realized that once the behavior (in the case of the tutoring) became compelling (CUBPO rich) enough for these young people, they could put additional conditions on continued participation. When participation is rewarding enough, young people are willing to meet otherwise onerous conditions. This same phenomena has been found at schools and states that have implemented "no pass, no play" eligibility requirements for school athletic programs. It is amazing to see the standards of citizenship, academic performance, and attendance that students will voluntarily commit to, when and if, these behaviors allow them to participate in CBUPO-rich activities. The key factor is affording the student the opportunity to experience the CBUPO rich behavior first. In many elementary schools the same phenomena observed with "cross-age" tutoring can be found in other types of programs such as big brother and big sister initiatives and peer mediation programs (both of which are discussed in some length in Chapter 4 when we have a look at service learning).

However, if we demand demonstrations of good behavior and positive attitudes as prerequisites for initial participation in an activity, at-risk youth will almost always opt out. That phenomenon is discussed in greater depth in Chapter 9, where we discuss the "if you've got the name, you might as well play the game" syndrome.

A few years ago when Dick shared the impact of the cognitive dissonance phenomenon at a workshop, a teacher shared with him the following proverb to summarize the process:

"It is easier to act your way into a new way of thinking than to think your way into a new way of acting."

The following Think and Do exercise will provide you with an opportunity to examine your own classroom and/or school to see if and where you might use cognitive dissonance as a strategy to change a student's attitude and/or behavior.

Think and Do Exercise—
Relating Cognitive Dissonance to Your Work

Think of two situations in which you have seen the cognitive dissonance phenomenon play itself out in a school or classroom.

♦ Consider a time when you observed the power of role and attitude to be so great that it made behavior change almost impossible for an at-risk student.

♦ Remember a time, with another child, when a new behavior became so compelling that it caused the student to adjust long held attitudes and role expectations.

♦ See if you can think up strategies that might have created dissonance for the first child so powerfully that he/she might have altered long held behavior patterns.

Dominant Theories of At-Riskness

Before proceeding any further in this book, it is important to review several major theoretical premises that undergird most public school programs designed for at-risk youth. While, the precise causes of at-riskness differs for each individual student, it is, nevertheless, possible to categorize the predominant theories on at-riskness into these two categories:

♦ Perspectives that presume that a *clinical pathology* exists in the student or his/her home environment, and

♦ Perspectives that allege that at-riskness is the result of alterable *institutional insufficiencies*.

There is no single cause of at-riskness for all children. Without a doubt some children are at risk because of such things as organic disabilities and being raised in dysfunctional families. For this reason our interventions must be as varied as are our children. However, the ever-increasing population of the at risk should force us to look at the increasing problem of at-riskness as "educational epidemiologists." As epidemiologist's we need to be asking what are/is the cause of the exponential growth of the at-risk phenomena.

Clinical Pathology

The Medical Model

This is a perspective that informs most current efforts serving at-risk youth in schools. This perspective posits that where at-riskness is present, it must be because something is wrong with the child or the child must have inherited or caught a defect. For this reason, it is assumed that this pathology is the cause of the child's at-riskness.

When and if the pathology is viewed as internal it is usually assumed that the pathology is psychological in origin. Other times it is argued that the source of the problem maybe physiological, perhaps the consequence of a brain dysfunction or some other deep organic process that we aren't capable of pinpointing. The diagnostic terminology prevalent in special education offers a window into the clinical basis of these theories. Each year we see an ever-increasing number of inferred conditions: hyperactivity, attention deficit disorder, dyslexia, learning disability, etc.

Cultural/Environmental Deficits

A second category of clinical pathology is built on a view that the at-risk child has inherited or caught a condition from their family or through interaction with their immediate environment. Until it became politically incorrect this phenomena was labeled as a "cultural deficit." Those holding this perspective generally inferred that the problems manifest by the at-risk child were rooted in either inadequate preschool experiences or grew from deficiencies in the child's home environment.

The *environmental* or *cultural deficit* perspective differs from the medical model in that it posits that while the problem didn't grow organically inside the child, the child caught the disease through interaction with the child's environment. For this reason, it is assumed that these problems will be amenable to correction through environmental interventions, much like removing the infectious toxin from the child's environment.

It was stated that the public school's response to at-riskness has been most influenced by the clinical pathology perspective. While the terms we have used here (defect, disease, condition, deficit) are seldom used by school officials; one can observe their influence over program decisions by the actions these theories inspire.

When one supports a clinical pathology explanation for the rising tide of at-riskness, it follows that meaningfully addressing at-riskness will require clinical interventions. There is a belief that applying the appropriate treatment will ultimately cure the illness. In the case of really deep-seated problems, the proper treatment can minimallyat least be expected to help "manage" the problem. This is the rationale for the use of interventions such as *counseling, school psychologists,* and *special education.*

When the cause is suspected to be an environmental deficit the recommended treatments generally involve immersion into a more appropriate environment or a "proper" culture so that the child's cultural/environmental deficit can be replaced with appropriate experiences. The use of *school social workers* and the existence of early intervention programs such as *Head Start* are built upon this notion. These programs are based on the presumption that low-income/disadvantaged students have "missed out" on specific early childhood experiences that will become necessary for later success in school.

Regardless of the particular diagnosis, believers in the clinical pathology models are united in the belief that the source of the problem resides within the child or his/her immediate environment.

Institutional Pathology

These theories grounded in the social and behavioral sciences, are based on the belief that when individuals or groups consistently receive differential treatment by social institutions one should expect to see them behaving differently. Followers of this perspective generally see the rising tide of at-riskness as an indication that increasing numbers of kids are receiving improper or inappropriate treatment by the institutions where they spend much of their time. Holders of this perspective believe that institutions play a big role in development of their clients' identity. Clearly the two most significant institutions that impact youth are the *school* and the *family*. In contrast to the *clinical* theories, when people subscribe to this view, they are drawn to interventions focusing on altering the flawed institutions (the institutional causes) rather than the victims (the students) of the at-riskness.

Understanding the differences between these perspectives is critical because these orientations lead to vastly different programmatic decisions.

Programmatic Implications of the Two Theoretical Orientations

Depending on the theoretical orientation one holds on the cause of the at-risk phenomena, the interventions one advocates will be different. Because these theories are not discrete, and they tend to overlap, it is not unusual to be attracted to elements of both perspectives. Nevertheless, readers will find it helpful to identify the theoretical source of the interventions they are currently working with. In Chapter 10 (where we deal with program evaluation) the critical importance of a conscious awareness to one's theoretical orientation will be discussed at length.

Interventions Based on the Clinical Pathology (Medical) Model

Figure 1.4 lists the steps of the intervention process generally employed when programs are influenced by a clinical pathology perspective.

Figure 1.4. Clinical (Medical Model) Interventions

Internal Clinical Pathology

- ◆ Identify the defect
- ◆ Treat/cure the defect
- ◆ Student no longer at risk

It is no surprise that these interventions reflect a medical model. The first step is identifying/diagnosing the defect, just as one might do with a physical condition such as measles. For example, when we see the rash, the fever, and the listlessness associated with this malady, we infer that a disease must be present. We then proceed to consult an expert on how to treat the disease. If the diagnosis is measles, the doctor might prescribe medicine, bed rest, and fluids. With at-riskness, the experts frequently prescribe counseling, psychotherapy, special schooling, etc. The presumption operating in both medicine and school is that if the diagnosis is correct and the treatment appropriate, then the disease will be cured or at least arrested.

As mentioned earlier, these approaches are popular and well funded in contemporary schools. It seems that wherever at-riskness is on the rise the call is heard for more counselors, interventionists, and special education teachers. Has this worked? From the available data one would suspect not. Most teachers and administrators are unaware of the cure rate for the counseling and special education programs operating in their schools. If data on cure rate are not known or is unavailable then shouldn't one be asking the following question?

> Shouldn't we abandon the use clinical treatments in school that haven't demonstrated success in curing or ameliorating the problem they were designed to fix?

By suggesting the use of this question, we don't wish to denigrate the motives of the many fine professionals working as interventionists, special educators, or counselors. We do, however, question the assumptions upon which their solutions to the at-risk problem are built. After all, if the problem is rooted in a curable malady, shouldn't trained professionals be applying an appropriate treatment? And, if the treatment is appropriate shouldn't the student be cured?

If they are not, then perhaps it is because they have misdiagnosed the source of the problem.

Interventions Based Upon the Clinical Pathology (Environmental Deficit) Model

Figure 1.5 lists the steps that interventions built upon the deficit model tend to follow in their efforts to ameliorate at-riskness.

Figure 1.5. Deficit Interventions

Environmental/Cultural Deficits

♦ Identify missing experiences and/or skills

♦ Provide experiences

♦ Support the student during transition

♦ Student no longer at risk

Programs built upon the environmental deficit model are based on an expectation that the student will become "ready to succeed" once the missing pieces have been effectively put in place. If you are engaged in a program based on a deficit model it is worth asking what percentage of the students are, in effect, ready to perform successfully after involvement with the "appropriate" experiences? If the percentage is relatively low, then we ought wonder, why do these programs continue unadjusted?

As mentioned earlier many times the rationale for these programs, which overwhelmingly serve students from minority or low-income families, is to provide the "readiness" needed for success at school. In these cases the intervention strategy most often used is providing cultural enrichment for the child. Aside from obvious classist and racist implications (that while often not intended, are inherent in these programs), their frequent failure can often be attributed to the fact that these programs ignore the at-risk child's deep need for belonging. By arguing that there is an "appropriate" culture for school success, they are asking the child to reject, or at least ignore, their home culture (this will be discussed at length in Chapter 4 where our focus is building feelings of belonging). Rejecting the culture of your family and community is an awfully high price to ask a child to pay for school success. Is there another alternative? Many believe the institutional pathology model provides an alternative approach with real potential.

Interventions Based Upon the Institutional Pathology Model

When one looks at at-riskness as being the consequence of differential and inappropriate treatment by institutional forces, it causes one to look for interventions that focus on very different variables than those that would be addressed if one were following a clinical theory. Rather than focusing the change effort on the *student,* instead one focuses on changing the institutions and institutional practices that are placing the student at risk, e.g. the school program or a dysfunctional family. Because changing families is outside of the scope of our control as educators, we would be wise to focus on changing school programs. Figure 1.6 lists the steps of this process.

Figure 1.6. Institutional Interventions

Institutional Pathology

- ♦ Organizational practices produce differential treatment
- ♦ Differential treatment places students at risk
- ♦ Change organizational practices
- ♦ Support student during transition
- ♦ Student no longer at risk

When one presumes that at-riskness results largely from organizational/structural mistreatment then it beckons for something to be done to correct the underlying systemic mistreatment. For example, if we are convinced that our economic system produces poverty and that low income students are more prone to at riskness due to the deleterious effects of poverty, then if we truly wish to eradicate at-riskness we ought to focus our efforts on changing an economic system that results in so much child poverty.

Or, if we find that success of non-white males are at our school is dependent on their learning to "act white," then it is both logical and fair to change our system to be more accommodating and appreciative of African American maleness. Furthermore, if we believe that it is deep-seated racial attitudes that are causing differential treatment of African-American males in our school, and we understand that such treatment is negatively impacting the self-image of those students (thereby placing them more at risk), then an honest attack on at-riskness would include an attack on all aspects of institutional racism.

While solving the problems of poverty and racism are beyond the scope of this book (and probably beyond any reasonable expectations of ourselves as individual practitioners), we still need to recognize that the institutions where we work, the public schools, often engage in practices that serve to disproportionately place particular children at greater risk of failure. For example, research evidence suggests (Slavin 1989) that students who have been retained one or more years are two times more likely to drop out prior to graduation than are students who were promoted along with their age-mates. And for years we have known that segregating special education students into special classes has had a deleterious impact on their self-images as well as their achievement (Dunn 1968). Yet, even with this information, support for the institutional policies of "retention" and "separation" continue unabated.

For all the above reasons, when we find ourselves drawn toward an institutional pathology explanation of at-riskness, we must do everything in our power to alter the dysfunctional organizational practices we control. When we make a concerted effort to do so, we can decrease the at-riskness of our students. While many at-risk students will need support and help during the creation of and transition to new organizational structures (because their past experiences likely have left them with little self-confidence) once we build schools and institutions where one can legitimately expect success for all, then we can say we have addressed and hopefully eliminated a major "cause" of at-riskness.

Three Program Prototypes

There are three categories of at-risk programs currently predominating the public school landscape:

- ◆ treatment programs,
- ◆ pacification programs, and
- ◆ prevention initiatives.

This is a good time to review the programs you are most familiar with. Are they attempting to fix at-risk students with counselors, social workers, and remedial programs? If so, they should be classified as *treatment* programs.

Are they trying to care for and manage at-risk students (rather than totally cure them) by housing them in alternative schools or classrooms along with other at-risk students? These could be classified as *pacification* programs, because while they may moderate some of the more unpleasant symptoms of at-riskness, they are rarely expected to fix the problem and restore the student to non-at-risk status. While one often sees students enjoying these programs, e.g., they don't deface the buildings, they enjoy going to school, and they don't gather on unsightly street corners, they are also unlikely to become the educated, self-assured youth we profess to desire. In the words of the Supreme Court "separate is inherently unequal" (*Brown v. Board of Education*, 1954).

Are the programs that you work with trying to alter school practices in a manner that will ensure that all students experience success in the mainstream? In the public health sector that type of approach is called *prevention*. For example, when one practices proper dental hygiene he/she will be less likely to need dental surgery later in life. Likewise, if we organize our schools and classrooms to prevent at-riskness now, then our students will be less in need of treatment later.

The Think and Do exercise below will give you a chance to examine the at-risk programs that you are most familiar with in an effort to understand both their orientation and focus.

Think and Do Exercise—Program Analysis

Using the worksheet presented below in Figure 1.7, analyze the programs that operate in your school to determine if they are treatment, pacification, or prevention efforts.

Figure 1.7. Program Analysis Worksheet

At-Risk Program Analysis

1. Think of the programs in your school that were designed to meet the needs of at-risk students.

2. List all of the programs you can think of and the resources being spent on them.

3. Finally classify each program as either treatment, pacification, or prevention.

Before we end this chapter it is worth noting that individual teachers can, and frequently have, a tremendous impact on their students. Many of us have felt tears forming in our eyes after hearing about the heroic successes of a Marva Collins or a Jaime Escalante (Mathews, 1998). In a remarkable study reported in the 1978 *Harvard Educational Review*, Eigil Pedersen, T. Faucher, and W. Eaton reported on a first grade teacher they called "Miss A," who had a remarkable preventative impact on her students. *Newsweek Magazine* reported on their study:

Thank You, Miss A.

If you have more years of formal education, a better house, and a higher-paying job than many of your contemporaries, your first-grade teacher may deserve a large share of the credit. That's the conclusion of McGill University professor of education Eigil Pedersen, who studied 59 adults from an unnamed elementary school in a Montreal slum district. At the outset, Pedersen wanted to identify the causes of IQ changes that occurred during the grade-school years. But the emphasis of the study shifted when Pedersen discovered that those who had been taught by one particular first-grade teacher (called "Miss A") attained significantly greater success as adults than others in the group.

Pedersen and his associates systematically considered a number of other possible reasons for the success of Miss A's pupils. In the end, however, Pedersen concluded that the difference had to be Miss A herself. "She believed every child could learn," he said. "In the 32 years she taught there, education went through a whole series of vogues. It didn't matter which method she used, the outcome was always superior."

According to Pedersen, whose report appeared in the Harvard Educational Review, the impact of a first-grade teacher should never be underestimated. The child has no academic awareness, and it's up to the first-grade teacher to start the ball rolling by teaching the 6- or 7-year-old pupil how to read. If nothing else, Pedersen's study bolsters a cheerful belief that has recently suffered some erosion—that a teacher's best efforts may indeed significantly help children from poor urban neighborhoods (*Newsweek*, June 5, 1978).

The techniques used by Miss A, Marva Collins, and Jaime Escalante and other outstanding teachers of at-risk students will be analyzed and discussed throughout this book. We will do so not just to extol the virtues of these pioneers but to make the point that each of us can replicate their success.

References

Brown v. Board of Education. 347 U.S. 483, 495 (1954), and 349 U.S. 294 (1955).

Cohen, P. A., Kulik, J. A., & Kulik, C. C. (1982 Summer). Educational outcomes of tutoring: A meta-analysis of findings. *American Educational Research Journal*, 19 (2), 237–248.

Collins, M., & Tamarkin, C. (1990). *Marva Collins' Way: Returning to Excellence in Education*. New York: J. P. Tarcher.

Conrath, J. (1986). *Our Other Youth*. Gig Harbor, WA: Our Other Youth.

Dunn, L. M. (1968). Special education for the mildly retarded—Is much of it justifiable? *Exceptional Children*, 35, 5–22.

Edmonds, R. (1979, October). Effective schools for the urban poor. *Educational Leadership*, 37(1), 24–27.

Festinger, L. (1954). *A theory of cognitive dissonance*. Stanford, CA: Stanford.

Frymier, J., & Gansneder, B. (1989). The Phi Delta Kappa Study of Students At-risk. *Phi Delta KAPPAN*, October, 142–146.

Mathews, J. (1988). *Escalante: The best teacher in america*. New York: Henry Holt.

Ogbu, J. U. (1989). The individual in collective adaptation: A framework for focusing on academic underperformance and dropping out among involuntary minorities. In Weis, L., Farrar, E., & Petrie, H. G. (Eds.) *Dropouts from school: Issues, dilemmas, and solutions* (pp. 181–204). Albany: SUNY Press.

Pearl, A. (1972). *The atrocity of education*. St. Louis: New Critics Press.

Pedersen, E., Faucher, T., & Eaton, W. (1978). A new perspective on the effects of first grade teachers on children's subsequent adult status. *Harvard Educational Review*, February, 48:1.

Slavin, R. E., Karweit, N. L., & Madden, N. A. (1989). *Effective programs for students at risk*. Boston: Allyn & Bacon.

Wehlage, G. G., Rutter, R. A., Smith, G. A. et al. (1989). *Reducing the risk: Schools as communities of support*. Philadelphia: Falmer Press.

2

ISSUES REGARDING ASSESSMENT AND THE UNIQUENESS OF LEARNERS

The Appropriate Role of Assessment

The Standards Movement is filled with benefits, as well as unintended consequences for the at-risk learner. On one hand the high stakes testing, the public airing of data on schools and students, and the accountability spot-light that standards place on schools makes it increasingly difficult for school systems to ignore the long-term trends of inequitable student performance. A few years ago a lead editorial in USA Today pointed out,

For years there was an unspoken agreement between schools and middle-class parents:

♦ Schools prepared the higher performing students for college, a job, and another round of middle-class life,

♦ and the rest of the students were kept out of the way. They were passed from class to class, grade to grade, and eventually handed a diploma that nobody looked at when they applied for a job at the mill, or signed up for welfare as a teen mom....

♦ those kids who could remain invisible 10 years ago, many of them black and Latino, now need a real education to survive. And they aren't getting it.

♦ The proof is in the standardized tests that most school systems are now administering....

♦ Yet state after state report a distressing gap between the performance of white and minority students. In Texas, black and Latino children fail at twice the rate of whites....

♦ That's why high stakes testing is so important. It forces action. Based upon such tests, New York City plans to send 250,000 children to summer school this year. Chicago has sent 20,000 children to its summer program for each of the last 3 years....

♦ Such moves...dispel the notion that it is OK for schools to fail minority students as long as nobody notices (*USA Today*, May 30, 2000, p. 16).

However, one would be wrong to think that these reforms are without flaws. In response to that editorial, Janell Byrd-Chichester of the NAACP Legal Defense and Education Fund argued:

In the 1960s when black children sought to desegregate the schools of Macon County, Alabama, the white schools adopted a new admissions requirement: standardized tests. Likewise after James Meredith moved to desegregate the University of Mississippi, the state adopted the same tactic, barring 70 percent of its black students from the best-funded schools for the next 30 years.

Today under the banner of "improving standards" high stakes testing is sweeping the county. The civil rights community fought for standards based reform: high academic standards for all children incorporating assessments aligned with high quality curriculum and instruction, teacher training, and adequate resources. Unfortunately we are getting high stakes testing—a simplistic method that's grinding educational reform to a narrow and punitive edge... (*USA Today*, May 30, 2000, p. 16).

For those of us concerned about narrowing the achievement gap between the advantaged and the at-risk, it simply isn't enough to let the political pressure build as more and more disadvantaged students fail to achieve their potential. Hopefully, *USA Today* is correct in that by taking the scandal of inequitable achievement out of the closet, disadvantaged students will reap a benefit. But, Ms. Byrd-Chichester is also correct that our job as educators is to ensure that disadvantaged children attend schools with "high quality curriculum and instruction" from teachers who have received top-notch "teacher training." It is imperative that we do everything within our power to help *all* our students succeed at the tasks placed before them. At the opening of the 21st Century one of the most compelling and "high stakes" tasks that our students will encounter are state mandated proficiency tests.

This is why it is imperative that we develop skill with classroom assessment. Those teachers who are able to effectively and efficiently assess their students' strengths and weaknesses, with regard to the outcomes measured on state mandated evaluations, will be far better equipped to coach their students to high levels of performance on those exams. Conversely, if during instruction we aren't able to accurately take our students' pulse and assess their educational vital signs, our students will become hostage to the winds of fortune when the state tests are administered.

But, preparation for high stakes evaluations is not the only reason why we, as teachers of those at risk, should invest in becoming skilled classroom assessors. An equal, if not more important reason to focus on assessment, is the role assessment can play in building a student's sense of "potency." The resilient students, those children who believe in the very depths of their soul that they will prevail, didn't develop those attitudes through attendance at a "positive image building assembly." Rather, those attitudes grew from having credible data on their own past accomplishments. The more formative experiences children have with quality feedback on their work, the more likely it is that they will develop confidence in their ability to persevere and ultimately achieve success.

Educators often talk about the difference between "intrinsic" reinforcement (deriving satisfaction from the joy of doing the work) versus "extrinsic" reinforcement (effort which is motivated by the expectation of tangible rewards), we will argue in this book that the use of extrinsic reinforcement can be justified as an appropriate, but *interim strategy*. That not withstanding, like most educators and parents, it is our fervent desire to see our students motivated through internal mechanisms rather than external devices. The best classroom assessment practices, in our opinion, are those that enhance the students' ability to monitor their own learning and to initiate changes, when and if, the *student* feels adjustments are warranted to achieve goals of *personal* value.

According to Rick Stiggins (2000) there are five principles that should guide educators when working with classroom assessment:

- ♦ Clear thinking and effective communication
- ♦ Teachers in charge
- ♦ Students as key users
- ♦ Clear and appropriate targets
- ♦ High quality assessment

A discussion of the first four characteristics and their relevance for working with the defeated and discouraged learner follows. In Chapter 6 we discuss building quality authentic assessments.

Clear Thinking
and Effective Communication

Oftentimes we talk in a very different language or use professional vocabulary when addressing students. This may explain why frequently we think we said something while the students are equally convinced that we didn't. We need to be careful that we aren't talking past our students. When we use language that is incomprehensible to our at-risk learners, our defeated/discouraged learners will logically infer that we neither expected nor cared if they learned the material. Once a student draws that conclusion it is almost certain that they cease trying.

Teachers in Charge

Ultimately it is the teacher who decides what is to be taught and how it will be taught. Consequently, it is the teacher who decides what the purpose of a lesson is and what the student should be expected to learn from a classroom experience. If students become accustomed to seeing a clear alignment between what they were taught, what was expected by their teachers, and what was assessed; they will tend to take the assessments seriously. Conversely, if the assessments appear to bear little or no resemblance to the work the students completed and which the teacher taught and graded, then it is unlikely the student will invest much energy in completing the assessment or reflecting upon the results.

Students as Key Users

One characteristic of defeated/discouraged learners is that they tend to see themselves as victims (this will be discussed in greater depth in Chapter 7 where we discuss "potency") not as empowered actors. Often they have concluded that they are simply pawns for others to move around, anything but key players in the system. Students who hold this perspective tend to see "assessment" as something that is being done to them for someone else: a report for the Board of Education, for the State or the Federal government, or as part of a report card "for their parents." As a result no one should be surprised to find that these students could care less about how well they do. Any teacher who has tried to motivate their alienated students to give their best effort on mandated standardized exams knows how difficult a task this can be!

However, if and when students see personal value in an assessment they will tend to take the entire process far more seriously. If you doubt the truth in that assertion, just watch a young person playing a video game or learning a new skateboarding trick. You will note that they care very deeply about the data on their performance and the feedback they are receiving. Why? Because the ardent video-game player and skater knows that attending to this "feedback" inevitably helps improve performance!

Clear and Appropriate Targets

Anyone who has ever prepared for a test has probably wondered aloud, "I wonder what will be on the exam?" If we stop and reflect on that question it is hard to escape the underlying absurdity. Should a school exam be a test of students' mind-reading ability or their ability to predict what card will show up at the top of the deck? Of course not. The purpose of an exam should be to help the interested parties (generally the student and the teacher) ascertain if a particular skill/knowledge was acquired. If we go to a golf instructor and ask for help straightening out a slice, we know what the test will be before we start. The test will be hitting golf balls to determine if we can hit it straight. Confusion over targets diverts the learner's energy away from the real purpose of instruction which is learning and instead focuses it on guessing. The big problem with this is not just that it is inefficient, there is much in our lives that fails on the efficiency scale. No, the terrible thing about the guessing game for our students with an external locus of control (this concept is discussed at length in Chapter 7) is that it breeds frustration, alienation, and giving-up. As the student finds it increasingly difficult to predict what trivia will appear on the test it becomes rational to conclude, "Why bother?"

We are sure many readers will be able to identify with the following statement. Tanis Knight (1998) frequently asserts, "Any student (or any teacher for that matter) can hit any target, providing they can see the target and the target will stand still long enough." If we had a dollar for every time we've heard a frustrated teacher complain about the state assessment saying, "Why don't they just tell us what they plan to test the kids on," or "It sure would be nice if we could keep the same test or use the same curriculum for more than 2 years!" we'd be rich.

If one reflects on it, it isn't hard to see why so many teachers lack an internalized belief in their ability to prevail. How could someone possibly be confident that they will be successful when they don't even know what it is they are supposed to be succeeding at?

Stopping to Look Down the Road

Later in the next chapter when we discuss mastery learning we will suggest strategies to assist students in becoming clear on our achievement targets. At this point we simply want to introduce this topic by suggesting one simple task. Before engaging in any major learning activity or beginning any unit of instruction, stop what you and the students are doing, and ask yourself (or them) what exactly are we/you trying to accomplish?

Dick recalls vividly a day several years ago when he was teaching a basic writing class to high school sophomores. Feeling that modeling was a powerful technique, he decided to teach his students the skill of peer editing by having them take a crack at revising a journal article he had been drafting. Dick gave each student a copy of his first draft, asked them to read it, and answer a set of questions on an "editor response sheet." The first question asked,

"In one sentence restate the author's main idea."

No sooner had the students settled into the assignment when Dick realized how great an idea this lesson was. He had never seen this group of students so on-task. Smugly, Dick thought to himself, this "modeling" thing is good stuff, they really are into it!"

After a few minutes Dick asked, "OK, who would like to restate my main idea in one sentence?" Instantly a sea of hands went up. Eagerly Dick called on a particularly excited student.

The student began, "I think you were trying to say…"

Dick responded, "No, that wasn't what I was trying to say, someone else?"

Another student jumped in, "What I thought you were trying to argue was that…"

Again, Dick responded, with a noticeable drop in excitement, "No, not exactly, that wasn't my main idea.…any body else have an idea on what I was trying to say?"

Another brave soul piped in, "Did you mean to say that…?"

"No," Dick, disappointedly added, "I don't think you got it, anyone else?"

Then a frustrated student shouted out, "Obviously we didn't get it. So what was your main idea?"

Sadly, Dick had to acknowledge that the student's question was quite reasonable. By now all the hands were down and clearly no one was confident of their ability to discern the main idea. So Dick shared, "What I was really trying to say was…"

No sooner had he finished when another student yelled out,

"THEN, WHY DIDN'T YOU JUST SAY THAT!!!"

Ah, out of the mouths of babes! The students were absolutely correct. Dick was working so hard trying to impress his readers with his "scholarly voice" that his ideas had become lost in his slavish attention to polysyllables. Dick learned two things from this episode. First, now when he writes he tries to be clear and concise and make use of plain English (at least in his opening paragraphs). Second, and probably more importantly, he now realizes that readers, like learners, appreciate knowing where it is they are going!!

Think and Do Exercise—Clarifying Targets

- Without prompting ask your students to write down (or tell a neighbor) what precisely they believe *you* want them to be able to do/demonstrate at the conclusion of the current unit/lesson.

- Or, if you are using a constructivist methodology, ask your students to write down or tell you what it is that *they* expect/hope to learn or be able to do at the conclusion of the project/activity they are currently engaged in.

Review the Responses

If it was a teacher directed activity and your students were clear on the target that you were directing them toward, then the ideas, (if not the precise words), written by each student should be almost identical. If not, it means your students lack clarity on the target you are asking them to hit.

If you were having your learners construct their own educational experience, react to the targets they shared:

- Were they meaningful?
- Will they contribute to the student's attainment of valued outcomes?
- Will this performance translate to high performance on state/district assessments?
- Does the quality of the targets differ by categories of students (gender, race, etc.) and/or is everyone pursuing valuable leaning?

Before we move too deeply into the "how to" portion of this book, it will be helpful to pause and consider some key differences between learners.

The Uniqueness of Our Learners

The act of teaching, as with all the true professions, requires constantly making choices. Occasionally this is easy. Solving routine problems (such as taking and maintaining attendance records) simply requires the use of one accepted method. However, what separates professionals from other workers is the nature of the decision making that is required. If and when, the problem encountered is non-routine; i.e., when the patient doesn't respond to the treatment prescribed by the doctor or when the student fails to learn even though the teacher is using a "proven practice," professionals turn to the knowledge base in an effort to help understand the problem and deduce a solution.

Now let's apply this to a teacher with defeated and discouraged learners in their classes. Hopefully the discussion earlier in this chapter (where we focused on assessment) provided a rationale on why your students need to determine if, when, and to what extent progress was being made. Whenever our data tell us that all of our students are thriving under the current circumstances, the wisest thing for us to do is "stay the course." But, this book is premised on the fact that most teachers find that their classrooms contain some students who aren't thriving and that contributes to the student's at-riskness. In the preface we introduced the notion of competing theories on learning. When we find ourselves confronting the student who isn't succeeding as professionals, we are wise to see alternative theories as "possibilities worth considering," not as competing possibilities forcing us to choose sides.

Returning to the medical analogy, while a doctor may not be a particular fan of a certain approach and consequently may rarely make use of that particular protocol with patients that are responding well to the preferred treatment regime, the doctor might still choose to employ another less conventional approach when and if a patient isn't responding adequately to the routine regime. Other times the doctor decides to use a nontraditional approach at the outset of treatment. This often occurs when the physician spots something about the patient that suggests that he/she would do better with another approach than the one normally favored.

Retention of Learning

Retention should be the goal of all of our educational pursuits. Here we are not talking about holding children back from their age-mates, rather we are talking about the learner's ability to apply a skill or access knowledge that was taught/learned at a previous time. What influences a learner's retention of knowledge and skills?

While there are many factors that play a role in whether information or skills are retained, one of the more important factors, which is always at the teacher's command, is the match between the instructional approach and the student's dominant learning style.

Building Mental Trellises

Dick recently returned from a trip to Spain. The Spanish love flowers and the exterior of many homes are decorated with an incredible array of beautiful plants. Upon examination one can see that much of this ornamental horticulture owes its success to the trellises or frameworks that the vines and branches were once attached to. When the plants mature, it is often impossible to see the trellises, in some cases the trellises have even decayed and disappeared. At this point the plants have become self-supporting.

One way to think of our work of developing student knowledge and skills is that we are helping our charges build trellises onto which they can attach each new learning. However, the experience of many teachers, as well as many gardeners, has shown that *all* students can't and won't use the same trellis.

That brings us back to Dick's recent trip to Spain. He was looking forward to this cycling tour because while he had never been to Spain, he had taken other excursions with the tour operator, and was pleased with those experiences. But, the most important consideration was that the dates of the tour fit an open spot on his calendar. What is important for the reader to know here is that Dick is what is called a "concrete" learner. This doesn't mean he is dense, hard headed, or any of those other things his wife accuses him of, rather it means that he learns best through concrete or direct experiences.

The Tour Company, assuming that Dick (and all their customers) were abstract learners, did a wonderful job of sending material to all the participants. This material arrived through the mail. It was fair to assume that Dick and the other riders would read it, comprehend it, and have a good idea what they were about to experience.

As Jerry Conrath (1986) points out people like Dick aren't reluctant learners, considering all the money that Dick spent to enroll on the tour revealed he was anything but reluctant. However, whenever he tried to read the material, it read like so much gobble-dee-gook. Consequently, when Dick arrived at the starting point for his "Camino de Santiago," all he knew was that they were going to ride a route that Pilgrims had traveled since the 12th Century. Apparently, all this had something to do with Saint James and shaving some time off one's stay in Purgatory. The bottom line was that Dick went to Spain without a clue, or in other words, without a *mental trellis*.

In fact, on the first evening when the tour group met, Dick felt rather awkward. Some other riders were asking detailed historical and geographic questions that held no meaning for Dick. This wasn't because he didn't care, it was because he had no trellis upon which to hang this information.

Well, as it turned out Dick not only had a marvelous time but now has more than a little detailed knowledge on the geography of the Castille, Leon, and Galicia provinces. He has a sense of the flow of Spanish history from the Middle

Ages forward and a growing appreciation for some very abstract concepts—spirituality and the evolving role of the Church in the life of the Spanish people over the last 500 years. Did he learn all this on a 10-day bike trip? No, he isn't that perceptive! Yes, he did learn a lot through his experience on the trip, but, if all we know is what we personally experience, we would be awfully ignorant people.

Dick's learning *started* with the concrete experience of pedaling along on paths that had been used for centuries and visiting breathtaking Cathedrals, but that was only the beginning. For a learner like Dick, concrete experience is most helpful in building a trellis. Once that trellis was established, Dick found he was able to read the material from the tour company and hang it where it belonged on his framework. As of this writing, he has read all the material originally sent by the tour operator, several books he purchased along the way, and other works he acquired on his return.

Enough of this talk of exotic foreign travel. It is probably only making the reader jealous! Let's return to our classrooms and our defeated and discouraged learners. Students like Dick succeed best when they can build a trellis from direct or concrete experience and then augment it with more abstract material. Dick is the kind of kid who often appears disinterested in class when library or text material is used to introduce a topic. But, when a unit of study begins with a field trip, it appears he is more motivated. Conversely when abstract learners are asked to begin a unit of study with a field trip or other concrete experience, they often become uneasy. Why? When the abstract learner engages in an experience without a mental trellis to attach the experiences to, it can seem like a waste of time. These abstract learners are the kids who are constantly asking, "Why are we doing this?"

The Think and Do exercise that follows is a strategy you can use to better understand the "trellis" building process.

Think and Do Exercise—Building a Mental Trellis

1. Think of something you truly enjoy and have a certain degree of expertise with.

2. Reflect on how you first became interested in this topic or pursuit. Was it through an experience, trying something out, going someplace, doing something? Or were you stimulated by something you read or heard about?

3. Now ask the students in your class to do the same thing.

4. Have a class discussion on the results.

5. Now ask yourself: Do all my students build mental trellises in the same way and how difficult is it to initially learn and retain material without mental trellises?

The Curriculum and Instruction Battle Fields

Increasingly students of education are told that there are wars going on in the schoolhouse. No, we aren't referring here to school violence. Rather, we are talking about the great pedagogical wars raging in many elementary schools and even a few secondary schools.

The Reading and Math Wars

When it comes to literacy the battle-lines are usually drawn this way. One side (often labeled *whole language*) argues that both the skill and the motivation to develop language skills begin with experience. Children might be encouraged to sing familiar verses, write, utilizing their own vocabulary, even inventing words. The notion is to invite having fun with language, recognize all the places where it's used to help them find ways to personally connect with the need/desire to write, speak, listen, and read. Educators in this camp might argue that once the children have built a literacy trellis then they will be ready, willing and able to do the hard work of developing the precision and discipline of critical readers, proficient writers, careful listeners and persuasive speakers.

Other educators argue that reading and writing are skills that are made up of critical discrete skills that need to be taught, learned, and mastered in a predetermined sequence if proficiency is to be attained. These folks would argue that it is those specific skills that form the trellis the learner will need as a prerequisite to the creative use of language.

In math the lingo is different, but, the battle is really quite similar. On the one hand, we find those who feel children need to master their basic number skills, develop confidence in using the standard algorithms to solve problems and achieve high levels of accuracy with their computation before they will understand the concepts. These folks might argue that only when the child has the confidence that comes from mastery of basic math skills could they understand the logic and meaning behind equations.

These teachers find themselves battling colleagues who argue that in an age of computers and calculators what is most critical is thinking with math. They are more concerned with children working through a problem and being able to explain the logic and decision making behind their strategies than coming up with a correct answer that is not fully understood by the student. To these folks an unconventional way to solve a problem is evidence of a child's development as a mathematician, which these educators feel is of greater importance than mastery of algorithms.

In Chapter 5 when we discuss the need of *belonging* we will discuss the issue of learning/teaching style at length and offer more guidance in choosing appropriate teaching strategies.

The reason for introducing this topic in Part 1, the introductory portion of the text, was to get us on the same page regarding several key factors. Specifically, we wanted to share why we feel it is so essential to begin planning instruction recognizing that students learn in different ways and that those differences must be addressed if our goal is universal success.

Why learn a skill or acquire knowledge if not to retain it? Even if you find yourself teaching in an environment marked by high-stakes testing, you will be doing yourself, your school, and your students a disservice if you allow them to believe that we are only teaching the curriculum because they are expected to know it for the exam. The cynicism that this will breed with students will create an ever-escalating motivational problem as students move through the system.

By contrast if students begin to see that each piece of learning, each skill or attribute is, in reality, one more branch on an ever evolving and more complex and beautiful trellis, we will be creating a motivational accelerator. Instead of expecting to forget or lose a skill and returning to point zero, students can begin seeing themselves as becoming ever more powerful with each additional learning.

If the goal of *retention* is for all students, then the goal of *building a conceptual framework* (a trellis) where each new item can be hung is essential for every student.

However, the process for building a mental trellis will differ from learner to learner. What we ask of you, the reader, at this point is simply this: When a strategy is introduced, don't ask yourself,

- ♦ "Do I like this?" or

- ♦ "Is this the way I'd like to learn?"

But rather, ask yourself, would this be a strategy with potential for helping *some* of my learners build a mental framework that will ultimately lead them to greater retention and excitement regarding this material?

Just as none of us wants our doctors to be wedded to a single treatment regime (regardless of its power for helping others), our students deserve to work with professional teachers who come equipped with the knowledge and skills necessary to administer the proper instructional protocol at the right time for the each of the students they are working with.

References

Stiggins, Richard J. (2000). *Student involved classroom assessment*, 3rd ed. New York:Prentice Hall.

Knight, Tanis. (1998). *But are they learning? A common sense parents guide to assessment and grading in schools.* Portland: Assessment Training Institute.

Conrath, Jerry. (1986). *Our other youth.* Gig Harbor, WA: Our Other Youth, Inc.

McTighe, Jay, & Wiggins, Grant. (1998). *Understanding by design*, Alexandria: ASCD.

3

THE "C" OF CBUPO: BUILDING STUDENT FEELINGS OF COMPETENCE

In this chapter we will begin discussing on developing feelings of competence. There is much truth to the old adage asserting "success breeds success." However, this holds true only when people believe they were responsible for their own success. Because of this essential truth, one of our top priorities should be committing ourselves to ensure that each child leaves our classrooms possessing credible evidence of their own capability and continuous growth in skills.

The Importance of Developing One's Feelings of Competence at School

The bricks that make up the foundation upon which self-esteem is built are feelings of competence. While schooling has numerous purposes, i.e., socializing the young into a common culture and developing social consciousness, it is widely agreed that our main purpose as public school educators is the creation of autonomous, knowledgeable, self-assured students.

Before many of our students even entered the first grade a significant number had internalized the viewpoint that there are two types of people in this world. There are those who can easily memorize all of the stuff required and are therefore destined for success, and then there are others, unable to make sense of the onslaught of academic expectations, who have been sentenced to a school experience that will be marked by failure. More importantly even young children believe that one's school experience is a good predictor of the life they will live as adults. Because many students hold this perspective, repeated experiences with success or repeated failure has profound repercussions.

As mentioned above, successful students come to believe that school success is a logical and necessary precursor to bigger and better things down the road. Conversely, unsuccessful students, those whose past history of failure has put them at-risk, logically conclude that their performance in school foreshadows a host of future failures on the job, in society, and perhaps even in their interpersonal relationships.

Those internal scripts produce expectations that echo the preschool story of the "little engine that could." This children's classic provides a helpful metaphor for the powerful self-image building capacity of the schooling process. Children who repeatedly receive feedback that they are learning continue to learn. For them the moral of the "little engine that could" story is proven daily. Their success indeed does breed future success. However, those other children, those who subliminally hear themselves repeating the line, "No I can't, no I can't!" over and over again are building what, for them, will likely be a lifelong legacy of doubt.

In the preface we introduced two "generic" instructional models.

Model 1: Classical Positivism

Instructed Skills → Success → Application → Meaning

Model 2: Developmental Constructivism

Meaning → Construct/Invent Skills→ Application → Success

In Model 1, skills are mastered (regardless of whether or not they held meaning for the learner). Then, after the learner has mastered a set of prerequisite skills, the learner is encouraged to discover and explore real world applications for the foundational skills mastered. Ultimately the learner is encouraged to integrate all of this learning through a project with personal meaning.

In Model 2, the learner first engages in finding meaning in an area of study. This process begins with the child's natural curiosity setting the stage for learning. Then later, once the learner's curiosity has been aroused and the child has developed "an internal need to know," the child can construct/invent the necessary critical skills and use these to construct further knowledge.

A deliberate and appropriate use of each of these models for the right student, in the right circumstanc,e and at the right time can significantly influence their development of academic self-esteem. In this chapter we will discuss the *positivist model* (Model 1) and its value in building feelings of competence. Later, in the next chapter, we will explore *developmental constructivism* and its potential for developing this most critical component of resilience.

Both of the models discussed throughout this book are means to get a learner to the outcome of becoming an enthusiastic lifelong learner. However, a careful reader will see that these two models are based on quite different views of knowledge, how knowledge is acquired, and consequently, the strategies used to help students develop proficiency as learners.

Mastery Learning as presented in this chapter is based upon the use of a specific set of instructional strategies organized for the learner by the teacher. One of the strongest arguments for using a mastery approach is its ability to *quickly* and *efficiently* get a learner to proficiency with an academic outcome. Mastery learning provides students with quick objective evidence of their success with learning. When at-risk students are provided with irrefutable data on improved performance, it inevitably creates *productive cognitive dissonance*.[1] (The productive use of cognitive dissonance was discussed in Chapter 1.) This is because the concrete evidence of their new-found success stands in sharp contrast to the student's earlier feelings of incompetence, impotence, and uselessness. Once students possess objective evidence on their capacity to learn, they cannot help but see themselves differently.

Mastery Learning: An Objective View of Knowledge

In Chapter 1 we reviewed three clusters of theories that provide the foundation for most of at-risk programs in our schools. The instructional interventions used most frequently with at-risk students are those grounded in the *environmental deficit* perspective. Remedial programs, ability grouping, and other forms of tracking are all built from the environmental deficit model. Unfortunately these practices result in the at-risk student being placed in a lower track and experiencing a "dummied down" curriculum (Oakes, 1985; Wheelock, 1992), consequently, it should be no surprise that remediation models seldom prove motivational for the at-risk student. Self-esteem simply cannot be built through the accomplishment of trivial or grossly simplistic tasks. In fact, it is the very reverse that is true; high levels of academic self-esteem result from repeated success with meaningful and high-level challenges.

One thing that has commended mastery learning to policy makers is that it is a mechanism, which, when properly implemented can enable *all* students to succeed with a singular rigorous curriculum. This feature of mastery learning fits nicely with standards-based systems that seek to produce universal student success with a mandated curriculum (schoolwide implications of the mastery

---

1   See discussion of the productive use of dissonance pages.

learning process are discussed in Chapter 8 where we expand our discussion to focus on standards-based reforms.)

For mastery learning adherents, "knowing" is defined as becoming proficient with the facts and skills sought through a lesson or unit and then later being able to apply this knowledge in novel situations. Success with knowledge is demonstrated via the recall of appropriate facts and procedures and the ability to utilize the correct algorithms in appropriate circumstances. When teaching in the mastery learning mode, we expect our students to be capable of following accepted proven procedures and best practices to arrive at a "correct" answer.

This is why mastery learning has been shown to be such an efficient way to achieve quick success with the objectives measured by most standardized testing programs. Beyond reaching proficiency on mandated objectives, mastery learning also packs a powerful motivational punch. This is because once students have repeatedly experienced success and have demonstrated high achievement on objective assessments; they cannot help but internalize an empowered view of their potential. As a result students cease to question whether or not they "can do the work."

The Mastery Learning Model

Low self-esteem need not be a life sentence for our "at-risk" students. Considerable bodies of research as well as the experience of many teachers have given testimony to the fact that success in a traditional school curriculum does not have to be limited to a select and privileged few. In fact, the preeminent mastery learning researcher, Benjamin Bloom, argues that when provided with the proper instructional processes, "Anyone can learn anything," given that the learner is motivated, enough time is available, and appropriate instruction is provided.

Bloom (1976), of the University of Chicago, began the modern mastery learning movement with his book *Human Characteristics and School Learning*. In this book he pointed out that when four variables are taken into account, the learning of any content is within the reach of any of our students (providing they have normal brain function). Equally important for at-risk students, he found that the instructional strategies most likely to be successful in accomplishing the mastery result work in whole class, group-based instructional environments. The importance of investing in group instruction rather than individualized remedial instruction is discussed extensively in the next chapter where our focus is on enhancing feelings of belonging and affiliation.

When one examines the methods used by such celebrated teachers as Jaime Escalante, the high school teacher portrayed in the film "Stand and Deliver," and Marva Collins, the elementary teacher featured on the CBS program "Sixty Minutes," one finds the techniques and technologies of mastery learning. Figure 3.1 contrasts the performance that research tells us is obtained in mastery learning classrooms with conventional classrooms.

Figure 3.1. Mastery and Conventional Expectations

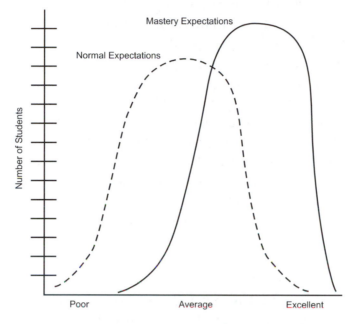

This graph illustrates a profound distinction between the expectations of the bell-shaped curve, in which only a few students are expected to do outstanding work (while an equal number do poorly, usually our at-risk students), and the overwhelming majority does average work, and the *mastery expectation* in which almost everyone performs at what is considered an "exceptional" level.

The two most important aspects of this difference are, first, poor performance is reduced to the point of elimination, and, second, the levels of high performance that were once just the province of a select few, can now become the norm. Blooms research demonstrates that, u*nder mastery learning conditions, 50 percent more students will perform at the level currently attained only by our A and B students.*

To produce this result, four variables must be considered and attended to. It is now important for us to take a look at these four factors which, when properly addressed, produce the gestalt that makes for such a dramatic difference in student achievement.

The Four Variables

The four critical variables (motivation, prerequisite skills, quality of instruction and adequate time) which enable all learners to be successful, may at first seem obvious, but on closer examination both the complexity and power of these variables becomes apparent. Once we accept the importance of these four factors we are forced to abandon old assumptions regarding the existence of innate intelligence and its alleged relationship to learning. When a conventional teacher accepts the power of these four variables he or she inevitably undergoes a powerful paradigm shift!

Variable 1: Motivation

Just as a "horse can be led to water, but not made to drink," likewise a student must want to learn if he or she is actually going to learn. The student who sees no purpose in acquiring mastery over certain material, or who has other priorities, won't be made to learn even when exposed to the most gifted teacher. That fact notwithstanding, we shouldn't despair. Jerry Conrath (1986), one of the nation's leading experts on at-risk youth, observed that of the several thousand at-risk students he's interviewed, he has yet to meet a single one who held a lifetime goal of remaining ignorant. In fact, he argues with much conviction that it is natural for all human beings to be curious and are born with an innate desire to learn and grow intellectually.

When we accept the logic of Jerry's observation, we are left with several searing and soul searching questions. For whenever one of our students argues that they won't do what it takes to learn our curricula, we must ask why? Had we made the purpose of the unit clear enough? Had we made its relevance known? Apparently we hadn't, or why would this otherwise rational student be choosing ignorance over knowledge? Those questions lead us to ask, "What could we have done differently to make possessing these skills or acquiring this knowledge a desirable end for this innately curious child?"

Once we commit to doing all we can to have the student see the mastery of our curricula as a desirable end, then we can move to consideration of the second variable, *prerequisite skills.*

Variable 2: Prerequisite Skills

Frequently, we place barriers before students that need not have been in their way. Much has been written about the fact that Jaime Escalante took hundreds of students through advanced placement calculus even though they hadn't yet mastered the math skills that many educators saw as prerequisite experiences for attempting that advanced curricula. Clearly, Escalante was right and most of the nation's math teachers were wrong. Among the things that the Jaime Escalante's experience should have taught us as educators was to avoid selling our students short by accepting excuses for poor performance. Because of his example we should always critically ask of each skill that is alleged to be a prerequisite "Is this really an essential building block to learning this material?" In many cases, we may find that *gatekeeper* competencies are merely superfluous obstacles. They work like boulders placed in the road to keep students from gaining access to higher level learning. But in other cases the "essential aspect" of prerequisite skills will be real and must be addressed.

For example, if we are trying to teach our students the algorithm for long division, we soon will acknowledge the essential fact that the students must have mastery of multiplication and subtraction prior to mastering long division. This is because multiplication and subtraction are critical sub-components of the long division algorithm. The student who can not perform those operations with some degree of precision will surely encounter frustration and failure when attempting long division. Whenever we have clear and convincing evidence (as with long division) of a prerequisite relationship, it absolutely behooves us to teach first things first. Otherwise we are setting up our most at-risk students for more failure. It should be noted that the need to have at-risk students master prerequisites is not a call for slower paced remedial classes. Just the opposite, what at-risk students need is to be placed in "accelerated" programs where they can pick-up the missing prerequisites in record time. (The concept of "accelerating instruction" is discussed more fully in Chapter 9.)

As mentioned above, the four key variables for mastery may seem obvious. Thus far we have seen that a child who does not want to learn (lacks motivation) or does not have the essential building blocks (prerequisites) for learning, is a student who will not and should not be expected to master a skill. But what of the other two variables?

Variable 3: Quality Instruction

Suppose you have a class of motivated students possessing the skills necessary to attempt the next challenge. Your students will still need top quality instruction. It is our job as teachers to provide this for them. But, suppose we don't. Suppose our teaching lacks clarity and precision leaves our students confused and bewildered. Suppose we don't answer their questions clearly, or we teach using ambiguous materials and language. Should we still expect our students to master the material? We think not. Any learning that occurs in those circumstances is more likely the result of luck than of our teaching.

If it truly is a new skill that we want our students to acquire and if they possess all the necessary motivation and prerequisites, they still will need assistance from their teacher. Moreover, the nature of that instruction must be appropriate for them. It must respect their learning style, their culture (learning style and culture are discussed in the next chapter) as well as their cognitive level. When the instruction provided meets all those criteria, then our students will have received *almost* all that is necessary for success.

However, possessing prerequisite skills, being motivated, and having access to quality instruction are not enough to ensure mastery of new material. Because once all of those factors have been provided teachers need to attend to the one true and significant difference between learners: *their learning rate*. This brings us to the fourth variable, providing students with enough time to learn.

Variable 4: Adequate Time

Almost everyone in modern society has been brought up to believe that learners differ by virtue of their intelligence (IQ). Furthermore, many of us have been told, and have incorporated into our belief systems, the view that intelligence is innate, God given, or inherited. Such a world view allows us to look into classrooms and conclude that some material is simply beyond the capability of certain learners. Likewise, we may conclude that other youngsters have been endowed by their creator as especially able or gifted.

Bloom (1976, 1984), Escalante (Mathews 1988), and numerous teachers have supplied us with evidence that quashes those assumptions. In fact, research in over a dozen countries and covering all subjects in grades K–Graduate School has shown that, excluding the organically brain damaged, all of our curricula are within the reach of all of our learners, given the motivation, prerequisites, and effective instruction, provided only that the learner is given adequate *time* to master the skills or acquire the knowledge. Once a teacher accepts this perspective, the teacher can begin seeing the students' and his/her role of teacher differently. No longer will the class be seen as differing in innate capacity, rather they are seen as a collection of children differing primarily on a continuum from slower to faster learners.

We must keep in mind that learning rate is not a euphemism for intelligence. While we were told that intelligence as measured by IQ tests, is universal and generalizable, the same is not true of learning rate. Learning rate appears to be content specific. Your fastest math learner may actually be your slowest reader. Your fastest artist may be your slowest mathematician. For example, I can master the content of the sports page faster than most of my adult friends, but for me to comprehend the intricacies of the international economic system, such as the relationship of exchange rates to domestic inflation, will take a great deal of time! If you doubt this is true take a moment to complete the Think and Do exercise that follows. It should help you see that there is some degree of giftedness in nearly all of our students. This led Harvard Professor Howard Gardner to the concept he refers to as multiple intelligences (Gardner, 1993). The concept of multiple intelligences and its many implications for instruction are discussed later in this book.

> ### *Think and Do Exercise—A Classroom Strength Inventory*
>
> Students' academic self-esteem is enhanced when classroom instruction builds on their strengths. Therefore, it is helpful to be cognizant of the learning strengths of each of our students. A classroom strength inventory is a valuable tool to make use of when designing lessons that will motivate all your students.
>
> First, list on the left-hand margin of a sheet of paper each of the students in your classroom.
>
> Second, by each child's name list a skill or attribute that this child possesses better than most of his/her peers (note that the skill or attribute does not need to be school related, e.g., exceptional motocross racer, skateboarder, dancer, comedian).
>
> Were you able to find a strength (gift) possessed by each of your students?

The finding, from the mastery learning research, regarding the variability of learning rate is fully compatible with the findings of Howard Gardner (1993) and Robert Sternberg (1997) regarding multiple and varied intelligences. Many wonderful consequences flow from accepting the findings of the mastery learning research on learning rate. The teacher can feel professionally confident when she looks at her students this way. She can know that they will all learn each particular element of content; it may just take some students longer than others. And she can tell the "slower" learners with confidence, that their learning rate is not a reflection on their intelligence, because she knows that in fact, they are speed demons with other material.

For example, in a typical math classroom, variations in learning rate could mean that the ratio between the fastest and slowest student would be as much as threefold. In other words, the slowest child in the class might need to devote as much as three times the time that the fastest student must invest to master the same concept. Finding and utilizing this additional time will call for much creativity. (In Chapter 8, when we discuss *standards-based education* we will review some of the more creative approaches schools have used to address the time dilemma.) Armed with an understanding of the four variables, we can approach our classes confident that when our students: 1) want to learn, 2) have the necessary prerequisites, 3) are provided with appropriate instruction, and 4) are given enough time to learn, then each one of them will be able to master the essential course objectives. This will be the case whether we find ourselves teaching basic arithmetic or calculus.

As stated above, mastery learning research provides us with a belief system regarding learning that is built on an objective view of knowledge. While the precise instructional process of mastery learning provides teachers with a framework for lesson and unit design, it still leaves a great deal of flexibility in adapting this approach to fit different teaching personalities and styles. We now present two approaches for implementing the instructional process of mastery learning in the mainstream classroom.

Two Approaches: The Deluxe and the Economy Models

Several years ago Dick's wife and he were engaged in a friendly professional rivalry. She was working with a long-term, well-financed, and federally funded mastery learning project (Project Write), while Dick was teaching 9th graders in a typical public high school. While both were deeply committed to making the Bloom model work, she had far more tools (and money) at her disposal. For that reason Dick came to describe the approach she used as the deluxe "Cadillac" model and his more modest homegrown approach as the economy "VW Bug" model. Both will be presented in this chapter. Readers should keep several points in mind. First, each of these models (or a hybrid containing the best of both) can be expected to produce results predicted by the mastery learning researchers, because they both remain faithful to the theory. However, anything less than the "economy" model will likely neglect at least one or more of the crucial components of mastery learning theory. If that is the case then the outcomes obtained may fall short of those predicted by research.

On the other hand, over time, a classroom teacher or a team of teachers who began with the "economy model" can systematically add to their programs until they have all of the components of the deluxe model in place.

The Deluxe Model

Figure 3.2 displays the deluxe mastery learning model. You will note that there is nothing radical in the first three steps of this approach. As teachers we have students assigned to us; we make it a point to know their skill levels; we provide them with instruction; we frequently divide our instruction into discrete and sequential units. Also, as mentioned earlier, mastery learning requires us to teach our students as a group instruction mode. Thus far nothing should sound particularly unusual. In fact, the next step in the model, following instruction by giving the entire class a unit test, is also pretty much par for the course.

However, in most conventional classrooms the results from these end of unit assessments are also predictable. Several students will demonstrate mastery of the material. (In the context of mastery learning, the term *mastery* usually means responding correctly to 80–90 percent of the questions.) The only errors one should expect to see from students demonstrating this level of mastery are either the result of sloppiness or oversight. Predictably, however, we will see another set of students who may appear to have learned some of the material, but have done so in a weaker fashion (scoring 60–80 percent). Finally, and unfortunately, we will find somacademically at-risk students scoring below the 60 percent level, who have not learned the material very well in contrast to their peers.

If we were using a conventional format, we would approach this state of affairs with a certain degree of resolution. We would continue to endeavor to make the percentage of students reaching mastery high, and hopefully, have the number that are failing comparatively low. But, regardless of the proportion of students in each category, the ship of learning would be required to move on. And it is the at-risk students who would be usually left at the dock with their feelings of competence and self-esteem once again diminished. Not so in a mastery learning classroom! It is at this point that the mastery classroom begins to look different.

At this stage immediately after the unit test the teacher creates a two-day time-out. As illustrated in Figure 3.2, the class now is now divided into at least two groups. The first group, those that have demonstrated mastery of the material, are directed toward enrichment activities. These are often called *extensions*. They might include applying the recently mastered material to more complex problems or it might involve things such as having peers tutor students who have not yet achieved mastery.

The second group, those whose performance on the first unit test did not approach mastery levels, will be assigned to work on *correctives*. Correctives are alternative learning experiences designed to give students more time and additional opportunities to acquire mastery. When selecting correctives for individual students, it is assumed that mastery will require the use of different instructional methodologies than the ones that proved inadequate the first time around. Examples of correctives which might be assigned are:

- One on one tutoring
- Additional drill and practice
- Computer simulations
- Alternative materials suited to particular learning styles. (The learning style issue is discussed in greater length in Chapter 4).

In classrooms where the teacher is implementing the deluxe model, the teacher could be expected to have a bank of file cabinets with at least one drawer for each instructional unit. Each file would contain dozens of alternative correctives and extensions for any imaginable type of student. In such classrooms we might expect to see a variety of learning stations, parent volunteers and appropriate media for each type of learner. If this doesn't sound realistic for your school or classroom, don't despair. We still have the economy model for you!

Figure 3.2. The Deluxe Mastery Learning Model

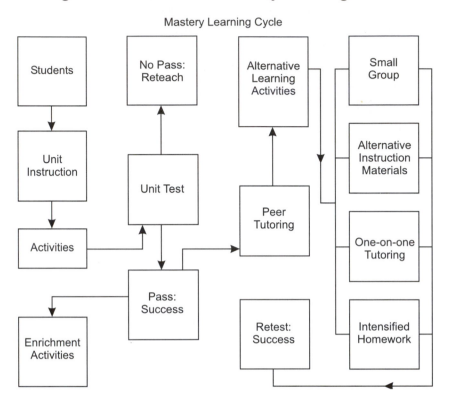

Now let's return to the flow chart in Figure 3.2. After the two days of "time-out" for correctives/extensions a second assessment is given. At this point all or almost all students should have acquired mastery. Finally, after a thorough in-class review of the second test, the class as a whole should be ready to move on to the next unit.

As the entire class moves ahead, every student has become a "little engine that could." Contrast this with the traditional classroom in which many students will be expected to approach the second unit with the conviction that they are bound to fail again, just as they had in unit one. Unfortunately, because they have internalized from infancy the truism that "the past is the best predictor of the future," the prediction will likely be realized!

The Economy Model

Functionally, the economy model is the same as the deluxe model with a few notable whistles and bells omitted. This is not unlike our automobile analogy. The Volkswagen bug and the Cadillac are functionally the same. Each has all the components required to get a passenger from one place to another, only the Cadillac does so with far more comfort. The economy model of mastery learning, as implemented in Dick's classroom, is illustrated in Figure 3.3.

Figure 3.3. The Economy Mastery Learning Model

Mastery Learning

1. Teach one unit at a time
2. Preview
3. Instruction
4. Check test
5. Retesting
6. Retesting
7. Next unit

Note that when using this approach, the formal pretest is abandoned in favor of the preview. While a pretest can help a teacher with diagnosis and prescription, it also adds several time consuming steps. First, the pretest requires the preparation of an additional test. Furthermore, to be of any use, the pretest must be scored and analyzed promptly. Finally, for pretesting to be of value there must be a readiness to adjust already planned instruction in response to the results. As much as Dick accepted the virtue of pretesting, he realized he simply did not have the time. (Of course, his wife did. The Federal Government, her rich benefactor, provided her and her colleagues with all the planning time they needed.)

However, the alternative to the pretest, the *preview*, is critical. Dick told his students that their mastery learning classroom was based on an old advertising slogan, "The Best Surprise is No Surprise." He told his students that in other classrooms students might find themselves playing the guessing game, "What's going to be on the test?" But in their mastery learning classroom, no one needed to waste time and energy on sleuthing. He told them they would know at the outset exactly what was going to be on every unit test. In previews, which he'd write out for his students (teachers of younger students deliver their previews orally) exactly what to expect on the final exam. He would make sure they understood by responding to a question. This is important foreshadowing and should always be stated clearly before the first moment of instruction.

For Example, for a high school Government class (the unit on the Presidency):

Prompt and Question: *You will be expected to learn the five constitutional powers of the president and the 3 extra-constitutional powers. Now class, what will be on the exam?*

Answer: *The five constitutional powers and the 3 extra-constitutional powers.*

Teacher: *Correct!*

For a 3rd grade basic writing lesson (unit on end punctuation):

Prompt and Question: *We will be learning the use of three end punctuation marks: the period, the question mark, and the exclamation point. Now class what will be on the exam?*

Answer: *The period, the exclamation mark, and the question mark.*

Teacher: *Correct!*

What is made clear with these previews is that the objective of the class is to help students learn academic material or to acquire skills, not learn to be the Amazing Kreskin or another world famous mind reader. As one can see when using mastery learning, we make no apologies about teaching to the test. If self-esteem is built on evidence of success why shouldn't students be given the same benefit we provide for ourselves when we take golf, tennis, or piano lessons. In those endeavors, we always know the target, we are being taught for mastery, and we get feedback on our successes!

Another major distinction between the deluxe and economy models lies in the type and number of correctives and extensions provided. As a teacher using the mastery approach, Dick committed himself to three additional tasks for each unit he taught. He needed to think through and construct a preview as well as two criterion-referenced tests for each unit. However, he decided that constructing a dozen alternative lessons for each unit on top of that was more than he could manage. Therefore, he settled for a comprehensive one-day "review" that would be given the day following each unit test. This review served as a combined *extension/corrective* for the entire class. Dick felt that it never hurt a student to quickly go over material that was already learned, and that often this type of deliberate review was all that was needed as a reteaching opportunity for those students who didn't achieve mastery the first time. Therefore, in place of the beautifully, preplanned, and artistically tailored extensions his wife had available in the deluxe model, in Dick's economy model still provided students with additional access to their teacher, an opportunity to review their previous work, and the opportunity to use additional time, (much of which they were required to get at home), to prepare for the retest, which was usually given the following day.

While the compromises inherent in the economy model aren't perfect, Dick learned that most motivated students, regardless of their past academic history, could still hit the mastery criteria on the first retest. (See the Jill Jones story at the end of this Chapter to understand why.)

As powerful as the mastery model appears, because many students don't come into our classrooms passionately ready to learn, we, as real world teachers, have learned (often through painful experience) that we need to structure extrinsic rewards into our classroom routines. For that reason we thought it would be helpful to share the approach to classroom management and grading that Dick used with his middle school social studies students to promote motivation for engagement. This approach can be readily adjusted to suit the needs of high school or primary students.

Management and Grading

In a perfect world where all the children have been treated to outstanding schools and teaching, the motivation that inevitably comes from academic success would be all that would be needed to sustain a mastery learning classroom. Unfortunately, none of us is teaching in such a perfect world. The use of extrinsic rewards such as grades, as problematic as they are, is something most of us have had to live with and will be living with for the foreseeable future. Furthermore, many of our students (and their parents) have become so addicted to self-validation through grades that even with the purest of instructional models, extrinsic benefits are often needed to stimulate and sustain student effort.

When Dick introduced the concept of mastery learning to his students, they frequently asked:

1. What if I don't master every unit?
2. Will I have to master everything taught?
3. What if I only learn the mastery material?
4. What are my rewards for going beyond mastery?

There are, no doubt, an infinite number of answers teachers could give in response to those questions. The grading and management system Dick implemented in a 9th grade social studies classroom, was successful. While clearly not perfect, it illustrates many of the compromises and procedures that worked for him. Hopefully seeing how he responded to those predictable student questions will provide you with a starting point. At the end of the chapter we have provided a planning sheet for you use when creating mastery learning lessons (Figure 3.4). When you design a mastery learning lesson, we suggest you craft your own responses to those same questions.

Figure 3.4. Sagor's Grading Policy

Premises:
- All essential objectives must be mastered.
- Everything expected in class has value.
- Intensity of effort is expected.

Requirements:
- To receive credit, the objective portion of each test must be completed with 80% proficiency.
- 90% of all participation grades must be (+)'s
- "A" and "B" grades are earned through performance on the application/analysis assignments or tests.

As shown in Figure 3.4, there were three overriding values that Dick wanted to promote through his grading process. Experience taught him the value of making these three values explicit for his students.

Premise 1: *Everything in class has importance*—Dick began class by telling his students that while only certain things would be tested on the unit exams, everything that was done in class was purposeful. They were told, for example, that their classmates and their teacher valued their input in class discussions, that the insights they might draw from films were also of value, and that their teacher believed that the scope of "world affairs" was much bigger and more important than the small pieces that would be captured on the unit test. For that reason they were told that the teacher expected their full attention and energy on anything and everything done in class as well as with everything assigned as homework!

Premise 2: *Mastery of all essential objectives is expected*—Dick told his students that he had reviewed the course curriculum to discern which specific knowledge and which skills he believed were truly essential for their future roles as citizens and students. Because he deemed these to be essential (e.g., prerequisite for further success) he insisted that they must be mastered. Therefore, the students were told that if they failed to master even a single objective, credit would be withheld until mastery of that objective was achieved. Needless to say, this requirement was often greeted with groans from the students.

Premise 3: *Intensity of effort is expected*—As a teacher Dick had long felt that nothing undermined a classroom culture for at-risk students as much as off-task and low energy behavior. Allowing lacksidaisacal behavior implies to the student (who is deciding whether or not to try) that the task at hand doesn't call for his or her full commitment. Tolerating off-task or low intensity work undermines the self-esteem of the dedicated student and it can make the classroom something less than a meaningful workplace.

Those three core values, therefore, gave rise to his three-part grading system. The system is designed to reward *participation, mastery, and creativity* simultaneously.

Part 1: *Participation*

Everyday and on every assignment students were given a participation grade (+ or –). When a student was present for the entire period, cooperated with classmates, and did as expected with vigor, the student was awarded a "+" for the day. If for any reason a student failed to meet all of the expectations they were granted a "–." These participation grades were prominently posted in the back of the room, identified by student number for purposes of anonymity, at the end of each class session. Homework and all non-mastery assignments were also awarded participation grades. Students knew that in order to pass the course 90 percent of the recorded participation grades must be +'s. This requirement was Dick's principal mechanism for enforcing his desire for intensity and participation in all aspects of the class.

Part 2: *Mastery of the Essential Objectives*

All unit tests had a mastery section that had to be passed (using a criterion level of 85 percent). The mastery section could be retaken as frequently as necessary; however, a student would not be deemed to have completed the unit (and satisfactory completion of every unit was essential for receiving course credit) unless and until that student had reached the 85 percent criteria on that unit.

Part 3: *Learning Beyond Mastery*

This part of the grading system served to reinforce the value of learning beyond mastery. Letter grades were assigned to student work on extension assignments and extension sections on tests. Each unit test had a second section that featured extension/analysis questions. These questions can only be successfully addressed once a student had acquired a foundation of mastery. They were purposefully left open ended and were constructed to be both doable by every student while providing sufficient challenge for the most creative and analytical. The political philosophy test shown in Figure 3.5 is an example of a unit test from a 12th grade government class Dick taught.

Figure 3.5. Political Philosophy Test

You, Law, and Politics Political Philosophy Exam 1A

Name: _____

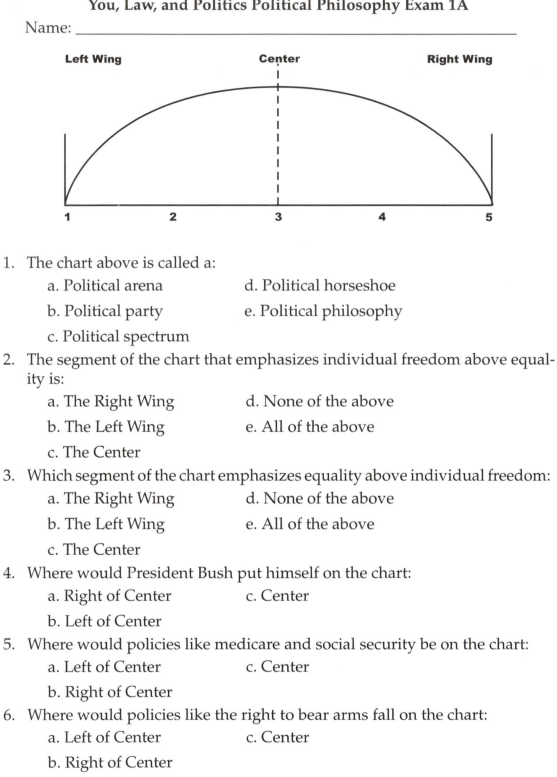

1. The chart above is called a:
   a. Political arena   d. Political horseshoe
   b. Political party   e. Political philosophy
   c. Political spectrum

2. The segment of the chart that emphasizes individual freedom above equality is:
   a. The Right Wing   d. None of the above
   b. The Left Wing   e. All of the above
   c. The Center

3. Which segment of the chart emphasizes equality above individual freedom:
   a. The Right Wing   d. None of the above
   b. The Left Wing   e. All of the above
   c. The Center

4. Where would President Bush put himself on the chart:
   a. Right of Center   c. Center
   b. Left of Center

5. Where would policies like medicare and social security be on the chart:
   a. Left of Center   c. Center
   b. Right of Center

6. Where would policies like the right to bear arms fall on the chart:
   a. Left of Center   c. Center
   b. Right of Center

7. Where would communist governments appear on the chart:

  a. 1   d. 4

  b. 2   e. 5

  c. 3

8. Where would fascist governments appear on the chart:

  a. 1   d. 4

  b. 2   e. 5

  c. 3

9. In the classical sense:

  a. Liberals would be on the Right Wing—conservatives on the Left Wing.

  b. Liberals would be on the Left Wing—conservatives would be on the Right Wing.

  c. Conservatives place the highest value on equality, and liberals place the highest value on individual freedom.

  d. There is very little difference between the moderate left and moderate right.

10. Which side would Rousseau be on:

  a. Right Wing

  b. Left Wing

MATCHING:

11. Rousseau	A. War of all against all
12. Hobbes	B. A Philosopher/King would make the best government.
13. Locke	C. The general should control government.
14. Aristotle	D. Governments should exist to protect individuals' life, liberty, and property.

15. Judicial Review is:

  a. A process that allows the courts to check the President and the Congress.

  b. A process that allows the Congress to check the courts and the President.

  c. A process that allows the President to check the Congress and the courts.

  d. A practice that has nothing to do with checks and balances.

  e. A process that allows the President and the Congress to check the judiciary.

16. Federalism in the United States means:

    a. That most power should reside in the federal government.

    b. That most power should remain with the states.

    c. That power should be shared between the federal government and the states.

17. The President can use his veto power to:

    a. Override decisions of the Supreme Court

    b. Check the power of the Congress

    c. Override constitutional amendments

    d. All of the above

    e. None of the above

MATCHING:

18. Civil Law	A. Regulates behavior between individuals
19. Criminal Law	B. Is the highest law of the land
20. Constitutional Law	C. Regulates the behavior of individuals and the state

ESSAYS

Answer either A or B and everyone should answer C

a. Some modern political theorists have argued that as population increases and civilization progresses governments will have to become more left wing to meet societies' needs. Do you agree or disagree? Be sure to demonstrate in your answer that you understand the difference between the left and the right.

b. Revisionist historians have had fun debating whether the American Revolution was a right-wing revolution or a left-wing revolution, or neither. What do you think? Make sure that your answer demonstrates your knowledge of the system of government that our founding fathers and mothers set up and that you understand what is meant by left- and right-wing.

c. What do you think should be the purpose of our government? What aspects of your answer might other people disagree with? How would you answer their disagreements?

Later in this chapter you will see a set of sample extension assignments that worked successfully with Dick's middle school students (Figures 3.7 and 3.8)

This grading system was designed to provide a guaranteed payoff for any student who was willing to put forth a sincere effort. In order to reinforce an internal locus of control, Dick was determined to avoid rewarding lackadaisical behavior. A grade of C was guaranteed to students who received 90 percent on participation and demonstrated mastery on all essential objectives. Grades of A and B were available to any student who earned it through their performance on the analysis/extension questions and assignments.

At the end of a grading period, most students fell into one of three categories:

♦ The student had mastered all the essential objectives, had done what was expected, and had over 90 percent "+" participation grades. This student received on the report card, the average of the grades received on the analysis assignments or a grade of "C," whichever was greater.

♦ The student had not yet mastered all of the essential objectives at grading time, but had done what was expected and had posted participation grades of 90 percent or better. This student received an incomplete on the report card, which would be replaced by the grade earned on the analysis assignments once the student retook the appropriate tests and met the 85 percent criteria level.

♦ The student had not mastered all of the essential objectives and chose to ignore what was expected in class, e.g., by earning less than 90percent "+" on participation. This student received some counseling from Dick. He was told that while he would not be penalized with a punitive grade (an *F*) because he had made some effort in the class, but because he failed to live up to his part of the bargain, he had forfeited his opportunity to receive credit. In these cases, the incomplete earned was made to stand and the course had to be retaken for credit.

The rationale behind Dick's use of this grading system is twofold. First, it fit the philosophy of mastery learning, but at least as important it helps him reinforce an internal locus of control. (Locus of control is discussed at greater length in Chapter 7.) Fundamentally, the only thing that distinguishes the student who receives credit from the student who had to retake the course was the student's *own* decision to do or to renege on his/her part of the bargain. In this system access to credit is not based on ability, learning rate, or cognitive development. Rather, access to credit is based solely upon the student's conscious decision to try! Figure 3.6 is a handout Dick provided to his twelfth grade government students at the beginning of the semester to outline his expectations. While the language on this handout should be adjusted, in our opinion most of the same issues could/should be covered with children from the third grade on upwards.

Figure 3.6. You, Law, and Politics Course Expectation Sheet

There is a great deal of material to be covered this semester in *You, Law, and Politics* and a variety of techniques will be used to present the information to assist you in learning all the essential concepts. In all probability the most valuable learning experiences will result from our class discussions and activities that are based on the reading assignments and class work. Therefore, the success of this class will be largely determined by *your* preparation and participation.

I will expect you to do the assignments, pay attention, and participate. In return, you should expect me to be prepared for class, to make sure the material and classroom activities are made as interesting as possible, and to be enthusiastic in my teaching.

Because I want you to feel at ease and enjoy the class my expectations and rules are few, but I expect them to be followed as though they were carved in stone.

1. Be in class and ready to work when the tardy bell rings.

2. Show respect to the instructor and the other members of the class.

3. Feel free to help your classmates but do not take credit for work that is not your own.

4. Maintain the same high standards of conduct and performance whether or not the regular teacher is present.

Grading

The grading system for this class is based on a philosophy called "mastery learning" and an assumption that by staying enrolled in this class you have committed yourself to being an active participant in the learning process. Mastery learning is based on the belief that anyone can learn anything if they give the effort, are given enough time, and are provided with adequate instruction.

If you promise (by signing this form) to put forth the effort and time that will be necessary to learn the material then I will guarantee you a passing grade.

To receive an A for the quarter you must

♦ Score at least 80 percent on the object portion of each test*

♦ Meet at least 90 percent of the participation requirements**

♦ Have an A average on the essay portions of the tests and projects.

To receive a B for the quarter you must

- ◆ Score at least 80 percent on the objective portion of each test*

- ◆ Meet at least 90 percent of the participation requirements**

- ◆ Have a B average on the essay portion of the tests.

To receive a C for the quarter you must

- ◆ Score at least 80 percent on the objective portion of each test*

- ◆ Meet at least 90 percent of the participation requirements**

To receive an Incomplete (Inc)

- ◆ Fail to score at least 80 percent on the objective portion of each test by the end of the quarter*

You, Law, and Politics

*   You will have the opportunity to retake every test until you reach a score of 80 percent

**   Participation requirements:

    A.   Be in class on time.

    B.   Do not cause a disruption of the class.

    C.   Complete assignments and tests.

For each day and on each assignment where the participation requirements are met you will receive a (+), if and when they are not met you will receive a (–).

Semester grades are computed as follows:

    First quarter: 40 percent of the grade

    Second quarter: 40 percent of the grade

    Final Exam and final project: 20 percent of the grade

I plan to achieve an _____ grade this semester in *You, Law, and Politics*.

_____(Signature)

High-Status Knowledge

One of the consequences of the way that we have traditionally organized schools is that students in the advanced tracks are exposed to a different (and according to researcher Jeanne Oakes (1985) and Anne Wheelock (1992), a more interesting) curriculum than are students in the general, vocational, or remedial tracks. This practice often begins subtly and early (often in the first grade). Most of the instructional time in the lower tracks is spent on the rudimentary basics, while the academically "elite" students get a chance to explore literature, current social issues, as well as scientific and technological matters of import. The cumulative effect of this can be enormous. Top students feel challenged, stimulated, and are given reason to believe that they are being prepared to take over the reins of society. Meanwhile low achieving students find their "basic" curriculum to be sterile and irrelevant to their young lives and with little promise to help them in the future. Ultimately many discouraged learners conclude that weighty matters of social concern are beyond them and more properly lie in the domain of those who are more academically advantaged. In too many cases this leads the discouraged learner to cognitively and then later to physically drop out of school. Perhaps worse, later in life these same individuals feel unable to meaningful participate in social affairs. Consider for a moment the low levels of political participation by adults who were once educated in our lower tracks. The hidden curriculum of tracking encourages both high and low achieving students to internalize a view of their "worthiness" as a consequence of their placement in our socially stratified curricula.

One solution to this dilemma is to educate all children in heterogeneous classes and to utilize the mastery learning approach to ensure success for all. However, unless we are careful this strategy can backfire. If the mastery learning strategy results in a skewing of the curriculum toward only "knowledge and recall" objectives, then we can anticipate several legitimate objections. For starters, if the curriculum focuses entirely on "knowledge and recall," the curriculum for the advantaged students will have become as sterile as the old tracking one was for the disadvantaged. Furthermore, the intellectual stimulation needed by the at-risk student will not be achieved by simply placing them in physical proximity to their advantaged classmates. Rather, the way to provide this is by immersing the at-risk student in the broad richness of the "high status" curriculum.

It is for this reason that we strongly believe that every mastery-learning unit ought to be followed by an enriching concluding assignment to be completed by all the students. Culminating assignments differ from the extension experiences completed by the faster learners during the two-day time-out periods following the check tests. When properly constructed, these activities require students to work at the top end of the cognitive taxonomy (analysis, synthesis, and evaluation) and there should exist no single correct answer to the problems posed. Figures 3.7 and 3.8 are examples of culmination assignments that Dick used successfully with his heterogeneous classes of 9th graders studying "World Geography."

Figure 3.7. Redrawing the borders of the Middle East

This activity is designed to give you the opportunity to review all your knowledge about the Middle East, analyze the facts at your command, and come up with creative solutions to regional problems.

In actuality, borders are developed a number of ways. The advances of conquering armies, the stipulations of peace treaties, natural barriers; such as mountains, rivers, and deserts, and nationalistic and cultural forces are but some of the ways boundaries are established for independent countries. Oftentimes the ways boundaries are set do not reflect the actual needs and desires of the inhabitants of a region and frustration and strife are the result.

Although your knowledge about the Middle East is not exhaustive, it should be sufficient to enable you to develop some theories and make some judgements on how countries might be rearranged to provide a more peaceful and prosperous region. In analyzing this problem, consider the things we have discussed in class, for example:

1. Nationalism and the location of different national groups

2. Languages

3. Religions

4. Natural resources, such as oil

5. Sources of water

6. Seaports

7. Agricultural land

You should also consider other factors that *you* think are significant, such as:

1. Population density

2. Physical barriers, like mountain ranges

3. History of the people

Use your textbook, atlas, and any other resources you think will be helpful. You may ask questions of your classmates; however, you must make your own decisions. As you think through these issues, you may want to do some tentative drawing on your map in pencil. After you have considered other factors, you may wish to rearrange some of your decisions and alter your map.

Make some notes for yourself about why you've drawn the borders that you have. Tomorrow, you will have to explain these decisions on your test.

You should add items to your map that help illustrate the reason for your decisions. For example, you may want to place cities and oil fields on your maps.

This is your opportunity to play *world-leader*. You can pull the strings. Use your wisdom and enjoy yourselves.

The assignment in Figure 3.7, "Redrawing the Borders of the Middle East," was delivered as a handout to a class of students along with a 2' × 3' outline map of the Middle East and a box of colored pencils. This assignment wasn't given until every student had mastered the locational and political "facts" (the essential objectives) of the region. Although the problem presented, producing a viable plan for peace in this troubled region, has eluded hundreds of highly capable world leaders, Dick found it was not beyond the capabilities of his 9th grade students, even those who were deemed "slow." Some of his more creative students prepared essays and maps that ought to have been sent to the UN Security Council, while other students produced products that reflected little more than an understanding of the status quo. Dick still delights in recalling one particular free thinker who decided to carve a 500-mile canal from the Red Sea to the Mediterranean, decided to line it with desalinization plants and consequently turned the Middle East into the bread basket of the world. While figuring out what was the appropriate grade for this piece of work was difficult, Dick sure enjoyed reviewing it!

The Congo River Trip assignment shown in Figure 3.8 is similar in its open-endedness.

Figure 3.8. The Congo River Trip

(This extension was assigned to students after they had demonstrated mastery on the geography of the Congo River basin.)

River Trip Paper

Below are some points to consider when researching and writing your imaginary river trip paper. You are free to use any procedure to research, outline, and write with that feels comfortable, however, I think you may find this suggested strategy helpful.

1. Feel free to work with other students in doing research, analyzing maps, and preparing to write your paper, however, each student must write their own report on the trip.

2. You might start out by tracing the route of your river from its source to its mouth on the attached outline map. Make a note of which countries and the parts of those countries that the river passes through.

3. Begin writing an outline by writing down the names of each of the countries that your river passes through and then leaving about a half page blank after each country. Whenever you find a fact that you will want to mention in your story, write that fact under the country to which it applies.

4. Use the index of your text to look up references to your river and the countries that it passes through. The text will give you a lot of information about the type of things one might imagine seeing from a river boat.

5. Find the course of your river on the maps on pages A6–A19 of the atlas in the back of the textbook. Those maps will give you a lot of information on the type of weather, vegetation, people, etc. that you may see on your trip.

6. Review the course goals and invent ways to use them in your story. Here is an example of Goal 90. "Africa has many natural resources largely exploited by foreigners." You might write, "As our boat slowly floated down the Zambezi River past the city of Livingstone we noticed a huge chromium mine in the distance. When the mine came into clear view, we saw a huge sign saying Minnesota Mining and Manufacturing Company. I turned to my companion and said "Mr. Sagor was right after all! Africa's resources are being exploited by foreigners!"

7. Once you feel that you've collected enough facts to write your story you should review your outline and number your facts in the order that you want to include them in you story.

8. You are now ready to write. Make your story creative and entertaining. Use your imagination but stay true to the geographical facts.

9. If your papers are exceptionally good, I'll send them to the Disney World in Ouagadougou to use when building their Jungle Boat Ride.

Note: When writing your papers, use your best English composition skills. Pay the same attention to spelling and sentence structure as you would in an English assignment.

Again students weren't asked to tackle this assignment until after they had already mastered the physical geography of the Congo Basin. At that point each child was deemed capable of tackling the same rigorous assignment. Although the students were only thirteen years old, even the students with the worst academic histories were able to take a stab at writing a creative journal of their river trip.

The virtue of these types of culminating assignments is that they have no top end. A James Michener would not have been bored by Dick's Congo River assignment (and Dick claims he wouldn't have been intimidated by his 1,500 page response) and Colin Powell would not have found the Middle East peace plan project to be beneath him. By integrating "open-ended" extensions into a K–12 mastery-learning classroom a teacher can get the best of all worlds, mastery of the basics, and the exploration of the high-status issues, which call for higher-level thinking. Furthermore, on a practical level these higher-level assignments provide a defense against the claim that heterogeneous mastery learning classrooms must include a "dummying down" of the curriculum. What parent of a gifted child could argue that assignments such as these are beneath their child?

The following Think and Do Exercise is an opportunity for you to explore the applicability of this approach for your classroom.

Think and Do Exercise: Developing a Mastery Learning Unit

The purpose of this exercise is to give you experience with the development of a unit of instruction utilizing the "mastery learning" process and culminating with a powerful "no upper limit" extension.

Using the worksheet provided in Figure 3.9, make plans for a unit that you will be teaching in the near future.

After completing the worksheet ask yourself these questions:

♦ Will all of my students be able to master the mastery objectives using this plan?

♦ Will all of the students find this unit interesting, challenging, and stimulating?

♦ If the answer to either of the above was no, how could the unit be changed to make it more successful?

Figure 3.9. Mastery Learning Unit Planning Guide

I.   Unit Topic:

II   Duration:

III. Learning objectives (what knowledge or skills must the learner possess at the conclusion of this unit?)

1. _____

2. _____

3. _____

4. _____

5. _____

6. _____

IV. Preview (how will you alert the students to the precise objectives listed above?)

_____

_____

_____

_____

V.   Initial Instructional Activities (What specific activities will the learner be engaged in during this unit?)

_____

_____

_____

_____

_____

_____

_____

VI   Check Test (how will you test for inital mastery? What will be the criteria for mastery?)

_____

_____

_____

_____

VII.   Correctives (What will you do to reteach the students who have not demonstrated initial mastery on the check test?)

_____

_____

_____

_____

VIII.   Extensions (What will you do to extend and enrich the learning of the students who achieved mastery on the check test?)

_____

_____

_____

_____

IX. Retest (What provisions will you make to retest the students who have not demonstrated initial mastery?)

_____

_____

_____

_____

X. Culminating Activity (What activity will you have the students engage in at the conclusion of the unit that requires the use of the mastered material? Is the activity open-ended? Is the activity at the evaluation, synthesis or analyis level?)

_____

_____

_____

_____

Before we end our discussion of mastery learning and its role in the development of feelings of competence let's examine the case of a discouraged learner who had her first experience with mastery expectations during her senior year of high school.

Mastery Learning and the At-Risk Student: A Case Study

Jill Jones was a nice enough senior girl. On the surface she appeared to fit in well at school. But, if one looked deeper one would see someone whose academic self-esteem was so low that she had all but completely disengaged from the academic learning process. Her transcript reflected a determined effort to avoid all academic challenges. She endeavored to earn all her required credits through remedial classes. Then, in the second semester of her senior year the computer threw her a mean curve. It placed her in a mastery learning section for the required government class. Jill was clearly not thrilled to have a teacher who was committed to the mastery learning approach.

Jill sat in the back corner, an emotionally safe spot in the room. Here she was safe from eye contact from her teacher and the knowing stares of her classmates. She endured the teacher's lectures on political philosophy and even passively participated in the simulations the teacher had designed for the class. Despite this surface compliance, a voice deep inside kept telling her, "This isn't working for me. I can't learn this!" So she sought the help of her counselor.

Ms. Hays, the counselor, was a kind and caring mother figure and it was easy for a student like Jill to seek her assistance. She approached the teacher expressing empathy and concern for this vulnerable student. She kindly pointed out that Jill was a very sweet girl who would really like to do well in class, but she was not very capable academically. In fact, Ms Hays shared that Jill suffered from a slight learning disability and consequently had been assigned to remedial classes throughout her school career. She said that Jill was convinced that this class was just too difficult for her. Ms. Hays ended her appeal by asking, "Is it all right for me to transfer her to an easier class?"

As a mastery learning zealot, the teacher took up this challenge with delight! The term "easier class" was to him like a red flag to a bull. It was obvious to the teacher that this well-intentioned counselor needed to be converted. Consequently, he proceeded to subject her to the same lecture he had given to his students the first day of class. In inspirational tones he invoked the words and intonations of a Jesse Jackson and told her how if one "could conceive it, and believe it, one could achieve it!" Before completing his sermon he explained his process for retaking tests with no penalty. Feeling rhetorically overwhelmed, the counselor retreated to the security of her office.

A week later, precisely one day prior to the first unit test, Jill approached her teacher, "Mr. Jones, I can't do this work. It's too difficult. I'm a "Special Ed" student." The teacher didn't flinch even though he was angered by her internalization of that negative academic stereotype.

He asked Jill if she had been paying attention. She said she had. He asked her if she had done the assignments. She said she had. Based on that information, he confidently assured her that if she simply studied from the study guide he had provided and reviewed her notes, she would do quite well on the exam. She looked at him with a mixture of intimidation and disbelief, but said, "O.K., I'll try."

The teacher was disappointed but not discouraged by Jill's 40 percent on the mastery portion of the unit test. After all, she wasn't the only one to bomb on this class's first "mastery" test. Based on the class's performance Mr. Jones suspected he hadn't taught the unit as well as he thought. After spending a class period going over the exam, he dismissed the class and Jill appeared at his desk. Her eyes were swollen and her light demeanor now seemed quite heavy, as she said, "I told you I was a "special ed" student. I can't do this stuff!" But as a "true believer" in mastery learning, Mr. Jones would not be dissuaded. He simply gave her a pep talk and told her to study from the material covered in the review and on her corrected exam. He assured her if she did that she could be confident of passing the retest. He was that certain that she would succeed the second time around! There was reason for his confidence. The retest he had designed was just a reorganized version of the first one.

However, even Mr. Jones began to have doubts when he saw Jill's second test. She posted a mere 45 percent. When she approached the teacher after class the day he returned the second exam, her eyes were filled with tears. What began as a noble instructional experiment was now taking a human toll. Somewhat shaken in his confidence, he mustered all the empathy at his command, and told Jill that he still had confidence in her. He knew she was trying and he truly believed that ultimately she would prevail. He asked her if there was a time when we could meet for tutoring. Luckily, the very next hour was Mr. Jones preparation period and Jill was working as an aide in the counseling center.

For twenty minutes Mr. Jones quizzed Jill. It was much like the use of flash cards in preschool. Once twenty minutes had passed Jill could recite the answers to the first two exams with perfection. Mr. Jones beamed and Jill looked relieved, but could she hit the 85 percent criterion on the third test?

Ten minutes later Mr. Jones entered the counseling center with test number three. He told Jill to relax, to remember what she'd learned, and do her best on this version of the same test she had failed twice before. Apparently, the coaching worked. Jill posted a 90 percent and she beamed like a cross between a child who just received her first puppy and someone who had won an Olympic gold medal, which in some respects she had. Remember, Mr. Jones had never low-ered his standards! She had learned that very material she had thought only a day earlier was too difficult and beyond her limited grasp. She now knew she could handle this "difficult material."

Jill stayed in Mr. Jones class for the entire term, ultimately receiving a B+, and she never once had to endure another retake. After that first experience studying became much easier for her. Her success occurred once she was able to silence the disconcerting static from a voice in the back of her head saying, "No I can't, no I can't!" Instead she could focus on the task at hand with the knowl-edge and confidence of *a little engine that could.*

References

Block, J. H. (Ed.) 1971. *Mastery learning: Theory and practice.* New York: Holt Rinehart and Winston.

Block, J. H., Efthim, H. E., Burns, R. B. (1989). *Building effective mastery learning schools,* New York: Longman.

Bloom, B. S. (1976). *Human characteristics and school learning.* New York: McGraw Hill.

Bloom, B. S. (1984). The search for methods of group instruction as effective as one to one tutoring. *Educational Leadership,* 41 (8): 4–18.

Conrath, Jerry. (1986). *Our other youth.* Gig Harbor, WA: Our Other Youth.

Knight, T. (1981). Mastery learning: A report from the firing line. *Educational Leadership,* 39 (2):134–136.

Gardner, H. (1993). *Multiple intelligences: The theory in practice.* New York: Basic Books.

Guskey, T. R. (1985). *Implementing mastery learning.* Belmont: Wadsworth.

Mathews, J. (1988). *Escalante: The best teacher in America.* New York: Henry Holt and Com-pany.

Oakes, J. (1985). *Keeping track: How schools structure inequity.* New Haven: Yale University Press.

Sternberg, R. J. (1997). *Successful intelligence.* New York: Plume.

Wheelock, Anne. (1992). *Crossing the tracks: How untracking can save America's schools.* New York: The New Press.

4

HELPING STUDENTS DEVELOP AND CONSTRUCT THEIR OWN FEELINGS OF COMPETENCE

A Constructivist View of Knowledge

Ralph Tyler, the noted curriculum theorist believed that all curriculum models needed to take into account the nature of the learner as well as the nature of the knowledge to be learned if it is to be effective (Tyler, 1949).

Additionally, to be effective, Tyler believed that instructional models ought to be consistent with the overall aims of schooling. To Tyler this meant above all else, being supportive of democracy. Although, you, the reader, may not wish to define the mission of schooling in this way, few will argue that one of the primary aims of schooling ought to be the development of students who see themselves as competent members of their society. To accomplish this goal, it is essential that students feel a sense of competence regarding their ability to function independently outside the confines of the schoolhouse.

The label most often attached to this outcome is "life-long learner." Every educator wants their students to continue to study and learn beyond the end of their formal education and do so for the sheer sake of knowing, rather than for the extrinsic rewards of a grade or the demands of an employer.

The difference between mastery learning and developmental constructivism can be traced to the two fundamentally different *views of knowing* on which they were built. Mastery learning proponents see "knowing" as a commodity that can be passed from teacher to learner while constructivists believe that knowing is an inherently individual process that cannot be transmitted, but, must be constructed by the learner him/herself.

Developmental constructivism, therefore, builds on the learner's interests, curiosity, and prior experience. One of the more powerful arguments in favor of this approach is that by building on the learner's interests and involving the learner from the outset in the decisions on the what's, when's, and where's of the unit, intrinsic motivation becomes much easier to achieve (Kohn, 1999).

Constructivist Learning Expectations: Subjective View of Knowledge

Constructivist learning, as we are presenting it, uses the child's innate interests and the learner's current level of understanding as the platform upon which further learning is built. For constructivists, the purpose of the classroom experiences is to help bring to light the thinking of the individual student, allow the student to be challenged, and ultimately have the student construct new and better understandings. It is believed that the "constructivist" process will consequently result in deeper understandings of the relationships present in the world (Piaget, 1973; Phillips, 1996; Kamii, 1989).

These deeper understandings will allow the child to go beyond recalling correct answers and instead invites the child to construct meaningful conclusions on their own. It is through this independent reconstruction that children come to see themselves as competent.

Unfortunately too many students fail to receive the benefits of this model because their teachers inadvertently overlook crucial key elements. It is understandable why this occurs. In recent years, the focus for many school systems has been on getting through material rather than on what the students should be expected to get from their educational experience. Whether teaching from a mastery learning or constructivist model, if our goal is having the student believe in his/her own competence then the focus of both the teacher and learner must continuously be on what the *child understands and is able to do independently* rather than what was *covered by the teacher*.

Often we teachers, feeling pressed for time, push ourselves to "cover" material rather than allowing "learning time" to be flexible. This is unfortunate as both of the instructional models presented in this text, to be done properly require that the time available for learning must be variable from learner to learner.

On the surface both constructivism and mastery learning appear to demand more time, than most teachers feel is at their disposal. Certainly it is true that a teacher can "get through" material faster when they are simply "covering it." If, however, our goal is to create opportunities for our students to experience genuine feelings of "competence," then we need to have our students develop high levels of proficiency.

As was the case in our earlier discussion regarding mastery learning, the focus here will be on the self-confidence building capacity of developmental constructivism and its potential for helping our students become enthusiastic life-long learners.

Developmental Constructivist Learning

Perhaps the foremost pioneer in the Constructivist framework is Jean Piaget. While working for Binet Laboratories on the design of IQ tests, he recognized certain patterns in the incorrect answers given by children at varying age levels. This became the launching pad for what later became his lifelong passion that forever changed the world of education. Prior to Piaget, children were seen largely as small adults with random incorrect ideas. Education's role, therefore, was to replace this random wrongness with correct thinking.

Piaget saw this model as flawed. He recognized that new ideas inevitably grow out of the previously held ideas of the learner. This is why he makes the point that all children begin their learning in an egocentric fashion, and only later become less egocentric. This broadening of perspective comes as the environment around them challenges their ideas.

Although Hollywood has not yet made a folk hero out of a teacher who based his or her teaching on developmental constructivist methods, we can still draw from the examples of the mastery learning teachers discussed in the last chapter (Marva Collins and Jaime Escalante) in order to compare and contrast these two models. Both Escalante and Collins came to know the children they were working with very well, including the knowledge that the students brought with them into the classroom. They used their understanding of the student's prior knowledge as a taking off point or, as a platform to teach from. Beyond these things, the methodology of these "mastery learning teachers" differs significantly from the practices employed by developmental constructivists.

Similar to the Mastery Learning Model the foundation of developmental constructivist pedagogy is the proposition that "all children can learn anything." However, where these frameworks part is how they address the four variables that were discussed as essential for mastery learning.

According to Piaget, cognitive development must precede learning. Therefore, until a child has developed the mental capacity to understand the relationships in the content, the child will be unable to truly make sense of those relationships. Therefore Piaget concluded, a child who lacks "readiness" would be limited to a mere memorization of contextually meaningless "facts." Researchers in both cognitive psychology and brain physiology have compiled significant evidence, supporting the idea that brain development leads to learning (Healy, 1990; Caine and Caine, 1997; Sylwester, 1995). We will discuss the implications of this at length in the next chapter, where our focus is on the development of belonging.

For now let's examine the four, key mastery learning variables and contrast them to other processes, specifically those employed by the constructivist teacher when endeavoring to assist the development of student proficiency.

Piaget used different terms than Bloom and Block when he discussed children's intellectual development. The four Mastery Learning variables (prerequisite skills, time, quality instruction, and motivation) are not mentioned directly by Piaget. While our constructivist colleagues will likely recoil at the use of these terms in our discussion of mental development, we felt that the best way to help you, the reader, in understanding the essential differences between these two models is by discussing both processes utilizing the same terminology. However, before we force Piaget's ideas into a foreign vocabulary, we feel it best to introduce Piaget's own terminology.

Assimilation and Accommodation

According to Piaget intellectual development occurs through the twin processes of assimilation and accommodation. We *assimilate* information into our existing understanding of the world. Everything that fits within that understanding is then learned easily, and later, given enough time, we are able to reconstruct this knowledge (that we already possess) in greater depth. That is to say that the knowledge that we have worked through in our own way and which we now see as consistent with our world view can be better understood. We suspect that all of us share the experience of attending a college class and leaving a lecture feeling that none of the material presented was truly new, but, rather it seemed as the same old stuff, repackaged. On such occasions we might feel that the lecture made sense to us even before it was delivered. Although some new information may have been offered, the relationships between the relevant information were quite predictable for us.

Contrast this to another experience that is also common, a lecture that seemed to turn our entire world on its head. For example, when the instructor presented ideas that fundamentally challenged the way we had seen our world. Such experiences force us to *accommodate* ourselves to this new perspective.

We now ask you to return to the example of the dissonance experienced by the high school students, discussed in Chapter 1, who while struggling with their negative views of school had to reconcile those negative attitudes with their new and very positive experience of tutoring the younger children. The high school students had a view of the world, which was well established (assimilated), but it didn't fit with this new data. The dissonance was created when they found it hard to "accommodate" a new more positive experience (with school). Human nature forced them to attempt to "assimilate" a positive experience into their previously established negative world view.

From their reactions—asserting to their friends that certain aspects of school were now "OK"—we can see that they had begun to accommodate a new more positive view of school.

Now having introduced the concepts of *assimilation* and *accommodation,* let's compare a Piagetian approach to the mastery learning process.

Motivation

Most Piagetians view discussions of motivation as implying a system of externally provided rewards and punishments. For this reason many constructivists will dismiss mastery learning as another purely behaviorist motivation model.

In the Preface we discussed the importance of intrinsic motivation (for the goal of building life-long learners) and we both strongly agree that learning is ultimately deeper and more meaningful, when and if, the learner is motivated from within. Clearly it takes considerable energy and effort to engage in the deep thinking that is necessary to *accommodate* new, or to construct more complete, ideas. Therefore, a critical first step is motivating the learner to invest their finite energy in the construction process.

In constructivist classrooms (our Model 2 approach) the teacher uses the child's prior knowledge/interests as the source of motivation. Most of us have had the experience of lying awake at night with our minds mulling over a problem that we very much want to solve. That experience illustrates that when learning matters deeply to us, we can be highly motivated, reflecting on it long after exiting the classroom. There are two sayings that Jonas is fond of invoking when discussing this with his "learning theory" students.

"All meaningful learning is voluntary" and

"All children can and do learn, they just may not learn what we want them to."

A Case Study

When Jonas thinks about student motivation he is reminded of a young man in his 8th grade physical science class. He was not usually actively engaged and often spent time daydreaming during class. One day the student began an activity involving the operation of electric circuits and seemed successful in figuring out how they worked. After he had discovered how to wire electric bulbs in a variety of ways (including parallel and series), Jonas asked the young man if he had a hallway at home where one could turn on the light from one end of the hall and then turn the same light off at the other end? Then Jonas asked if he could wire a similar 3-way circuit using a battery, a bulb, two switches, and several wires. The student worked on this problem diligently for the remainder of class and for the next two class periods. On Friday he asked Jonas if he could borrow the lab materials and bring them home for the weekend. When Monday morning arrived as Jonas was walking to class, the student, excitedly yelled down the hallway, "Mr. Cox I've got it! Without a doubt this child was feeling *compe*tent!

Later Jonas found out, from the boy's sister, that he had worked diligently on this project all weekend, ignoring invitations from his friends to go out and play. Apparently, he also missed several meals. It isn't often that we see students getting this excited about their schoolwork. To Jonas this illustrated the importance of finding engaging questions for his students. While we all know that intrinsic motivation can be a powerful force for learning. We often forget that it takes the right questioning, probing, and challenging from the teacher in order to activate this power. But, as this case demonstrates, when a child is motivated to solve a problem, he or she often brings considerable fortitude and mental resources towards finding a solution.

Prerequisite Knowledge

There is an important difference between the two approaches presented in this book (Mastery Learning and Developmental Constructivism) in their view of skills and knowledge. As you recall from the last chapter, when we were discussing Mastery Learning, the need for prerequisite skills was stressed. Here again we will emphasize the importance of prerequisite knowledge. This is because skills and knowledge in a constructivist classroom grow out of the student's need for a deeper understanding of the material and the content in which it is used.

Here, it is worth considering Kamii's work with children "reinventing arithmetic" (1989). Her students knew the answers to the math problems they were assigned. The teacher's goal was not to have the students find the right answers but to invent the right procedure. This would enable the learners to make greater use of the learning in the future. The children "reinvented" arithmetic by developing their own algorithms. By doing it this way they were able to apply their understanding in new and more difficult situations recognizing that the standard procedure was simply one way of solving problems rather than *the* way to solve problems. The skills they constructed grew out of both their need to know and their prior knowledge of the number system. Imagine the feeling of competence that develops when a child is able to apply their invented algorithm successfully with novel situations.

Like mastery learning teachers, constructivists believe that a child's ability to solve problems is contingent upon prior knowledge and, therefore, will be limited by what they do not yet know or do not yet fully understand. Where these approaches will differ is their interpretation of why pre-requisite knowledge might be lacking. Mastery learning teachers often argue that these deficiencies exist due to inadequate instruction (an institutional pathology), while developmental constructivists would posit that these knowledge gaps result from an absence of experience and reflection necessary for accommodation and assimilation or neurological immaturity (an environmental or clinical pathology).

To appreciate this distinction let's consider a classic Piaget interview; one regarding the conservation of liquid volume. Here the child establishes that two containers have the same volume of fluid (see Figure 4.1).

Figure 4.1

After the child agrees that there is the same volume in each vial, the interviewer then pours the contents of one of the vials into a taller and skinnier vial providing a strong visual miscue for the child (see Figure 4.2).

Figure 4.2

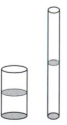

The child, who possesses an under-developed understanding of volume, will usually believe that the tall slender vial now has more water. This child has assimilated this information incorrectly into their framework. They believe that if it looks bigger (more volume) it is bigger. It takes time and experience for a child to overcome this egocentric perspective and accommodate themselves to a new understanding of the world. This perspective is not easily overcome as the following story will demonstrate.

Early in his career Jonas took a class in human development where he was asked to give conservation tasks to children of varying ages. He was interviewing his niece Cassia with his own son Aaron, looking on. Cassia being older and well along in her cognitive development answered that the two quantities were, in fact, the same. Even in the face of the visual miscue she held to this view. Aaron being much younger was foiled by the miscue in spite of the modeling of his older cousin, whom he greatly admired. He seemed embarrassed for her as he attempted to correct his older cousin saying "No Dad, this has more, look."

It is deeply held among developmental constructivists that conservation concepts in their various forms are not a pieces of knowledge that can be transferred to the child rather they must be constructed by the child. In fact if we tell the child he/she is wrong, that these are the same quantity, we are telling the child that he/she should not trust what they know to be true. The child will hear us asking them to abandon what they currently know to be true about the world and accept what he/she have been told. This hardly builds feelings of competence!

For this reason developmentalist's feel that rushing students to the accommodation of these basic concepts can be detrimental. (Kamii, 1998; Fischer & Kennedy, 1997; Fischer & Bidell, 1998, Phillips, 1999)

So, if directly teaching these ideas is detrimental to the child then what is the role for the teacher in cognitive development and learning? What should "high-quality instruction" look like in light of this danger?

High-Quality Instruction

Often constructivists are accused of holding a laissez faire educational philosophy. However when done well constructivist teaching provides a rich environment for the growth of young minds and the building of a sense of competence. However, if constructivism is implemented poorly, it will result in students failing to learn much of anything and takes on the look of child abandonment.

For this reason there are several things that teachers need to consider when planning to use this model.

- ♦ Considerable care needs to be given to structuring the learning environment, to building the right atmosphere for learning, and to carefully thinking through the structure of the discipline. Specifically, adequate teacher attention must be paid to the relationships between all the pertinent facts. Therefore, becoming a constructivist teacher requires developing a deep understanding of the relevant knowledge students are expected to acquire and as well as the skills to manage and guide student learning through questioning.

Take for example "classification," a skill that is deemed critical in most science curricula. Most teachers unfamiliar with the development of the concept of classification in children would not think to ask if there are more cows or more animals in a set of farm animals. It is too obvious for those of us who long ago came to understand part/whole relationships. We might answer by saying "of course there are more animals because cows are part of animals." Yet this part/whole relationship may not be understood by many primary school students (Phillips, 1996). In the same vein many adolescents struggle to understand more advanced forms of classification and serialization like matrices and Venn diagrams.

These pieces of knowledge or logical structure are potential land mines for an unaware teacher. Assuming that what is obvious to the teacher is also is obvious to the child is a dangerous mis-step. As stated earlier the unintended outcomes (frustration and feelings of incompetence) can be terribly detrimental to the students.

It is beyond the scope of this book to attempt to cover all of the details of cognitive development (see Phillips, 1996 for a more complete discussion). However, there are several things a sensitive teacher should be aware of that can be profitably discussed here.

- *First*, ask more questions of your students. In fact, try and answer questions you are asked with questions of your own and listen carefully to their responses.

- *Second*, if a student's response seems illogical to you, stop and consider what the child must be thinking, ask the child how he/she arrived at the answer, and then pose a question that challenges these assumptions.

- *Third*, whenever possible encourage students to find answers to questions by having resources at their disposal. For example we believe manipulatives in math class should be available to all students from pre-K through college. As adults we often need manipulatives, drawings, or other representations to assist when we are problem solving, yet as teachers we sometimes deny children these same tools.

- *Fourth*, don't treat the curriculum as a body of facts to be covered, many of those "facts" are, in reality, convenient fictions and half-truths that have been used to try and make sense of the world.

There are few facts that we all agree students need to know. While in this time of "accountability" it is important for the students to know the things that "state standards" expect them to know, we must also consider the cost of turning a kid off to school if we fail to make important connections to the students' views, interests, and cognitive abilities.

One of the first hurdles a constructivist teacher must overcome is student buy in. The students must understand that the rules of a constructivist classroom are different from the norm. Many traditional management systems, which many older students have come to expect, are based on manipulation. The teacher coerces the student to do things they might not wish to do in an effort to turn them into educated adults. How often have we heard a classroom teacher saying, "I know you don't want to learn this, but you will need this later when you are in...."

We are reminded of a time when one of Jonas' seventh grade students who, after listening to him explain that the students would be involved in setting classroom expectations, replied:

"No, Mr. Cox, That is not how it works, you are supposed to make the rules and then we are supposed to break them."

This child was reluctant to connect the learning environment to what he wanted out of life. This student was comfortable being disempowered (the critical importance of empowerment will be discussed in Chapter 7). For many reasons it is tempting at times to offer students rewards for buying into the classroom process. As we stated earlier, we are not such purists as to believe that an external reward could never be appropriate, however, there is no doubt that the excitement of gaining knowledge itself is always the strongest motivator in the classroom.

This is why it is essential for the teacher to find out what interests their students and then look for strategies that will connect those interests with the mandated curriculum. When we begin with their interests, connect the curriculum to things they are motivated to learn, there will be much less need for control. While much less control is needed in a "good" constructivist classroom the learning environment still needs structure. Jonas usually asks his students what structure they will need to maximize their learning in the classroom. A complete discussion of this issue takes time from class, but the two or three periods invested is time well spent! During a class discussion, the observant teacher will usually spot those instances when students are trying to pull one over on the teacher and can usually steer the discussion back to maximizing learning. It is absolutely crucial that a constructivist teacher always remains focused on what is to be learned within the classroom. They must assess and monitor constantly. This is done so the teacher can refocus the student's attention back to investigating the important relationships present in the content of the class. This may require constant negotiation and renegotiation between student interest and external curriculum demands.

Allowing Enough Time for Learning

No teacher who has been trained in Physical Education would expect a student who has not reached puberty to be able to lift heavy weights. Their muscles and bone structure simply are not physically ready for such a task. Fortunately, it is relatively easy to tell which students have begun this time in their lives and which have not, and then allowances can be made accordingly. Why then do we expect all children to be cognitively ready to be on the same page at the same time in mathematics or other academic classes? It seems clear that some will be developmentally behind others. In fact, there is considerable evidence that as students age the developmental lag among students of the same age will grow wider rather than narrowing. That is to say that the developmental spread among the students in first grade is less than the developmental spread a representative group of adult or in a "homogenous" high school classroom.

Reconciling Developmentalism with High-Stakes Testing

Differences in cognitive development ought to give pause to proponents of high stakes standards-based reform. If a student is not biologically capable of succeeding at a task, yet, state policy forces the school to label the child a failure because his/her brain has not yet had a chance to fully develop, the consequences can be both severe and unfair. Such actions can lead to feelings of incompetence and can place an otherwise capable child into the ranks of the at-risk. For this reason, we encourage educators in a position to control "high stakes" to be judicious when holding children accountable for skills and attributes for which they may not be developmentally ready.

Developmentally ready or not, each of your students will be engaged in high-stakes testing on a regular basis. So what is a teacher to do?

Guidelines for Reconciling with Standards and High Stakes Assessment

- ◆ *First*, review the pedagogical recommendations that the each of the national organizations made when they published their recommended standards. Many of these recommendations are in line with constructivist pedagogy.

- ◆ *Second*, for most of the year, *spend your time and energy teaching for depth of understanding using good constructivist techniques*. The time to cover the trivial details or what we call "factoids" that will be on the "state test" is just before the test itself (this is because isolated facts are quickly forgotten).

♦ *Third*, make certain that you teach test-taking strategies to your students. Go over the format of the test and all the tricks of good test taking.

♦ *Fourth*, do all you can to relieve as much of the stress as possible. Brain based research has demonstrated that high levels of stress is debilitating to student learning (Sylwester, 1995).

A Final Case Study: The Constructing of Scientific Knowledge

One day Jonas was speaking to his nephew, a precocious middle schooler at the time. He began asking the child about his understanding of science. Knowing that these particular concepts were difficult for his college students to grasp, Jonas was amazed at how well this young man was explaining the way the world worked. He explained how the tilt of the earth produced the seasons and how the mass of trees comes from carbon in the air. Jonas worked his way through many of the questions from a "science misconceptions pretest" that he regularly gave his university students. The 7th grader did remarkably well. In fact, he did far better than all but a few of Jonas' college students.

How is it that this child with less formal education and life experience dealt so readily with these concepts? Jonas asked his nephew how he knew so much and he said "When I hear something I compare it to what I already know and if it fits then OK"— "if it doesn't (fit what I know) then I have to change what I know to make it (the new idea) fit." Jonas was struck with what a succinct definition of *assimilation* and *accommodation* this was. Thrilled with what he was hearing, he pressed on. The next question was how we on Earth could visually see the phases of the moon. At first the young man stumbled explaining the shadow of the Earth as the cause of a new moon. Then he picked up three objects and labeled them the Sun, Earth, and Moon and proceeded to work out the relative positions of each body until he had explained all of the phases. An amazing demonstration of constructing an understanding of how the world works. Perhaps more importantly was the feeling of competence and pride that this young man derived from being able to explain the understanding he had "constructed" for his "old" uncle.

Mastery Expectations

Whether circumstances call for the use of mastery learning or using constructivist methods, our expectations for student performance should always be the same. If our goal is building feelings of "competence" then there can only be one criterion for acceptable work. Simply put, what we have told our students is that *no piece of work is done, until it is done well!*

This is what we mean by *mastery expectations*. We do not endorse punitive grading and for this reason neither of us uses the "F" grade. Instead we tell our students that we want them to produce work that they can be proud of. For this reason, we offer feedback, encouragement and coaching along the way. But, until the work meets a mastery standard, it is deemed incomplete. Only when we, the student and the teacher, can agree that it is a quality piece of work, will we award a grade or grant credit. Throughout this book when we use the phrase *mastery expectations* we are referring to these high standards not the mastery learning instructional model.

Concluding Comment

Our at-risk students develop their academic self-esteem through their experiences in our classrooms. In conventional classrooms many students learn the material and learn to have confidence in themselves as learners. But other students get left behind. For them schooling becomes a never-ending confrontation with their shortcomings. Once failure becomes a habit, the student has two options: drop out to avoid the pain and/or internalize low expectations for him/herself. This need not be the case!

When teachers adopt the belief that all students want to learn and can learn and then commit themselves to using strategies that will provide their students with concrete evidence of their proficiency, the students will be the beneficiaries. Whether circumstances call for the use of mastery learning methods or inviting students to engage in the creative construction of knowledge, the feelings of competence that result will provide students with one of the most powerful components of resiliency.

References

Caine, Renate, & Caine, Geoffrey (1997). *Education on the edge of possibility*. Alexandria: ASCD.

Fischer K. W., & Kennedy, B. (1997). Tools for analyzing the many shapes of development: The case of self-in-relationships in Korea. In E. Amsel, & K. A. Renninger (Eds.), *Change and development: Issues of theory, method, and application* (pp. 117–152). Mahwah, N.J.: Erlbaum.

Fischer, K. W., & Bidell, T. R. (1998). *Dynamic development of psychological structures in action and thought*. In R. M. Lerner (Ed.), & W. Damon (Series Ed.), *Handbook of child psychology: Vol. 1. Theoretical models of human development* (5th ed., pp. 467–561). New York: Wiley.

Healy, Jane (1990). Endagered minds: Why children don't think and what we can do about it. New York: Simon and Schuster.

Kamii, Constance (1989). *Young children continue to reinvent arithmetic*. New York: Teachers College Press, Columbia University.

Kohn, Alfie (1999). *The schools our children deserve*. Houghton Mifflin.

Phillips, Darrell (1996). *Structures of thinking: Concrete operations*. Dubuque: Kendall Hunt.

Piaget, Jean (1973). *To understand is to invent: the future of education* New York: Viking Compass Books.

Sylwester, Robert (1995). A celebration of neurons: An educators guide to human brain development. Alexandria: ASCD.

Tyler, Ralph W. (1949). *Basic principles of curriculum and instruction*. Chicago: University of Chicago Press.

5

THE B IN CBUPO: HELPING STUDENTS DEVELOP A SENSE OF BELONGING

As educators, our goal is to enable students to feel CBUPO (feelings of competence, belonging, usefulness, potency, and optimism) in every school experience. In the last two chapters we reviewed two curriculum models both of which have strong potential to help make the school experience more successful for students. Implementing those strategies ought to go a long way toward developing feelings of competence, the "C" of CBUPO.

In this chapter, we will focus on the "B" aspect of the CBUPO equation, as we shift our attention to building a sense of *belonging*. One would expect individuals to feel a greater sense of belonging in an institution in which they have had a history of success. Because of this, the curriculum models, discussed in the preceding chapter, could be viewed as tools for the development of a greater sense of belonging at school. That notwithstanding, we must remember that although some persons have been successful at school, it does not necessarily follow that they will feel welcome, valued, and come to believe that they are an important part of the social fabric of their school or community.

The Hidden Curriculum

Many factors, some deliberate and some coincidental, oftentimes conspire to deny children the feelings of belonging that all human beings innately covet. For example, when we segregate classes for at-risk students through "tracking" programs, clear signals are telegraphed about who belongs and who doesn't. Unfortunately, while de jure racial segregation may be a thing of the past, the isolation of at-risk and special needs youngsters continues to increase. Other subtle but observable patterns like the gender and race of the teaching and support staff also send powerful messages to students. Whether intended or otherwise, these messages form what is often called the hidden curriculum (Figure 5.1).

Figure 5.1. The Hidden Curriculum

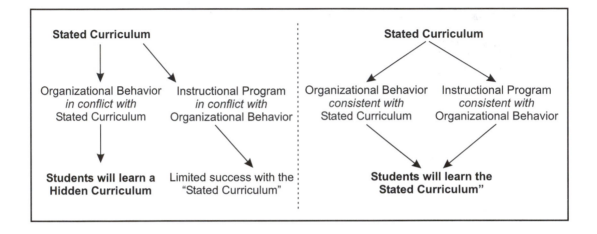

Figure 5.1 illustrates the effect that professional and organizational behavior can have on the outcomes achieved by our students. The mythology of schooling holds that learning flows cleanly from our stated objectives through our instructional strategies to learning the established curriculum. However, in reality, it isn't always that simple. Regardless of what our objectives may state about our values, our organizational behavior frequently is at odds with our stated goals. While we may want to believe that the intentions captured by our lofty goals are, in fact, realized by our students, we know this is often not the case. As the research on modeling powerfully reminds us, our students learn more from what we do than from what we say. The reality is that our stated goals are realized and understood *only* as they are experienced by our students as patterns of organizational behavior. For example, we may say that we want the children to feel cared for and valued, but if the institution of which we are a part treats students in an impersonal and officious manner, the insensitivity experienced by the children will ultimately teach more than our stated humanistic aspirations.

If we can't recognize our stated curricular goals in our students' behavior, it is usually because they have internalized the lessons of the hidden curriculum, not the stated curriculum. One of the things we know with some certainty about defeated and discouraged learners is that they don't feel part of the mainstream. Their alienation from school and from the school's predominant social system makes it unlikely these students will ever develop the feelings of *membership* that Wehlage (1989) and his colleagues found to be so essential for students' well being. Without feeling a sense of *membership*, the other two legs of Wehlage's success equation, *engagement* and *commitment* are hard, if not impossible, to develop and maintain.

For this reason, schools that wish to be effective in reaching at-risk students must consciously focus on how their students are experiencing and interpreting patterns of organizational practice. This is critical if we want to better understand the messages our organizational behavior is sending. For example, when school authorities agree to send at-risk students to separate and low-prestige pullout programs for special services and/or remediation, when they continue to staff math departments only with men and fill primary school faculties almost exclusively with women, they must recognize that they are continuing to teach future generations a particular and biased view of who belongs and who doesn't.

Michelle Fine and Nancy Zane (1985) conducted extensive research into the problems faced by low income women in the public schools. They found that the hidden curriculum posed some very specific problems for this category of at-risk youth. Their research helps us understand why these students tend to have high drop-out and low reentry rates. They pointed out that the values promoted by the school through its organizational structures and expectations force these young women to deny critical aspects of their selfhood. If and when those conflicts become too frequent and too great the students tend to feel alienated and disengaged. They concluded,

> For these same young women, attending public high school typically means learning to dismiss the material complexities and relationships which enrich and entangle their lives; ignoring the rich split consciousness with which they see the world and engaging instead in a single, linear view of mobility, progress, and justice; and practicing to protect (or not) their bodies from "invasion." These three meanings of public schools, unacknowledged and essential to institutional coherence, place low-income young women in positions of academic, economic, and social jeopardy. To presume any different is to reproduce the ideology which believes that those public institutions we call "public schools" are gender, race and ethnicity, and class neutral. Instead we must realize that those institutions serve in ways that could empower but that currently, more typically, betray those young women who most believe, who most need, and who most suffer from the absence of a high school degree.

Multicultural Education
and the Hidden Curriculum

Significant numbers of students from non-majority cultures experience problems similar to those documented by Fine and Zane (1985) in low income women. This is particularly the case when students from non-European cultures attend schools that appear to recognize only one cultural tradition, that of the European majority.

When the holidays, foods, language, and literature of only one culture are shared and glorified at school, and when those practices seem to exclude the experiences of a child's extended family, then for the non-majority child, attending school becomes a constant reminder of a child's outsider status. Such feelings won't and shouldn't be expected to lead toward increasing feelings of "belonging" or "membership" at school.

On the other hand, schools that have been successful at engendering feelings of belonging for all their students have found ways to rejoice in the cultural diversity represented by their student body. Several years ago Dick visited Ingraham High School in Seattle, a school that due to Seattle's desegregation program enjoyed a wonderfully complex multicultural student body. His student guide told him, "We celebrate New Years every week: Tet New Year, Cambodian New Year, Chinese New Year,...." The posters on the wall and the displays throughout the school paid tribute to the truth of that statement. Cultural diversity worked at Ingraham because it went beyond the superficial ceremonial trappings and was integrated into the academic program. Dick witnessed the inclusion of multiple perspectives in numerous classroom discussions ranging from world literature to social studies to science. At this school, being culturally different meant you were especially valuable and needed, since you had something unique to contribute to the education of the community.

In recent years it has become vogue to declare that schools should "celebrate diversity." However, many thoughtful observers have begun to question that premise. After all, they argue, celebrations are usually held to recognize what has been accomplished. Diversity in many schools is not evidence of an accomplishment; rather it is a simple reflection of demographics. Critics are now pointing out that the focus of our efforts should not be to declare that "we are good just because we are diverse," but our focus should be on making use of the potential benefits of diversity to help create a future that will make us better and different than we are currently. It was that type of *multicultural curriculum enrichment* that was being accomplished at Ingraham. All students could point out specific examples of how they were learning more and better as a result of the multiplicity of cultural perspectives in regard to art, music, history, literature, philosophy, etc.

Five-year-old children come to our schools having had their basic needs for love and survival met by their first teachers, the members of their immediate and extended families. If, at school, they do not recognize the culture of their home and neighborhood they will begin to feel as though they are being sent to spend six or more hours a day in an alien land. That feeling, if allowed to persist, has significant and far reaching consequences. These consequences can be most severe for children from African American, Native American, and Mexican American backgrounds when these children attend schools that are dominated by the values and artifacts of the majority culture. John Ogbu, an anthropology professor at the University of California, and himself of African ancestry, explains that the perspective of these groups differs sharply from that held by members of other "voluntary" immigrant groups. Ogbu argues that although the members of "voluntary" immigrant communities may desire to be accepted by the majority culture, they recognize that they have chosen their minority status and that they chose it for a reason (usually to improve their economic or political welfare). Furthermore, members of voluntary immigrant communities will likely contrast their experience in America with that of those that were left behind in the old country. This "old country" referent serves as a reminder that things "could be worse."

While Ogbu's theory holds true for "voluntary immigrants" he points out this is not the case for many African, Mexican, and Native American students. This is because these students don't come into our schools and other institutions with a referent to the old country. Rather, their referent is to the previous generation, a group that generally hasn't been treated very well by our schools or our other public institutions. If these students are going to "buy in" or commit themselves to "membership" in our schools they will need to be shown a compelling reason to do so. Otherwise they will resent and fight the fact that their mono-cultural school looks, feels, and acts differently from the culture that they have grown accustomed to at home, in Church, and in their neighborhoods. If they cannot recognize themselves, their elders, and their community in our classrooms, then why should they believe that these schools truly have their interests at heart? As any student of Maslow (1970) would point out, asking these children to abandon their community, the initial source of their foundation of love and security, is asking these vulnerable children to give up the impossible.

Extending Membership to All

Clearly, if the price of membership in school means abandoning one's culture, values, and beliefs, many youth will see those costs as too high. If we want these youth to see school as a place for them, we need to be prepared to respond to their issues. What are these issues? Minority youth come to school asking implicitly, even if subconsciously, two questions about us and our programs.

♦ Does this school understand and appreciate who I am and where I come from?

♦ Will participation in this school program help someone like me in the future?

The answers to those questions are provided through a gestalt of our materials, language, and behavior. But how should we manage this gestalt effectively?

Clearly the most powerful thing we can do to help students see their schools as reflective of and responsive to people of their cultural background, is having a fully integrated professional staff. When a student encounters elders at school who look, talk, and interact with them in a comfortable and familiar manner it helps them to see the school as an institution by and for "our" people. But, what if that is not the case? How can schools staffed by members of a majority culture still convey a truly "invitational" stance to minority youth? To answer that question let's examine each of the two key questions separately.

Does this school understand and appreciate who I am and where I'm coming from?

If individual students do not recognize themselves in their teachers' speech patterns, examples, assigned literature, or curriculum, then the students are left to conclude that either nothing in their background is of educational relevance or their cultural history is so unique as to be foreign to the school authorities. Either explanation makes students feel like strangers in a strange land. If, on the contrary, the students regularly encounter examples and illustrations from their own community, have their experiences regularly solicited and brought up and utilized to explain concepts, beliefs, and values, then the students are more likely to feel personally validated.

Ultimately, there is no substitute for having adults from the local ethnic community in the school collaborating with the staff. Students' behavior and attitudes change when their classrooms are filled with the same parents and community members whom they see outside of school. Often, school administrators are heard complaining about the difficulty of getting minority parents to come to school. The fact that it may appear difficult does not make it a goal worth abandoning. Parents will come to school when and if they feel welcome and needed. Overtures to parents from disadvantaged groups must be made personally, sincerely, and with respect for the constraints (financial and logistical) on their availability. Some schools have made arrangements for bus passes while others have developed car pools for parents without ready transportation. The key is letting the community know that the school will do whatever it takes to get these important people into the classrooms. Around the country many elementary schools have begun using "family literacy" programs whereby parents come to school to learn to read and use standard English alongside their school-aged children. Later in the day these same parents repay the system for their continuing education by assisting in the classroom as parent volunteers. That type of adult presence in the schools tells the child that the school is not an alien and hostile institution to people from his neighborhood and culture.

How can you tell if your classroom or school appears to be mono-cultural or multicultural? A place to start this examination is with a mini-cultural audit as described in the following Think and Do Exercise.

Think and Do Exercise—A Classroom Cultural Audit

This activity will help you determine whether your classroom is a place in which students from different cultures will feel a sense of belonging. This five-step activity can be done by teachers individually or by a faculty collectively.

Step 1. On a typical day tape record your lessons and collect all the instructional materials that you utilized.

Step 2. Review your lectures, explanations, and/or discussions, and your materials and handouts for examples and/or illustrations drawn from non-majority cultures.

Step 3. *This is optional.* Share your findings with colleagues in an attempt to see if there is a pattern of multicultural or mono-cultural perspectives in your school or classroom.

Step 5. If you are not satisfied with the inclusiveness of your instruction and materials, invite some culturally different parents to review your data and to make suggestions for incorporating multiple perspectives into your program.

This brings us to the second question on the mind of students from non-majority cultures.

Will participation in this school program really help someone like me in the future?

Many children from non-majority cultures enter our schools suspicious that commitment to our programs will not ultimately pay real dividends for them. As we may recall from our own childhoods, we operated on an assumption that our future lives would be much like the lives currently lived by our parents and extended families. Many children from what Ogbu calls the "involuntary immigrant communities" (people whose minority status is a result of exploitation, slavery, or conquest) come to school suspicious that joining up and pursuing the goals of the school won't provide any greater benefits for them than it did for their elders. As a result, many of these children see themselves paying a heavy price in committing to the school's expectations, especially if it means abandoning their peer culture. For example, African American males often share a very real fear that complying with school expectations will brand them as Oreos (black on the outside and white on the inside). They wonder if it's worth subjecting themselves to this ridicule only to be the subject of discrimination and blocked opportunity in the future. If we want these children to feel that they "belong" at school, these perceptions pose a very real problem, and if we wish to offset them, we will need very powerful solutions.

One radical and controversial intervention being proposed in several cities is the creation of single gender academies for the education of African American males. In these schools boys can be taught by African American men and are immersed in a culture of black male achievement.

Another less controversial alternative that has been employed successfully in Washington, D.C. is to make strategic and systematic use of adult classroom volunteers. In this project, schools have recruited successful professional men from the community to be regularly scheduled classroom helpers. The goal is to provide real concrete models of success for young African American students. When three times a week young children come in contact with black lawyers, stockbrokers, accountants, professors, social workers, and engineers, they can realistically grow to believe that these are goals and lifestyles that they too can aspire to achieve. When these adult African American models give testimony to the virtues of participation and commitment to school expectations that testimony will have a much greater chance of being perceived as legitimate.

At Charles Wingate High School in the Crown Heights section of Brooklyn, school authorities attacked the future payoff question aggressively. Wingate serves a 100 percent poor and minority population. It is a school where academic performance had historically lagged behind most of the city's other high schools. Now students who attend Wingate's "excelsior academy," a program for students who are reading more than three years below grade level, are, upon matriculation, placed in career clusters of their own choosing. Here they receive basic math and language instruction in the context of that career. For example, students in the medical careers cluster receive their math, reading, and language instruction on medically related issues in special classes reserved for students preparing for those careers. These classes are co-taught by employees at the King County Medical Center, which is across the street from the school. Consequently, students at Wingate are left with no question why they were studying what they were studying and where it might take them if and when they apply themselves and succeed. It is no surprise that Wingate has a drop-out rate far below the city's average and a college matriculation rate well above the norm.

Because many children of poverty and other at-risk youth come from homes and communities torn by strife, chemical abuse, and dysfunction, many in the school community have come to believe that the homes of these children have little to offer the child and even less to offer the school. It is even argued by some that the best thing we can do is to remove these children from their parents and communities and re-socialize them. This viewpoint, regardless of how sincerely articulated, is inevitably flawed. As Marva Collins once accurately pointed out to Morley Safer of CBS Television's "60 Minutes,"

"I have not seen a parent yet who wants to see their children fail. To the contrary, I know how proud these (poor black) parents are of their children. Invariably it is just the opposite, the very poor black parent wants their children to excel."

Even when at-risk children come from immediate families that cannot provide adequate physical or emotional support, that does not mean that the children cannot and will not benefit from the resources of their extended cultural family. If we want children to honestly feel and believe that our schools are for them, we will need to take affirmative steps to show them that the culture and experiences that they bring into the schools are valued and are utilized when we choose how to teach our curricula.

Valuing Students by Valuing Their Interests

One rarely discussed, but significant benefit of the constructivist model is that basing instruction around the students' interests, especially the questions they bring to the learning, helps a great deal in building a sense of belonging for our at-risk student population. We are making an empowering statement to our students when we meaningfully involve them in selecting the content they will be experiencing. By building curricula around matters of personal interest a natural connection is forged between the students and the curriculum. When this occurs the students begin to see the school curriculum as a means to acquire the type of knowledge they value; knowledge that will help them solve the problems they are facing now rather than offering them solutions to some anticipated issue they might face in the future.

As was illustrated in the Wingate High School example, basing classroom experiences on individual student interest often provides a huge payback in terms of student motivation. Managing this is easier to accomplish than one might think. When students are actively engaged in studying things of personal interest, accountability becomes less of an issue for the teacher. In traditional instruction accountability is almost always a teacher responsibility. Quality control is exerted from outside the learner.

In the constructivist classroom, where the students' questions provide the focus for learning, it becomes the students' best interest to hold themselves accountable. If students enter the classroom with a desire to learn, then teachers can allow their role to shift from taskmaster and quality control officer, to personal trainer. In this capacity, teachers' primary function becomes offering help and assistance to students so that the students can hold themselves accountable.

In this era of standards we often hear it claimed that we simply don't have the luxury of time to allow the focus of school to shift to the learners' interests. This is a realistic concern, since the officially sanctioned and tested curriculum may not appear (on the surface) to be of particular interest to the at-risk child. This creates a dilemma for the teacher. If we maintain a single minded focus on the officially sanctioned and tested curriculum the result will likely be increased student alienation. When students are alienated their minds disengage. Ironically, this often means the more we focus on the tested curriculum the less likely the students will learn the material.

While it may not be possible to cover as much material when we are building instruction around student interest, experience has shown that it is possible for students to emerge from a year of constructivist learning retaining a good deal more knowledge than if the same material had been covered without reasonable efforts to connect it personally to the learner.

We are reminded of an advertisement run by a company selling automobile auto filters. The add concluded with this comment "The choice is yours; you can pay me now or pay me later." The message of this commercial was that making a small investment on the front end often saves us a great deal on the back end. Following the steps of the Think and Do Exercise below, will help you prepare your students for state-mandated exams while still building their learning around individual student interest.

> ### *Think and Do Exercise—*
> ### *Reconciling Developmentalism with Standards*
>
> 1. List the concepts or skills that your students will be held accountable for on the mandated achievement test.
>
> 2. Share this list with your students and tell them that all of these concepts will need to be adequately addressed during this school year
>
> 3. Using broad parameters, invite your students to select an area of personal interest for their inquiry.
>
> 4. Using appropriate questioning strategies assist your students with the development of a plan for investigating their area of inquiry.
>
> 5. Have your students (if your students aren't old enough to do this themselves, you can do this for them) identify which, if any, of the concepts/skills on the "mandated list" will be addressed through the completion of their plan.
>
> 6. If several of the "mandated" concepts will be addressed, have the students indicate this with a checkmark on the list of the mandated skills.
>
> 7. If none of the mandated concepts will be addressed ask the student to see if their inquiry plan might be adjusted to include some of the mandated skills. Using your best questioning skills assist your students in finding ways to incorporate these skills into their plan.
>
> 8. Tell the students that later in the year you will have to conduct teacher directed mini-lessons focused on any mandated concepts that haven't been addressed in their individual inquiries. This is to alert them of the benefits of finding ways to address the mandated curriculum.
>
> 9. As the year progresses have the students monitor whether they are addressing all of the necessary concepts.
>
> 10. In the months immediately prior to the mandated test review all of the required concepts and directly teach the one's that were not addressed in the student inquiries.

In the last chapter we saw how the "pay me now or pay me later" phenomena works with mastery learning. Time spent gaining early mastery of concepts inevitably reduces the need for greater investments in remediation later on. In curriculum design we are confronting a similar issue. If we elect to save time initially by imposing content on the student, we will need to cope with the problems of low motivation and lack of retention later. However, if we invest in gaining student interest and commitment at the front end, there will be far less need for us to nag, prod, and/or cajole the students later. More importantly, the increased retention will reduce the need for extensive review and remediation later.

This condition is all the more true when dealing with defeated and discouraged learners. Consider how many of our at-risk kids know an enormous amount about Pokemon cards or have a mastery of trivia regarding their favorite musicians, bands, or athletes. This fact demonstrates that many of these students are not lacking in an ability to learn, more often they simply lack the desire to learn what they understand to be our official curriculum. The key challenge for us is to instill a sincere desire for learning the required material. This is often best done, by helping the learner to clearly see the connections between the knowledge the school wants them to learn and their own interests (this is the purpose of the strategy suggested in the above Think and Do Exercise).

But how one may ask, are students' interests in Harry Potter, Britney Spears, or butterflies going to help them learn the material that they will ultimately be tested on regarding Geography, the properties of light, or Newton's laws of motion? At first glance it might not seem that logical connections could be made among these items. But, this may be because *we* are lacking skills in "convergent thinking."

Each of the pieces of knowledge mentioned above (Harry Potter, Brittany Spears, butterflies, geography, properties of light, and Newton's laws of motion) can be connected. Even childrens' interest in short-lived pop phenomena can be used to illuminate important content. For example, Britney Spears travels all over the world and meets all kinds of people on her tours. Could her itinerary be an object of study? Where was she born and when did her ancestors immigrate here? Or, how does the lighting on stage affect how she looks? Are some hues of lights better for her than others? It this consistent with all singers? For the student interested in butterflies, could the migration routes of butterflies be the hook that gets the student interested in places around the world? Could insect flight be explained using Newton's laws of motion? The creative and caring professional can artfully bring even these seemingly disjointed pieces of knowledge together, though it does require time and energy.

Jonas was known for having many different animals in his classroom. Among them was a collection of snakes native to the Pacific Northwest. These snakes were a very high-interest item among his middle school students. Jonas often used their interest in the animals to lure the students into learning what they previously had thought was unimportant knowledge. Many defeated/discouraged learners found that they connected with the animals and through this interest they found a home in Mr. Cox's Classroom. One of Jonas' young Oregon geographers found it necessary to deeply examine a state atlas to find locations in Oregon where he might find a California King Snake. Another student was enticed to study temperature graphs after doing some reading on how to hibernate, breed, and incubate the eggs from various species of snakes. Many students who were hesitant to give public speeches enjoyed making presentations on what they found out about "their" animal to the lower grade students housed in a neighboring building. Other students found themselves constructing graphs revealing the food eaten and weight gained by different animals. Several students reported discovering important relationships regarding how energy moves through an ecosystem.

Every one of these skills and pieces of knowledge grew from the child's interests and then used that interest as a catalyst for motivation. By engaging students this way, they began working with a sense of purpose and developed a sense of connectedness with the school as a learning organization.

The most important thing we want the reader to take from this discussion is that when we ignore connecting the learners' interests to the learning expected, we are likely making things worse for many of our most at-risk students. As was discussed in Chapter 1, we already know that many of these kids come to school with doubts regarding whether or not they belong and consequently the traditional schooling process contributes to their feelings of alienation. If our approach to standards adds to our student's view of schoolwork as synonymous with doing someone else's work, it will only exacerbate any preexisting alienation. With motivation depending largely on one's feelings of belonging and having a sense of "membership" at school, then few instructional issues will be as important as helping our learners see that schoolwork is "their work."

Learning Styles and Developing Feelings of Belonging

Nothing may be more personal to an individual than the way in which he or she learns most comfortably. Our predominant learning style is such a natural and integral part of our being that we are seldom even conscious of it. But when our style doesn't fit the environment in which we are expected to learn, we infer that we don't belong.

If you are a student who prefers to learn in a manner that is compatible with the way your teacher teaches you most likely feel very much at home in class. In fact, school might feel so natural to you that you might even feel that classroom activities were designed with you specifically in mind. Conversely, if your natural learning style differs dramatically from your teacher's favored approach, you might very well feel like the proverbial fish out of water. No matter how hard the teacher tries, you just don't seem to understand.

Think and Do Exercise—Mini-Exploration of Learning Styles

Ask some friends the following questions, and note the differences in the responses you receive.

1. When going somewhere for the first time, do you

    A. prefer to have a map drawn for you, or

    B. prefer being given a list of directions.

2. When being evaluated for a grade in class, do you

    A. prefer to do a group project that will be holistically graded, or

    B. prefer to take an individually graded objective short-answer test.

3. When learning new material, do you enjoy

    A. doing simulations and role playing, or

    B. reading primary source material, viewing films, and following a study guide.

While question 1, the preference for maps or step by step directions, may seem to be merely an oddity, answering questions 2 and 3 frequently unleashes significant emotional reactions from colleagues. If we as professional adults consider being exposed to an uncomfortable evaluation system as alienating and/or emotionally frustrating, think of the impact that constantly being confronted with instructional strategies and expectations that don't fit can have on students.

Gregorc Style Delineator

Anthony Gregorc (1985) is one of a number of theorists who has analyzed the relevance of learning styles to school performance. His approach asks us to consider two dimensions to our style preference, each of which is relevant to the structuring of learning experiences. The first dimension is our preferred mode for taking in information. Here Gregorc makes a distinction between those who prefer to receive data initially through direct experience (concrete learners) and those whose preference is to acquire new knowledge through the use of symbols (abstract learners).

concrete ↔ abstract

The second dimension pertains to how we go about making meaning out of data once we have taken it in. Here the contrast is between those who prefer to organize data and ideas systematically in accord with an established schema (sequential learners) and those who are more comfortable constructing meaning through what may appear to be an idiosyncratic relationship amongst ideas and thoughts (random learners).

$$\text{sequential} \leftrightarrow \text{random}$$

Those two continua lead to four learning style preferences according to Gregorc: concrete-random, concrete-sequential, abstract-random, and abstract-sequential (Figure 5.2).

The concrete-random is a person who takes in information through direct experience and makes meaning of that data in an idiosyncratic fashion. The concrete-sequential also prefers to take in the data through experiential learning, but has a need for an established and clear framework in order to make meaning. The abstract-random is most comfortable acquiring information through symbolic representations (words, numbers, and pictures) and then draws understanding through personal associations. Finally, the abstract-sequential prefers data entry through symbols but wants to use an established structure to draw understandings.

Figure 5.2. Learning Style Diagram

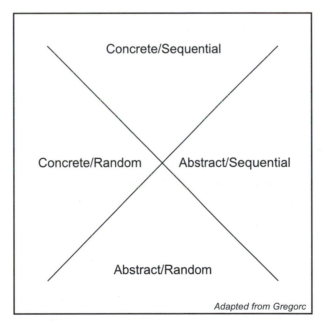

Adapted from Gregorc

You can see why sequentials have a preference for directions, while randoms feel more comfortable with maps.

Gregorc's research indicates that most people have a profile that emphasizes one of these preferences over the others although everyone has within them some facility with each style. Occasionally a person will have a profile that is absolutely and perfectly balanced between all four styles.

An Illustration—High School Physics

Regardless of what level we currently teach at, we all share the high school experience in common. If learning style seems irrelevant to you, try and recall the two physics courses taught in most large comprehensive high schools. One physics course is generally taught in the science department and is considered to be among the most academic and intellectually challenging subjects offered at the school. Students in physics generally hold the highest intellectual status in their schools. However, most of the objectives of the science department's physics class are also taught in the vocational education department under the lowly title of "auto mechanics." Although we are reluctant to admit to esteeming the academic proficiency of science students more than that of vocational students, everyone knows that we do. Yet, a case can be made that the principles studied, the mastery required, and the reasoning expected in both courses is fundamentally the same. The actual differences may reside more in the expectations regarding student learning style utilized by the instructors.

In the science department's physics class, the usual instructional process has the students beginning by reading a chapter from their texts. Having done so (generally as homework), the students are introduced to the mathematical formulae and concepts that explain the phenomena being studied, e.g., friction, pressure, temperature. After reading the chapter and familiarizing themselves with the key concepts, the physics students will be invited to witness a classroom demonstration performed by the teacher, applying the phenomena under study. As a culminating experience, the students might be asked to perform and write up their own laboratory demonstrations of the concept. Let's contrast this to the vocational student's experience.

In the auto shop, students generally begin their inquiry by tearing apart an internal combustion motor. Each student will have the opportunity to take apart a motor and move a piston up and down through the cylinder. Physically they will be able to experience the impact of loose or tight valves, fresh or worn seals, etc. Later, their teacher will take them through the technical manual, where what has just been directly experienced is illustrated and explained in a methodical step by step procedure. The culminating part of this sequence usually involves the teacher lecturing the students on the general principles and formulae that govern the delivery of power in the internal combustion engine.

When instruction is concluded both groups of students understand the dynamic relationships between temperature, pressure, and friction equally well, although the route that took them to that understanding was fundamentally different. Imagine what might have occurred if the typical "auto mechanics" student had been expected to learn this material in the manner of the "physics" classroom or vice versa?

Generally, we would predict that the vocational student would feel uncomfortable, perhaps even incompetent if placed in the physics class. Being asked to interpret abstract formulations independent of any direct physical referent would likely prove very difficult. Likewise, the physics student might well feel as though he were all thumbs if he found himself in the vocational class. Is this an artifact of intelligence or just an illustration of two intelligent young people who came to the study of the same material with fundamentally different learning styles?

Often it is observed that defeated/discouraged learners thrive in art and vocational classes. This is occasionally interpreted as evidence that the material in those classes is of greater personal relevance to the students. Furthermore, it may be inferred that the intellectual demands made of students in these disciplines are more modest than in the "academic" classes. It is worth considering that this may not be the case at all. It is more likely that in art, music, and vocational education, the experiential and practical learning style of these youth are legitimated, while in academic classes only the abstract learner's attributes are valued.

Another example is the child who has tremendous difficulty getting started on traditional composition assignments, but after a field trip to the zoo can write fluently about his experience.

Figure 5.3 illustrates some of the different instructional approaches that appeal to different learning styles when teaching a unit on advertising.

Figure 5.3. Alternative Learning Activities

Unit: Advertising

Goals: Students will:

1. Become aware of propaganda techniques.
2. Learn how to introduce and market an item.
3. Understand the five myths of advertising.
4. Become more aware of consumerism.
5. Become aware of careers in the field of advertising.

Possible learning activities for each learning style as presented by Anthony Gregorc.

Abstract sequential

1. Describe the history and growth of the advertising field in the past fifty years.
2. Interpret the meaning of the phrase *honesty in advertising.*

3. List myths about advertising.

4. Devise a theory for the recent changes in prime time commercials.

5. Research each advertising technique.

6. List careers in the field of advertising.

Abstract random

1. Create a taste test for the public on a new product.

2. Devise and conduct a survey about what consumers want in a fast-food restaurant.

3. Write a jingle for a product.

4. Write, then role play a commercial.

5. Design an bulletin board about advertising.

Concrete random

1. Brainstorm many ways in which advertising influences people in their daily lives.

2. Create and design a new product and its logotype.

3. Describe the types of products consumers might buy in the year 2004.

4. Write a poem or story about how toothpaste became popular.

5. Design a board game to teach facts and information about advertising.

6. Identify 25 products by their logotypes.

Concrete sequential

1. Design a storyboard using sequential procedures.

2. Write a computer game about advertising.

3. Design a wall display showing a past advertisement, a current advertisement, and a future advertisement for the same product.

4. Make a collage of advertisements from various magazines by classifying them according to an advertising technique.

5. Take a field trip to an advertising agency.

In his work with teachers of at-risk learners Jerry Conrath has inquired into the preferred style of teachers and students.

Conrath has been asking teachers at his workshops to identify their own learning preferences. Additionally he has asked them to identify the style preferences of the "specific" at-risk students in their classes who "appear to be the slowest, who achieve the least, and with whom they have the most conflicts." His findings, reported below, were startling.

	Teacher	At-Risk Student
Analytical	28%	7%
Intuitive	28%	20%
Practical	17%	54%
Experiential	27%	19%

Conrath points out that this means, "Over 50% of the kids who apparently learn best through practical applications, trial and error, and experimentation, are identified as slow, achieve the least, and get involved in more conflicts with their teachers." He adds that

These identifications are made by teachers K–12, who take classes and workshops on improving their skills in working with discouraged learners. What must the figures be from adults who want to keep avoiding these kids? (p. 25)

Helpful Responses to Learning Style Differences

Ever since educators became sensitized to the existence of different learning style preferences among their students, there has been discussion about how these issues could and should be addressed in instruction. In the early 1970s there was considerable interest in finding ways to assess student learning style preference accurately so that instruction could be tailored to fit all children's unique needs. On the surface there is much to commend this approach. Clearly, children who spend time in classes in which instruction fits their style like a tailored glove cannot help but feel comfortable in school and this no doubt contributes greatly to developing feelings of belonging. But there is also a down side to this approach. The instruments that are available for assessing learning style lack the reliability that we should demand for such high-stakes assessment. The results obtained by the most popular assessments are easily affected by one's mood, frame of mind, and other recent experiences. Scores and preferences for the same student have been found to differ remarkably from one day to the next. If educators were to construct a child's entire program around this type of unreliable data, the risk of error and educational malpractice would be far too great to be justified.

But more importantly, attempts to match teaching style to learning style would only further handicap our at-risk students. While Dick is a concrete-random and feels most comfortable when confronting tasks and assignments that fit his style, there is no guarantee that his department head or his publisher will choose to accommodate his style. In fact, Dick frequently comments that his department head and publisher are far too sequential for his taste. Yet it is for precisely this reason that successful adults (like Dick) need to be ambidextrous with regard to learning style. The more we are able to adjust comfortably to tasks and expectations that don't perfectly fit with our natural preferences, the more likely we will be to find success in all our future pursuits.

Bernice McCarthy's 4MAT System

Bernice McCarthy is an educator who has made a tremendous contribution to the field of learning styles with her approach called *4MAT*. McCarthy has struck a wonderful balance between children's need to feel that their style is accommodated and their need to stretch their style comfort zone. She proposes that teachers teach around the style circle (see Figure 5.4).

The terminology that McCarthy uses in the 4MAT System differs slightly from that used by Gregorc. Despite the challenges presented in translating between learning style theorists, a terminology correlation between McCarthy and Gregorc follows.

Concrete	=	Concrete Experience
Abstract	=	Abstract Conceptualization
Random	=	Active Experimentation
Sequential	=	Reflective Observation
Concrete sequential	=	Style 1
Abstract sequential	=	Style 2
Abstract random	=	Style 3
Concrete random	=	Style 4

McCarthy suggests that the solution to the learning style problem lies with the teacher varying the style of instruction systematically so that every child has the opportunity to feel both accommodated and stretched. She suggests that this could be accomplished by teaching around the circle. She has also theorized that each style preference is further divisible by right or left hemisphere strength. Holding such a perspective on student differences affords the teacher eight different lesson style formats to incorporate into unit planning.

If teachers commit themselves to constructing each daily lesson as though it were aimed at a different style, then individual students would have their personal style perfectly met once every four days (using Gregorc's four categories) or every eight days (when we add McCarthy's brain hemisphere considerations). In elementary classrooms the teacher might want to teach each subject in a different style format at different times. Such an approach would ensure that no student will ever feel style alienation for an entire day (like our hypothetical mechanics student in physics) and equally importantly, each student will get training with those styles, which, while alien and uncomfortable, must be mastered to some degree for future academic success. The Think and Do Exercise: Teaching the Different Styles will help you learn how to accomplish this.

Figure 5.4. The 4MAT System

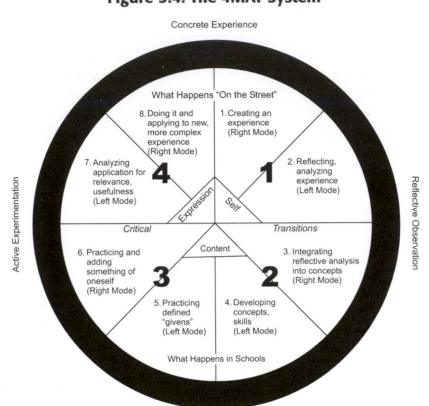

Think and Do Exercise—Teaching the Different Styles

A valuable exercise to develop skills as an ambidextrous instructor is to take a given piece of content and try to develop separate unit plans for each of the four categories of learning styles identified by Gregorc. Using the planning guides (Figures 5.5 through 5.8) provided on the following pages, construct plans appropriate for 5th, 8th, or 11th grade level for your choice of one of the following concepts:

The Civil War

The rain cycle

The food pyramid

Figure 5.5. Unit Planning Guide: Concrete Sequential

I.   Unit Topic: _____

II. Learning style: Concrete Sequential

III. Duration: _____

IV. Learning objectives (what knowledge or skills must the learner possess at the conclusion of this unit?)

    1. _____

    2. _____

    3. _____

    4. _____

    5. _____

    6. _____

V.   Instructional Activities (What specific activities will the learner be expected to engage in during this unit)

_____

_____

_____

_____

_____

_____

VI. Student Assessment (How will students demonstrate to you that they have individually acquired the knowledge or skills expected?)

_____

_____

_____

_____

Figure 5.6. Unit Planning Guide: Abstract Sequential

I.   Unit Topic: _____

II. Learning style: Abstract Sequential

III. Duration: _____

IV. Learning objectives (what knowledge or skills must the learner possess at the conclusion of this unit?)

    1. _____

    2. _____

    3. _____

    4. _____

    5. _____

    6. _____

V.   Instructional Activities (What specific activities will the learner be expected to engage in during this unit?)

_____

_____

_____

_____

_____

_____

VI. Student Assessment (How will students demonstrate to you that they have individually acquired the knowledge or skills expected?)

_____

_____

_____

Figure 5.7. Unit Planning Guide: Random Abstract

I.   Unit Topic: _____

II. Learning style: Random Abstract

III. Duration: _____

IV. Learning objectives (what knowledge or skills must the learner possess at the conclusion of this unit?)

    1. _____

    2. _____

    3. _____

    4. _____

    5. _____

    6. _____

V.   Instructional Activities (What specific activities will the learner be expected to engage in during this unit?)

_____

_____

_____

_____

_____

_____

VI. Student Assessment (How will students demonstrate to you that they have individually acquired the knowledge or skills expected?)

_____

_____

_____

Figure 5.8. Unit Planning Guide: Concrete Random

I.   Unit Topic: _____

II. Learning style: Concrete Random

III. Duration: _____

IV. Learning objectives (what knowledge or skills must the learner possess at the conclusion of this unit?)

     1. _____

     2. _____

     3. _____

     4. _____

     5. _____

     6. _____

V.   Instructional Activities (What specific activities will the learner be expected to engage in during this unit?)

_____

_____

_____

_____

_____

_____

VI. Student Assessment (How will students demonstrate to you that they have individually acquired the knowledge or skills expected?)

_____

_____

_____

_____

Teacher Expectations and Feelings of Belonging

Most educators are aware of the research that supports the need for high expectations. Beginning with the famous study detailed in *Pygmalion in the Classroom* (Rosenthal & Jacobson, 1968), educators have had evidence that students will perform up to the expectations we hold for them. Due to their history of poor performance, teachers tend to expect less from at-risk kids, and we find that they rarely disappoint us. If we want to change this it will not be enough just to pledge to expect more from underachieving youth. Rather, we will need to understand those mechanisms through which our expectations are communicated. Tom Good and Jere Brophy (2002) visited classrooms and systematically observed the students whom teachers had identified as either high or low achievers. They uncovered patterns of behavior that differentiated the treatment teachers provided to those students from whom more was expected and those who were expected to perform poorly. Figure 5.9 shows their findings.

Figure 5.9. Differential Teaching Behavior

- Seating slow students farther away from the teacher, making it more difficult to monitor these students or to treat them as individuals
- Paying less attention to slow students, by smiling and making eye contact less often
- Calling on slow students less frequently to answer classroom questions
- Waiting less time for slower students to answer questions
- Failing to provide clues or to ask follow-up questions in problem situations with slower students
- Criticizing slower students more frequently for incorrect answers
- Praising slower students less often for correct or marginal responses
- Giving slower students less feedback and less detailed feedback
- Demanding less effort and less work from slower students
- Interrupting the performance of slower students more frequently.

Excerpts from ASCD Research Information Service. (1981). Differential teaching behavior. *Educational Leadership*, 38, 5. Reprinted with permission of the Association for Supervision Curriculum Development. Copyright by ASCD. All rights reserved.

When at-risk students see that the students who are doing well are consistently receiving different treatment than they are receiving, it telegraphs low expectations that can have a devastating impact on their sense of belonging. If we want our students to believe that we are holding high expectations for each of them, we will need to find ways to treat the "lows" in the same manner in which we treat the "highs." The following Think and Do Exercise will help you assess your own teaching in this regard.

Think and Do Exercise—
Telegraphing High Expectations

Using the worksheet provided in Figure 5.10, conduct a self assessment. The terms on the worksheet correspond to the definitions from Good and Brophy found in Figure 3.9.

If you can't determine the answer to a question you should ask your students for their perceptions. If there are behaviors that cause you to perceive a difference in the way you respond to students, devise a strategy for improvement. For example: if you elicit responses differentially, your plan might be, "I'll call on students using a randomized deck of cards with the at-risk students' names on two cards, thereby increasing their involvement in class."

Figure 5.10. Expectations Worksheet

Do I differentiate between high and low performing students in:

1. Seating?   _____yes _____no
   If yes, what could be done to improve this?

2. Attending?   _____yes _____no
   If yes, what could be done to improve this?

3. Eliciting responses?   _____yes _____no
   If yes, what could be done to improve this?

4. Wait time?   _____yes _____no
   If yes, what could be done to improve this?

5. Follow-up questions?   _____yes _____no
   If yes, what could be done to improve this?

6. Criticism?   _____yes _____no
   If yes, what could be done to improve this?

7. Giving feedback?   _____yes _____no
   If yes, what could be done to improve this?

8. Praise?   _____yes _____no
   If yes, what could be done to improve this?

9. Providing feedback?   _____yes _____no
   If yes, what could be done to improve this?

10. Demands?   _____yes _____no
    If yes, what could be done to improve this?

11. Interruptions?   _____yes _____no
    If yes, what could be done to improve this?

The importance of the Good and Brophy's findings is that they focus our attention on certain specifics of our habitual teaching behavior rather than on our intentions. Much of the *differential* treatment that their research isolated probably had its basis in compassionate concerns. For example, as teachers, our instincts had us *calling on* our high-achieving students more frequently than our low-achieving students because we wanted to spare the low achievers the embarrassment of publicly giving a wrong answer or having to admit that they didn't know the material. Likewise, we both tended to avoid *staying with* the low achievers after they offered an incorrect response, and being too *demanding of production* from our disadvantaged learners. Each of those decisions appeared to be a realistic compromise based on our concern for the emotional well being of those students. However, this type of compromise can telegraph a message of personal unworthiness to at-risk students.

The Special Case of Wait Time

Of all the differential teaching behaviors, none may give our students as pronounced a message regarding whether they belong than *wait time*. Luckily, it is easily rectified. Wait time refers to the length of time we pause between asking a question and calling on a student for a response. Like most teachers Dick's adrenaline is pumping when he teaches and his pace quickens. As a result, he gets impatient and calls for a response as soon as a few hands are raised. Often this occurs in a matter of less than two seconds. Worse, when he does elicit a response perhaps only 3 out of 25 hands have been raised. Why is this so problematic?

Research by Mary Budd Rowe (1969) found that teachers tended to provide less than 1.5 seconds of wait time from the students whom they deemed to be low achievers while providing significantly more time on the average for those they thought to be more academically able. Now consider this fact. Each of our brains works something like the microprocessor in a computer. Some of us have microchips that can consider a question, scan our memory banks for all the relevant information and formulate an answer in less than a second. Others have microchips that take significantly longer. However, it is likely that this processing time is in no way related to intellectual potential, because, for example, brighter people might, in fact, be inclined to take longer to contemplate an answer as they go about considering a wide array of possibilities. Now imagine that we are in a class in which the teacher provides only 2 seconds of wait time. It is November and we have come to realize that he always calls on someone precisely 2 seconds after asking his question. We have also realized that we possess 4-second "mental processors" and, therefore, we are always in the middle of contemplating an answer when our teacher interrupts us with someone else's conclusion.

We are perpetually in the state we call *thinkus interruptus*. It doesn't take us long to decide to simply wait ourselves. We will subconsciously become mental dropouts from the class. After all, why should we start thinking and cognitively engaging with his question when the answer will be given before we have even fully examined what was asked? That realization produces two consequences, one cognitive and one emotional. In such a situation we will inevitably learn less. It is axiomatic that one learns more by doing than by passively observing. If we spend our time in class listening to others give answers (even if they are always correct) we will not be as productive or as intellectually valuable as constructing them ourselves. But, perhaps more importantly, when our teacher doesn't give us enough time to engage in the class we are likely to interpret that action as a statement that he doesn't care about what we have to say, contribute, or share. Being a 4-second student in a 2-second classroom can lead to feelings of intellectual rejection and being overlooked all year. And, as we learned earlier, a 4-second wait time has nothing to do with intelligence.

This expansion on the issue of wait time is here because it is one factor in our teaching practice that is easy to modify and experiment with. When we see the impact that comes from altering this particular differential teaching behavior it can serve to inspire us to address the other eleven. The Think and Do Exercise that follows provides a structure for you to explore the impact of altering your wait time.

Think and Do Exercise—Altering Wait Time

This activity will provide you with an opportunity to experience the impact of lengthening wait time in your classroom. It has two parts. Part one deals with wait time 1, how long we wait after asking a question, and the second part deals with wait time 2, how long we wait before injecting ourselves into a classroom discussion.

Part 1: Wait Time 1

Select a lesson that you were going to teach that calls for eliciting student responses. Experiment with expanding the time you pause between posing a question and calling on a student for a response. Using the chimpanzee counting method—*chimpanzee 1, chimpanzee 2, chimpanzee 3, chimpanzee 4, chimpanzee 5*—count 5 full seconds before calling on a student for an answer.

Hints:

♦ Count to yourself. Your students might think you are crazy if they hear you counting chimpanzees out loud.

♦ Make sure your students know to raise their hands and not call out with answers.

♦ Conduct this lesson for at least 20 minutes. It will take a while for your students to adjust to your new cadence.

After 20 minutes ask yourself whether any students engaged in this lesson that had been sitting in the shadows before? What happened to the number of hands raised as the lesson progressed? What appeared to be the impact on your at-risk students?

Part 2: Wait Time 2

When you hold a class discussion during which you want to have students piggyback on each other's answers, you will need to employ wait time 2. This refers to the time between a student contribution and a teacher response. Using chimpanzee counting, discipline yourself to withhold your contributions until at least 5 seconds of silence have elapsed after a student's contribution to the discussion.

At first you will note that students will look at you after each comment, they will want to see your reaction. Don't despair. By remaining quiet you will be conveying that you are interested in what each of them has to say.

After 20 minutes ask yourself, did this discussion involve students I hadn't heard from before? Did more students seem to feel as though their contributions were appreciated and valued?

Nothing tells people that we value them quite as much as giving them time and space to participate in our lives. Not giving someone the chance to participate in a discussion, whether it is in our private social lives or in our classrooms, tells people that we don't care. What is important about differential teaching behaviors is not that they grew out of an intent to convey an uncaring message, but that they result in telling some students that their contributions are of less value than are the contributions of others. Over time such patterns will deny a sense of belonging to many of our most at-risk students.

Intelligence Reconsidered

Perhaps no concept in the history of education has had a more deleterious effect on students' sense of belonging than the belief that there exists a general category of aptitude called intelligence or IQ. As discussed in the previous chapter, when one holds the view that capacity to learn is innate, limited, and measurable one effectively sentences all but a handful of students (those who test high on IQ exams) to limited opportunities to learn and realize their future potential.

The history of this erroneous belief system would be humorous were it not so tragic. Stephen Jay Gould (1981) traces the futile and frequently ill-intended efforts to measure and categorize intelligence in his classic *The Mismeasure of Man*. He traces the history of crainiometry, a pseudo-science that posited that the shape and size of the skull determined an individual's capacity to learn. In today's parlance, students with large skulls were considered "gifted" and small skulled students would be the learning disabled. By this method, incidentally, women were also "shown" to be less intelligent than men. Gould does a credible job of showing that the correlations that support the Stanford-Binet and other intelligence tests are no more reasonable measures of intelligence than were comparisons of skull size.

In recent years two psychologists Robert Sternberg (1997) of Yale and Howard Gardner of Harvard have received considerable attention for their theories of multiple intelligences. Gardner (1983) argues that there are at least nine separate intelligences: linguistic, musical, logical-mathematical, spatial, bodily-kinesthetic, intrapersonal, interpersonal, naturalistic, and existential. Goleman (1995) has now added a tenth called emotional intelligence. Researchers have since provided numerous examples of individuals who were gifted in one of these areas while seemingly quite ordinary in others. Those findings are now bringing into question the very concept of intellectual capacity as a single immutable attribute.

At the Key School, an elementary school in Indianapolis, Indiana, the academic program is based upon Gardner's multiple intelligences. In this school the teachers regularly collect data using videotapes, personal observations, and student portfolios to track individual progress in each of these domains (Olson, 1988). Periodic student–parent conferences are held to review the performance data and diagnostically plan future activities. The exciting finding from this work is that each of these intelligences can apparently be learned and developed. They are not innate and immutable. The Think and Do Exercise below will help you apply these concepts to your own classroom.

Think and Do Exercise—Looking for Signs of Multiple Intelligences

Refer back to the "Classroom Strength Inventory" you developed in Chapter 3 (Think and Do Exercise p.). Now using Gardner's nine intelligences:

- linguistic
- musical
- logical-mathematical
- spatial
- bodily-kinesthetic
- interpersonal
- intrapersonal
- naturalistic
- existential

Try to identify the intelligence area displayed by each of the student strengths you identified.

Now look at the lessons you designed for the coming week. How many of the intelligences will be utilized, tested, and rewarded?

Gardner's work has had a profound impact on educational practice in America and the field has been well served through the challenge to the single intelligence model. However, it would be sad indeed if we codified these types of intelligence as though they fully defined mental capacity as we once assumed of the old IQ scores. We simply do not understand enough about the human mind to make these sorts of declarations. In Chapter 3 we shared evidence that the bell curve was not an accurate depiction of human mental capability. The mastery learning research has confirmed that most everyone can learn most anything, with the only significant difference between learners being learning rate. Lezotte and Jacoby (1990) points out that the mastery expectation of performance then should not be drawn as a bell but as a "J" (see Figure 5.11).

Figure 5.11. The J curve of Success

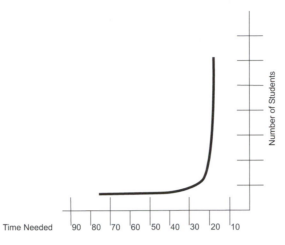

Number of Students

Time Needed   '90 '80 '70 '60 '50 '40 '30 '20 '10

The "J" Curve of success shows us that learning rate is not the same thing as aptitude or capacity to learn. Those of us who took three times as long to learn to drive and several trials with the road test are now as competent as those who learned it in a matter of hours and passed the test the first time out. If this were not the case we would have laws prohibiting us "slow learning drivers" from being on the road under hazardous conditions. On the face of it, such a law would be silly. We all know it is where one ends up that is the mark of genius, not how long it took them to get there. Michelangelo is not marked down for taking "too long" to complete the Sistine Chapel. Likewise, neither should the student who takes longer to master the quadratic formula or the form of the Shakespearean sonnet be labeled as less smart or less capable.

Building Belonging with Constructivist Learning

When students cannot make sense of the content in class it is difficult for them to believe that they truly *belong* there.

Certain critical differences among students can be revealed when we assess them from a constructivist perspective. Students will often bring very different ideas to the learning environment. This is due to differences in development as well as experience. Constructivist theory obligates the educator to be cognizant of the student's thinking in contrast to the structure of the discipline so that errors in student thinking can be challenged and hopefully modified.

Many learning theory texts have erroneously asserted that Piaget's theory of development predicts that students of a particular age will make use of concrete manipulatives when learning certain concepts in math and science. This theory holds that most adults would not need manipulatives, because adults have already moved into formal operational thinking. However, it has been demonstrated empirically that this is not so. Indeed, every time Jonas is teaching a science or math methods course he encounters mature, even highly successful adults who still need manipulatives to solve and understand basic math and science relationships. This lends credence to the premise that it is less a matter of maturity and broad experience and more a matter of specific experience in the particular area being studied.

Students need to have the option, without public ridicule, of messing around with objects so they can gain the concrete experiences they need to make sense of the relationships present in the content of the class.

Why is this important? Stop for a moment and consider the impact on a learner who lacks the necessary concrete experiences, yet, is being held accountable for material they are not able to understand. Without the concrete experiences it will be difficult to make much sense of the abstract relationships presented in readings or classroom discussions.

We should expect some of our students to have had prior experience with the content we are studying and this will prove beneficial for them. However, other students (because of their lack of experience and therefore lack of reflection on those experiences) often will not be able to benefit from the activities planned. It is important, therefore, to have optional activities that are easily entered and easily exited, meaning that students can move in and out of them with little or no prior instruction or downtime. It is also beneficial to have activities that can be engaged in without a full understanding. Sink or Float was an activity Jonas used in his middle school science classroom that is a good example of this process.

Sink Float Example

The instructions given to the students were

- Take a dish tub and fill it with water.

- Take a piece of tin foil and try to get it to float.

- Then see how many weights you can get the floater to hold

Students can move into and out of the activity with little attention from the teacher, providing that the proper groundwork for the activity has been laid earlier. This model allows for those students that need to mess around with notions of weight, displacement, and volume can gain the experience they need. Others in a typical classroom may understand these two notions separately but may not have yet connected the two ideas and found the relationship between them, specifically the concept of density.

The students who have been able to construct the notion of density will be able to work on generalizing these notions with different liquid mediums, such as oil, salt water, or different boat building materials such as clay, plastic, or plaster. Additionally this activity will introduce other content such as shape, symmetry, volume, surface area, and surface tension. Jonas has successfully used this activity to engage learners from third grade to graduate school. Each time it provided the concrete experiences students needed to develop and test their ideas about the way nature works.

To develop curricula consistent with this approach Jonas uses a model involving the following five questions:

Five Questions for a Constructivist Curriculum

1. What are the *big ideas* in this area?

2. How will I *assess* what my students already know about this area?

3. How will I get my students *actively involved* in constructing or refining their understanding?

4. What *questions* can I ask them to assess what they have learned?

5. How will I *evaluate* their answers?

Think and Do Exercise— Teaching in a Constructivist Framework

A valuable exercise to gain experience in developing an activity based curriculum aimed a helping students construct important relationships, is to take a given piece of content and try to develop lessons plans using the four questions listed above. These questions have proven useful for all grades and in any content area. For this exercise you may pick 2nd, 5th, 8th, or 11th grade students as your target audience and any concept from any discipline normally taught to that grade level.

As a guide we are providing this example from a lesson Jonas used in his class.

States of Matter

1. The *big ideas* in this area are:

  ♦ Water changes to a water vapor and forms the bubbles in boiling water.

  ♦ Water does not split into hydrogen and oxygen as water boils.

  ♦ Science requires testing ideas, gathering evidence in support of a conclusion

2. I will *assess* what my students already know about this by:

  ♦ Asking them what the bubbles are made of when a pot of water boils and giving them the following options:

Air

Space

Steam

Hydrogen

Oxygen

3. My students will be *actively involved* in constructing or refining their understanding by:

    Designing an experiment testing to test to see if their answer to the above question is correct.

4. I can I ask them these *questions* to assess what they have learned.

    ♦ What are the bubbles made of?

    ♦ What evidence have you found to support your idea?

    ♦ Have you examined your evidence in light of what others have found?

5. How will I *assess* their answers?

    The answers they arrive at need to be a logical connection of the data they have collected. If they have arrived at an answer that is not in keeping with current scientific theory or is not supported by evidence they have gathered then they should be challenged accordingly.

It should now be clear that the measure of an individual's capacity is simply a factor of time invested and their passion to succeed. Where enough of both are present it appears that nothing is beyond the reach of any of our students. If, however, we construct school tasks in such limited ways that only a few will succeed and then promote an ideology that argues that the success they experienced was preordained by innate attributes, we will have ensured that many children will continue to feel alienated and disengaged at school. If, on the contrary, we organize curriculum so that it affirms and includes the interests of our children and takes into account how they learn, and allows for the expression of their innate curiosity, we will have made our classrooms places where all students can truly feel they belong.

References

Collins, Marva. (1979). *60 Minutes*, CBS Television.

Conrath, J. (1986). *Our Other Youth*. Gig Harbor, WA.

Fine, M. & Zane, N. (1985). "Being wrapped too tight: When low income women drop out of high school." In L. Weis, E. Farrar, & H. G. Petrie (Eds.), *Dropouts from school: Issues, dilemmas and solutions* (pp. 23–54). Albany, NY: SUNY Press.

Gardner, H. (1983). *Frames of mind*. New York, NY: Basic Books.

Goleman, D (1995). *Emotional Intelligence: Why it can matter more than IQ*. New York: Bantam Books, 1995

Good, T., & Brophy, J. (2002). *Looking in classrooms*, 9th ed. Boston: Addison-Wesley.

Good, T., & Brophy, J. (1981). Highlights from Research on Teacher Expectations and Student Perceptions. *Educational Leadership*, February.

Gould, Stephen J. (1981). *The mismeasure of man*. New York: W. W. Norton.

Gregorc, A. F. (1985). *Gregorc style delineator: A self-assessment instrument*. Columbia, CT: Gregorc Associates.

Lezotte, L., & Jacoby, B. (1990). *A guide to the school improvement process vased on effective schools research. Okemos, MI: Effective School Products*.

Maslow, H. M, Frager, R., and Fadiman, J. (1987). *Motivation and personality*, 3rd ed. New York: Addison, Wesley.

McCarthy, B. (1987). *The 4MAT System: Teaching to learning styles with right/left mode techniques* (rev. ed.). Barrington, IL: EXCEL.

Ogbu, J. U. (1989). The individual in collective adaptation: A framework for focusing on academic under performance and dropping out among involuntary minorities. In Weis, L., Farrar, E., & Petrie, H. G. (Eds.). *Dropouts from school: Issues, dilemmas, and solutions* (pp. 181–204). Albany: SUNY Press.

Olsen, L. (1988). "Children flourish here", *Education Week*, January 27.

Rosenthal, R., & Jacobson, L. (1968). *Pygmalion in the classroom*. New York, NY: Holt, Rinehart & Winston.

Rowe, M. (1969). Science, Silence, and Sanctions. *Science and Children*, 6, 11–13.

Sternberg, R.J. (1997). *Successful intelligence*. New York: Plume.

Wehlage, G. G., et al. (1989). *Reducing the risk: Schools as communities of support*. Philadelphia, PA: Falmer Press.

Phillips, Darrell. (1996). *Structures of thinking: Concrete operations*. Dubuque: Kendall Hunt.

6

HELPING STUDENTS BUILD FEELINGS OF USEFULNESS

In the last chapter we focused on the issue of creating sense of belonging for *all* our students. The importance of being cared for, understood, and appreciated as unique and sensitive human beings should never be underestimated. However, simply inoculating students with feelings of belonging will not be sufficient to build resiliency and ultimately hold off at-riskness.

As teachers we sometimes want to believe that if we just love our students enough everything will be alright. Unfortunately, creating self-actualized learners and building self-esteem requires much more than that. Several years ago in a reflection on the state of America's honored high schools Dick observed,

"In 20 years we've witnessed a formal institution, the American high school, with a singular and rather narrow academic focus, evolve into a complex of formal and flexible social structures which are at least as concerned about the emotional and psychological well-being of their clients as they are with their academic development or acquisition of skills."

"The evidence of this change can be seen in almost every community and in practically every one of our nation's schools. The presence of alternative schools, work experience programs, expanded activity programs, alternatives to suspension, and guidance departments which have personal counseling as a major, if not paramount, goal have not only changed the appearance of our schools, but have provided vast improvements in school holding power, graduation rates, and reduction in the frequency and degree of such self-destructive behavior as substance abuse and mindless violence."

"The student-teacher relationship in most high schools has changed radically. The stodgy authority figure whom students rarely saw out-

127

side the school building and whom a teenager wouldn't dream of approaching with any problem more personal than solving a quadratic equation, has been replaced, by and large, by the nurturing adult who is a mix of mentor, adviser, and friend."

"The 273 secondary schools that my colleagues and I visited for the Secondary School Recognition Program were universally noted by students, parents, and staffs as caring places. In each school students reported that there were many adults whom they "felt comfortable going to with personal problems," and in each case they described many teachers as "friends" and their schools as "caring.""

"I personally visited several schools whose primary goal was enabling each student to feel cared for and to develop a sense of belonging. The programs in these schools reflected not only tremendous creativity, but produced outstanding results both in terms of student attitudes and behavior."

"As a profession we apparently became determined that it was important to expand our mission to include nurturing the emotional development of our charges. We deserve credit for addressing that problem in such an exemplary fashion. Unfortunately, all our other efforts have not fared as well (Sagor, 1986)."

That trend is still apparent today. Although too many secondary schools remain large and impersonal environments, the overwhelming majority of students in our elementary schools do get to experience six or more years of nurturing and caring adult supervision. Nevertheless, many of these same youngsters end up frustrated, alienated, defeated, and/or discouraged. This is partly because while they may be affirmed by their teachers as beautiful, unique, and worthwhile, they may not have internalized any significant feelings of competence. However, if we attend to a mastery orientation and maintain consistently high standards (Chapter 3) we can go a long way toward ameliorating that concern. Alternatively, if we empower our students to construct their own learning of higher order concepts we will have provided them with evidence of their emerging competence. However, even if we have assisted our students to feel competent and a acquire a sense of membership at school, there is still another crucial psychological need that must be satisfied in order to positively influence our students' views on who they are and who they will become.

That need exists in the psychosocial domain and consequently exerts great power over the development of one's self-concept. We are social animals; we live, work, and recreate in groups. The social groupings we live and work in supply us with status, reinforcement, and reaffirmation of our value. Therefore, our feelings of *usefulness* will be derived or denied as a direct result of both the quantity and quality of the interactions we have with others.

Ironically, some of our more sincere efforts to improve and modernize schools have added to problems in this area rather then providing a solution. The abandonment of the one-room school house triggered an evolution of schooling practices that in all likelihood have hurt children's development more than helped it.

In the one-room school the teacher knew she couldn't do it all. Each child was expected to study a dozen subjects, and the teacher needed to manage as many as twelve different grade levels in one small room. Only a super-human teacher could be expected to have the ability to direct all that learning simultaneously. As a result, teachers created mini communities in their classrooms. Olders taught youngers, the more skilled tutored the less skilled, and the classroom became an extended family. Children learned to depend on one another as well as their teacher. With our large urban schools and their "economies of scale," we have perpetuated another sort of poverty, a poverty of neglect. It should be no surprise that the recent rash of school shootings have all occurred in large secondary schools.

Too many classrooms have become places for individualistic and competitive work, without opportunities for productive codependency; places where the sharing and developing of feelings of usefulness have been diminished. While this is unfortunate for all children, it is our at-risk students who have been the prime losers in this transition.

In recent years the conditions of the individualistic competitive classroom have become a concern for many educators as well as numerous progressive social theorists and national educational organizations such as the National Council of Teachers of Mathematics (NCTM, 2000) and the American Association for the Advancement of Science (AAAS, 1993). It is repeatedly pointed out that the more successful workplaces in the private sector are not characterized as much by individual competitiveness as they are by group cohesiveness and orchestrated collaborative effort toward the attainment of shared group goals. The traditional "me against the rest of the class" mode has been proven to be counterproductive not only in the public school classroom but in the workplace as well (AAAS, 1993; Johnson, & Johnson, 1990; Ouchi, 1981, Peters & Waterman, 1982; Senge, 1990).

In the push for "standards based reforms" educators have focused so much on the "objective" measurement of academic outcomes that other outcomes have often been overlooked. The current reform climate has all but ignored the "process" recommendations of some of the same national organizations who authored the standards teachers have so enthusiastically adopted. Chief among these recommendations are the utilization of *cooperative learning* and constructivist teaching methods including *problem-based learning* and *student directed inquiry.*

Problem Based Learning and Student Directed Inquiry

These two methods ask the students to do the organizational work necessary to solve a problem or to launch an investigation. While the degree of teacher involvement varies from classroom to classroom, both of these methods are built on the need to move away from direct instruction to an approach, which is more student directed. Jonas recalls a time while teaching middle school science when he was organizing worksheets to guide his students through a lab. It suddenly dawned on him that most of the organization of the lab was already included in the worksheet. Indeed, much of the learning he had hoped that the students would gain from the lab had been done for them. Consequently, all that the students had to do was read the worksheet and respond to the questions. No real thought and probably no significant learning was required on the part of the students. Jonas then mentally reviewed the labs he had created in the past and realized that he, personally, had learned a great deal as a result of the thinking involved in developing the lab activities. He realized that by organizing the labs so well, he had inadvertently, but effectively, removed the opportunity for the students to experience the same learning. By reserving the intellectual work for the teacher, Jonas had learned a lot of science, but in doing so, left little for his students to discover.

Thinking through the issues associated with a discipline and designing and carrying out activities to test one's ideas and hypotheses requires a different type of lesson planning than preservice teachers are generally taught. Delegating aspects of the planning to students will provide meaningful opportunities for at-risk students to shine. However, because of the complexity of the issues that will be encountered, this type of planning requires skills with holistic problem solving, continued tinkering, and lots of trial and error. Often, ultimate, success requires the contributions of many minds and perspectives. Because this type of work calls for dialogue and give and take, it is best accomplished in cooperative groups. As you will see throughout this chapter, it is our belief that participating in meaningful cooperative learning inevitably results in enhanced feelings of usefulness for our students.

Usefulness is not something that is experienced in isolation but rather in relationship to others. Usefulness makes no sense in a context of isolation, because it begs the question: useful for whom? In real life usefulness could be defined simply as "service to others." It doesn't matter if this service is being paid for or if it is voluntary. Either way, usefulness brings a sense of self worth well beyond what any extrinsic reward could ever convey.

These ideas aren't new. It is no longer the exception to see (elementary) classrooms with desks arranged in clusters or circles as opposed to the traditional set-up of students in rows, all facing front. Unfortunately, the 1995 TIMSS study indicates that passively listening to lectures and/or engaging in competitive individual work are practices still alive and well in most American high schools. On the surface, seeing elementary teachers circulating and children working in dyads, triads, and other groupings seems quite positive, however, some caution is called for. This is because a poorly managed cooperative learning classroom can place an at-risk student at an even greater disadvantage than before the cooperative model was introduced.

We will start by exploring the crucial importance of helping youth establish a sense of usefulness. In doing so we will explore the basic principles of cooperative learning and provide some guidelines for creating an *accountable* cooperative learning classroom. The chapter will conclude with a discussion of *community service* as a powerful means for developing a student's sense of usefulness.

Two Dimensions of Utility

When it comes to work, there are two dimensions of utility that apply to adults as well as youth. One has to do with qualities inherent in an assigned task and the other has to do with the value others place upon a completed product.

Busy Work vs. "Real World" Work

In the first chapter we examined the need of many defeated and discouraged learners to see the practical applications of their school tasks. Young people, like adults, seem to have an innate dislike for busywork. So when a task is filled with what students label as "real world" utility, it becomes intrinsically more motivational. This is another reason why production oriented classes such as wood shop, art, music, and journalism have historically maintained their popularity with at-risk youth.

Frequently, a question that is asked (directly or implied) through the behavior of at-risk students is, "Why should I do this?" On the surface it seems that the answer they are seeking and the one we most often supply relate to the benefits that completing the task will provide for them personally. Consequently, we are often heard telling them that, "Doing this will make you a better worker, thinker, or student." However, there is another dimension to usefulness, and this one often provides far more motivational value. It has to do with the value that others place on our work. This is often referred to as *social utility*.

Social Utility

Because we don't live alone, we depend on our relationships with others for hints as to who we are. Consequently, the value our work contributes to others can have tremendous impact on our self-esteem. If other people need us and value our assistance, it affirms our worth in a way that a 1,000 smiley-face stickers could never approximate. Conversely, when workers toil on impersonal assembly lines, they tend to become alienated from the end product of their labor. If workers are unable to see their unique contribution reflected meaningfully in the final product, it shouldn't be a surprise when they neither care about nor identify with the outcome. On the other end, the artisan who designs, produces, and signs his own work, ultimately putting it on the market for potential patrons to assess, will find their persona intimately tied to the outcome of the labor.

One need only watch a football, baseball, or basketball game and observe the team responding to a touchdown, home run, or clutch basket to see reaction of a worker to an act that has been appreciated. In our efforts to create feelings of usefulness in our classrooms that is precisely the reaction we should be after. Our goal should be to produce internal and external "high fives" for all our students, particularly the defeated and discouraged learners, those who deep down fear that they have nothing meaningful to give to others.

Cooperative Learning

It is not surprising that the concerns discussed above have led many educators over the past 20 years to explore mechanisms to get students to work more productively and successfully in inter-dependent group settings. This category of strategies has been labeled *cooperative learning*. In this chapter we will reflect mostly on the work done by Robert Slavin and his associates at the Johns Hopkins University, because the body of work they've created has demonstrated significant success with at-risk students in heterogeneous environments. Before we do so, however, it will be helpful to review the basic premises and the underlying principles of the other well known approaches to cooperative learning.

Group Investigation

One of the earliest approaches to cooperative learning was the "Group Investigation" approach promoted by Shlomo Sharan and his colleagues at the University of Tel Aviv. Their group investigation process involved six stages that typically occurred over several weeks or months. The six stages are:

1. The topic to be investigated is identified and students are organized into research groups. The teacher presents a broad topic to the whole class. The topic should be multifaceted to encourage diverse reactions and stimulate interest.

2. Students and their teacher plan the investigation. Group members determine which aspect of the subtopic each will investigate and then decide how to proceed and what resources will be needed.

3. Students carry out the investigation by using diverse sources to learn more about their subtopic.

4. Each group prepares a final report. Students analyze and evaluate the information they have gathered, synthesize the parts into an integrated whole, and plan a presentation that will be both instructive and appealing. Presentations can take the form of an exhibit, a model, a learning center, a written report, a dramatic presentation, a guided tour, or a slide presentation.

5. Groups present their final reports to the class. The purpose is for all students to gain a broad perspective on the topic and to involve classmates in each other's work.

6. Evaluation includes individual and/or group assessment. Evaluation of students' higher-order thinking, application of knowledge to new problems, and ability to use inference and draw conclusions is emphasized (Sharan, summarized in Rapp 1991).

Jigsaw

Around the same time, Eliot Aronson (1978) began promulgating an approach to group work called *Jigsaw*. The fundamental innovation in Jigsaw was that Aronson suggested dividing up the assigned content among several members of a group. Later, participants would become responsible for teaching their portion of the assigned material to others in the group. The key feature of Jigsaw was the creation of structured *interdependence* in order to learn the material.

Circles of Learning

Probably the best known and most widely disseminated approach to cooperative learning is the work of David and Roger Johnson from the University of Minnesota. A complete description of the processes employed in their model can be found in their book *Circles of Learning: Cooperation in the Classroom* (1990). In this book the Johnsons outline 18 steps that constitute their process. The Johnson and Johnson model allows for significant teacher adaptation, and teachers are encouraged to exercise discretionary options at each step. The 18 steps are:

1. Clearly specify the instructional objective.

2. Decide on the size of the group. Cooperative learning groups tend to range in size from two to six.

3. Assign students to groups. Maximize heterogeneity in terms of ability, sex, and ethnicity. Occasionally, homogeneous groups may be used to master specific skills.

4. Arrange groups to facilitate communication. Circles are usually best.

5. Instructional materials should be used to promote positive interdependence among students. Three ways of doing so are materials interdependence, resource interdependence, and structuring competition among groups.

6. Assign roles to ensure interdependence. Roles might include a summarizer, a checker, an encourager, a recorder, or a time keeper.

7. Explain the academic task so that students are clear about the assignment and understand the objectives of the lesson.

8. Structure positive goal interdependence. This can be accomplished by asking the group to produce a single product, report or paper, or by providing group rewards.

9. Structure individual accountability for learning so that all group members participate and contribute.

10. Structure intergroup cooperation.

11. Explain criteria for success. Evaluation needs to be criterion-referenced and established for acceptable work rather than grading on a curve.

12. Specify behaviors that are acceptable and desirable within the learning group.

13. Monitor students' behavior continually for problems with task or collaborative efforts.

14. Provide task assistance by clarifying instructions, reviewing important procedures and strategies for completing assignments, answering questions, and teaching task skills.

15. Intervene to teach group skills. Teachers may suggest more effective procedures for working together and more effective behaviors for students to engage in.

16. Provide closure to the lesson, using summaries by students and teacher.

17. Evaluate the quality and quantity of students' learning.

18. Assess how well the group functioned, using ongoing observation and discussion of group process (Johnson, Johnson, & Holubec, summarized in Rapp, 1991).

Besides the schedule of instruction just described, the Learning Together method emphasizes five other elements (Johnson, Johnson, & Holubec, 1990).

1. Face-to-face interaction: Students work in two- to five-member groups.

2. Positive interdependence: Students work together to achieve group goals.

3. Individual accountability: Students must show that they've individually mastered the materials.

4. Group processing: Students evaluate how they did both in the area of content acquisition and with group skills.

5. Interpersonal and small-group skills: Students must be taught effective means of working together.

Cooperative Structures

Finally, Spenser Kagan of the University of California-Riverside took another tack with the express goal of getting students to work cooperatively. Believing that the other popular models were too restrictive, he came to the conclusion that teachers would be better served by having an array of "cooperative structures," which could be used as needed in a wide variety of contexts, grade levels, and disciplines. In his book *Resources for Teachers* (1989) he delineates twelve structures which have shown promise for teaching students to work collaboratively in groups. They are:

Characteristics of Informal Cooperative Structures

1. Numbered Heads Together

   The teacher asks a question, students consult to make sure everyone knows the answer, then one student is called to answer.

2. Color Coded Co-op Cards

   Students memorize facts using a flash card game. The game is structured for maximum success, moving from short-term memory to long-term memory.

3. Pairs Check

    Students work in pairs in which one student solves a problem while
    the other coaches. After every two problems, the pairs within the
    group of four check to see if they have the same answers.

4. Three-Step Interview

    Students interview each other in pairs, first one way, and then the
    other. Academic discussions could include reactions to a poem or
    conclusions drawn from a unit of study.

5. Think-Pair-Share

    Students think independently about a topic provided by the teach-
    ers; they pair up with another student to discuss the topic; they then
    share their thoughts with the class.

6. Team Word-Webbing

    Students write simultaneously on a piece of chart paper, drawing
    main concepts supporting elements and bridges representing the re-
    lationship of ideas in a concept.

7. Simultaneous Roundtable

    Each student in turn writes one answer as a paper and a pencil are
    passed around. With Simultaneous Roundtable more than one pa-
    per and pencil are used at once.

8. Inside-Outside Circles

    Students stand in pairs in two concentric circles. The inside circle
    faces the outside circle. Students use flash cards or respond to
    teacher questions as they rotate to each new partner.

9. Partners

    Students work in pairs to create or master content. They consult with
    partners from other teams they then share their products or under-
    standing with the other partner pair in their team.

10. Jigsaw

    Each student on the team becomes an expert on one topic by work-
    ing with members from other teams assigned the corresponding ex-
    pert topic. Upon returning to their teams, each one in turn teaches
    the group. All students are assessed on all aspects of the topic.

11. Round-Robin

    Each student in turn shares something with his or her teammates.

12. Corners

Each student moves to a corner of the room representing a teacher-determined alternative. Students discuss within corners, then listen to and paraphrase ideas from other corners (Kagan, as cited in Rapp, 1991)

Cooperative Team Learning

Robert Slavin and his colleagues at the Johns Hopkins University Team Learning Project decided to replicate the dynamic social structure of a friendly playground softball game inside the academic classroom. Observing the motivational value of team competition and the way that the strong and weak players on the same team naturally supported and assisted each other, they sought to translate that type of collaboration to the achievement of basic skills. Because they were working with schools that were attempting to mainstream handicapped children and to affect positive results in newly desegregated classrooms, they were particularly concerned about developing a system that would not only work in, but would actively support, heterogeneous grouping.

The Johns Hopkins team has since developed many applications of the cooperative team learning approach; however, the initial three models, Teams Games Tournaments (TGT), Student Teams Achievement Divisions (STAD), and Jigsaw II lend themselves particularly well to local teacher adaptation. For this reason those three models will be discussed in some detail, and an example of a hybrid adaptation that Dick used in his classroom will be shared to show readers how easily these structures can be modified to fit any context.

Teams Games Tournaments

Teams Games Tournaments (TGT) was the first of the cooperative team learning models developed by the Johns Hopkins team. It is used at the elementary school level and is particularly useful when teaching basic skills and knowledge level objectives.

The first step in using TGT requires the teacher to divide the class into heterogeneous teams. The aim here is to make the teams as balanced as possible (by race, gender, training challenges, etc.), but most particularly in terms of past performance with this content. For our discussion let's assume that the teacher is using TGT for instruction in spelling. The development of team rosters requires taking into account the previous performance of each of the students, thereby allowing each team to have an equal number of strong, moderate, and weak spellers. This grouping process produces teams with the same diversity as would the selections made by two softball captains on the playground.

Once having assigned the students to groups, the teacher informs the students that she will be conducting a six week competition between teams and announces that prizes, certificates, or other rewards of the teacher's or students' choice will be awarded to each member of the most successful teams. Students are then grouped with their teammates to choose names for their teams. We are not exactly sure why, but the very act of naming a team serves to bond group members together in a most powerful fashion! In any case, team naming is a step that is always a fun ice-breaker for students and teachers alike.

The teacher then proceeds to teach the assigned spelling words in whatever manner has been most successful in the past. When using TGT one often sees no difference in instructional strategy until the fourth day (Thursday), when at spelling time the teacher tells the students to work as teams for group study. During group study each member of the class is given an identical worksheet with pictures on one side and a space to write the word that the picture represents on the other side.

Working in their mixed ability teams, students jointly study and practice the spelling problems posed on the worksheets.

Friday is the first tournament day. On this day when the students enter their classroom, after recess, they find that their chairs and tables have been rearranged to create four tournament tables (Figure 6.1).

Figure 6.1. Assignment to Tournament Tables

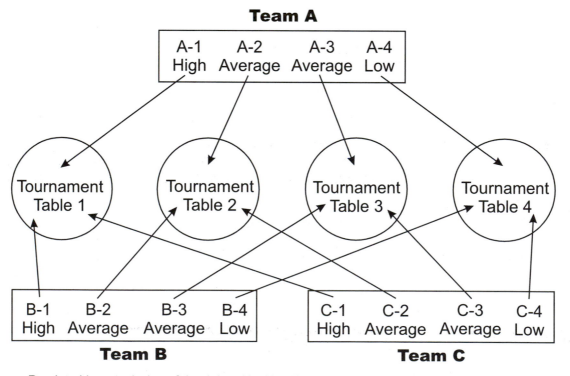

They observe that their teacher has placed a placard at each tournament table with the names of the students assigned to compete there. The students soon recognize that each table contains only one representative from each team. Moreover, table assignments were made to create "a level playing field." One table has been assigned to the top spellers from each team, while another table has the weakest spellers from each group assigned to it. The other two tables have been assigned to the middle ability spellers.

At each table there is an identical deck of cards. The cards bear a striking resemblance to the worksheets used the day before. In fact, they are basically a deck of flash cards constructed from those same worksheets. On one side of the card is the picture and on the back is the word properly spelled. Each table is also equipped with a die that is rolled to see who will go first (usually the student rolling the highest number).

When the teacher gives the signal to begin, the first student takes the deck and tries to spell the word that's illustrated on the top card. The card is then turned over. If the student was correct, she gets to keep the card. If she was in error, she places the card back in the center of the deck and the deck moves clockwise to the next contestant. This process continues at each table until all the cards have been won.

Tournament day ends with all students giving the teacher their cards and the teacher recording the number of cards won and compiling them as team points. For example: five cards earned equals five points for the team. One can see that this process would force a team's top speller, for example Robin, to work every bit as hard as the team's weakest speller, Pat. Equally important, Pat has as great a chance of emerging as the team MVP as does Robin. That positive codependence is accomplished by having the teams being maximally heterogeneous yet, having the actual competitions occurring in separate, performance ranked, flights.

On Monday when the students return to the class the teacher presents them with a newsletter containing the results of the previous day's contest. Figure 6.2 shows an example of a TGT newsletter.

The type of reward that is typically bestowed upon the winning team(s) after about 4 to 6 weeks of competition is often as simple as a pizza party with the teacher or the awarding of certificates (Figures 6.3 and 6.4).

Figure 6.2. TGT Newsletter

The Weekly Planet

4th Week March 28

FLASH! Fantastic Four Sweeps Language Arts tournament!

The Fantastic Four was the winning team this week with a total of 55 points. John T., Kris, and Alvin put in outstanding performances for the Four, each contributing sixty points to their team. Their victory brings the Four to second place in the National League standings, only six points behind the leading Giants! Mary said, "We won because our team works well together."

Hot on the heels of the Fantastic Four were the Brain Busters with 52 points. Anita and Tanya helped the team out with victories at their tables, while Peter tried for first at his. The Brain Busters are still in third place in National League competition, but are moving up fast! Darryl was overheard telling Peter, "We really learned to cooperate with each other."

Third this week were the American League Geniuses with 44 points. They were helped out by Kevin and Lisa A., both table winners. Mark told his teammates he had more of a chance to help others this week.

Other table winners were Lisa P. of the Daredevils and Mike of the Grammar Haters.

THIS WEEK'S SCORES

1st—Fantastic Four		*2nd—Brain Busters*		*3rd—Geniuses*	
John T.	60	Anita	60	Mark	40
Mary	40	Peter	50	Kevin	60
Kris	60	Darryl	40	Lisa A.	60
Alvin	60	Tanya	60	John F.	40
				Dewanda	20
	220		**210**		**220**

Daredevils		*Giants*		*Chipmunks*		*Grammar Haters*	
Lisa P.	60	Robert	40	Caroline	50	Sarah	20
Henry	20	Eric	20	Jerry	20	Willy	20
Cindi	40	Sharon	20	Charlene	30	Mike	60
Fred	40	Sylvia	40	James	20	Theresa	20
						John H.	20
	160		**120**		**120**		**150**

SEASON'S STANDING FOURTH WEEK

National League		*American League*	
Team	**Season Score**	**Team**	**Season Score**
Giants	195	Grammar Haters	185
Fantastic Four	180	Geniuses	162
Brain Busters	165	Daredevils	142
Chipmunks	147		

Figure 6.3. Certificate A

Reprinted by permission of the Johns Hopkins Team Learning Project Center for Research on Elementary and Middle Schools.

Figure 6.4. Certificate B

Reprinted by permission of the Johns Hopkins Team Learning Project Center for Research of Elementary and Middle Schools.

Student Teams Achievement Divisions (STAD)

Of the three most often used approaches to cooperative team learning, Student Teams Achievement Divisions (STAD), requires the least alteration in a teacher's normal routine. STAD works particularly well from the intermediate grades up through high school with any subject area/discipline that is amenable to objective testing.

As with TGT the teacher using STAD should begin by placing students into mixed ability teams. The students are then given an opportunity to give their team an identity through the naming process. Like TGT the instruction can employ whatever procedure the teacher deems appropriate. This could include group discussion, lectures, trips to the library, guest speakers, reading from the textbook, etc.

Business as usual continues until the day before the unit test. On that day the students are placed into team groups for a session of team study. They are told that team points will be awarded based on the number of points each student achieves on the test in excess of their previous average. In other words Pat, who had a previous average in geography of 65 percent can score 15 points for his team if he can post a score of 80 on the unit test. Robin, on the other hand, with a 90 percent average will have to really produce a great test if he is to produce any points at all for the team. (Many teachers have decided to award a 20 point bonus for a perfect test as a special incentive to top students like Robin.)

The following day the exams are taken individually by the students and are scored individually by their teacher. The teacher, however, still has one additional mathematical and clerical task ahead: the computation of team points. This is accomplished by having another class roster in the grade book (arranged by team) and recording the points achieved by each student and then producing team totals (Figure 6.5).

At this point all that remains to be done by the teacher is the announcement of results and the awarding of prizes. In our experience the intrinsic fun of STAD competition is as powerful a motivator as any extrinsic prize. Dick has used prizes as simple as bonus points (5 additional points to every member of the first place team, 3 to each second place team member, and 1 extra point to each third place team member). Other teachers have used certificates, popcorn or pizza. Some choose to distribute awards after each contest (test) or after a series of 4–5 competitions. These, as well as other variations of STAD are all within the discretion of the individual teacher.

Figure 6.5. Quiz Sheet (STAD and Jigsaw II)

Student	Date: Quiz: Base Score	Quiz Score	Improve-ment Points	Date: Quiz: Base Score	Quiz Score	Improve-ment Points	Date: Quiz: Base Score	Quiz Score	Improve-ment Points

Reprinted by permission of the Johns Hopkins Team Learning Project Center for Research on Elementary and Middle Schools

Jigsaw II

The third most commonly used format for cooperative team learning is Jigsaw II. Jigsaw I was the strategy successfully introduced by Aronson (discussed earlier) and was later adapted to fit the group competition aspect of the team learning environment by Slavin and his colleagues.

Jigsaw II works best in the upper grades as it requires increased sophistication as well as responsibility on the part of each team member. It is tremendously versatile and can be utilized with almost any piece of academic content.

The teacher prepares the class for Jigsaw II in the same manner as with STAD. Teams are created, names are chosen and instruction is ready to begin. But the teacher approaches a Jigsaw lesson fundamentally differently than a conventional teacher directed lesson. The teacher takes the instructional unit to be studied and divides it into a set of separate and discrete pieces. Let's assume, for example, that the teacher is going to use Jigsaw for instruction on a unit about Japan in a world geography class. The course syllabus states that instruction will cover religion, politics, government, and the economy. The teacher then literally tears up the unit into a jigsaw puzzle as illustrated in Figure 6.6.

Figure 6.6. Modern Day Japan

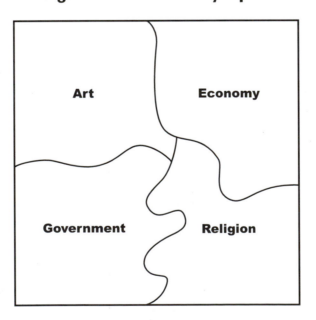

The teacher then approaches each team and assigns to one person on each team one segment of the content. Therefore, each team will have one student studying Japan's economy, each has one looking into its religion, and another looking at its politics (occasionally we might double assign one or two topics thus requiring the creation of five or six member teams).

Each student is given a study guide appropriate to their piece of the puzzle and the next few days are spent learning the material in whatever manner the teacher deems appropriate. Perhaps a trip to the library is in order, or reading from the text, or viewing a film, or interviewing community members.

Once the teacher believes that each student has had ample opportunity to learn the assigned material, she devotes a class period to the convening and deliberations of *expert* groups. The students are told that they are to assemble in separate corners of the room with all the other students who have been studying the same aspect of Japan as they have. If we visited the classroom on a day reserved for expert groups, we would find in one corner the experts on politics, another would contain the religion experts, a third the economy buffs, and the fourth corner would have the art specialists. The task for expert groups is the development of their individual confidence regarding their understandings of the particular content for which they have been given responsibility. This is a fun day for the teacher, but it requires significant self-discipline. Students who are not used to cooperating will want you to answer each of their individual questions. The teacher, while circulating around the room, must follow a basic rule of cooperative learning, *the only questions the teacher should answer are group questions.* This means that you, the teacher should not enter into the discussion until the *entire* expert group is confused or the group is deadlocked.

The following day when students come into class they are told to gather together with their teammates for team study. Each member of the team is then given copies of all four study guides by the teacher. However, they will have to rely on the experts in their group to learn the content. Generally several days are devoted to group study because each student will need to learn as much as 75 percent of the required content from their classmates.

After enough time has been provided for team study, the teacher gives the class a test on the material learned. Each student's test will be individually scored, and individual grades will be entered in the teacher's grade book. However team points will be computed in the same fashion as with STAD. Each point in excess of a student's previous average will become a point for the team. Appropriate rewards and prizes are awarded for team accomplishments.

An Example of a Hybrid

When using cooperative learning or other instructional approaches, teachers are wise to avoid orthodoxy. Each model should be seen as a beginning structure, a place to start. The content that one is teaching, the unique character of the class, and the context of the instructional environment should be allowed to inform lesson planning decisions. All a teaching model provides is a starting point and some guiding principles. Often creative teachers will chose elements from several models to craft an experience that will work for their students. To illustrate this type of customizing we'll share an example of a Jigsaw/STAD hybrid that Dick puy together for his senior government class a few years back.

Just forty minutes before class time, he found himself with the previous day's test not yet corrected and his new unit not yet planned. Consequently he was in dire need of a one day lesson plan, but a week-long unit certainly wouldn't have hurt. As he scanned his memory for viable ideas, it struck him. The night before, his department head had just reminded the faculty that with the school's mock election coming, they all needed to cover the election issues and the use of the voter's pamphlet. The teachers were informed that an ample supply of voter's pamphlets were available (a 100-page affair) in the departmental office. Remembering that discussion was all Dick needed to be off and running.

His first stop was the departmental office to collect a classroom set of pamphlets. Having secured them he spent the next twenty minutes selecting twelve races and twelve ballot measures that merited the students' attention. He wrote them longhand on a sheet that looked much like the election issues in Figure 6.7.

Figure 6.7. Election Issues

Attorney General	Governor
State Superintendent	Congress 1st Dist.
U.S. Senate	Congress 2nd Dist.
Ballot Measure 1	Ballot Measure 4
Ballot Measure 7	Ballot Measure 8
Ballot Measure 10	Ballot Measure 12

Fortunately, his class was already divided into six teams as he had been using STAD for a number of weeks. Dick then ran to the copy machine and made 36 copies of his worksheet thirty were put into one pile as a study guide and six more were taken to the paper cutter to be made into six decks of cards (one deck per team) each card contained one of the races and/or measures. This left Dick with just enough time to take a deep breath, grab his green and gold (the school colors) cowboy hat in one hand, the voters' pamphlets, study guides and cards in the other, and head off to class.

After a brief apology about not getting their tests corrected, he reminded the students of the upcoming election and provided a five minute pep talk on the importance of casting informed ballots in both the "real world" and in their school's mock election. He then told them to get into their teams. Dick now proceeded to visit each team, placing a deck of cards in his cowboy hat, and had each team member select four cards.

Dick then went up to the board where he wrote the directions shown in Figure 6.8.

Figure 6.8. Voter's Pamphlet Directions

Using the voters pamphlet, periodicals, and personal interviews (if appropriate) you are to compile the following information on the two positions assigned to you.

If it's a candidate:

Two key positions taken

Two major differences with his/her opponent

If it's a ballot measure:

Two arguments in favor

Two arguments against

Get to work

The rest of that class period was spent assisting students in learning the proper use of the voter's pamphlet and responding to group process questions. The next day's class was productively spent moving between the classroom and the library. The following day was spent putting the students into expert groups where the rule was "no teacher help unless the entire group is stumped." Dick intended to allow only one day for group study; however, based on the earnestness of their work and the scope of the assignment, he determined that two days would be necessary, and so the plan was adjusted. On the sixth day he gave a test. Students took it individually, yet, Dick also scored it for team bonus points. Just as he had told the students, he awarded each member of the first place team 5 bonus points, three points were given to each member of the second place team, while one point was awarded to everyone on the third place team.

Five days of learning and a test, all created out of less than 40 minutes of planning. Not bad! We say that only somewhat tongue in cheek. Obviously, we feel that quality lesson planning is important and in many cases cooperative learning requires more planning time than conventional instruction. Certainly, Dick should have been more organized, and he was lucky to have had a unit (the election) in the wings with which he was already familiar, and for which he had readily available materials. On the other hand, this story illustrates another important point. By empowering the students to serve as their own teachers, Dick was able to provide five days of meaningful and intellectually invigorating work without very much direct teacher input, coaching yes, but direct instruction, no.

To this day Dick contends that this was the hardest lesson for him to learn about cooperative learning. The students often learned more and learned it better when he took a back seat and had them become more dependent on each instead of their "expert" teacher!

What is important about each of the cooperative team learning structures is that all students, regardless of past level of performance, are capable of producing points, contributing to the team, and becoming valued by their peers. In fact, with cooperative team learning, the weaker students (in terms of past performance) have an even greater opportunity to generate team points. With cooperative team learning there are two factors that influence individual productivity: the degree of effort expended and the degree of cooperation engaged in. This is the beauty of using these structures with at-risk students. In order to gain feelings of competence, belonging, and usefulness all the student needs to do is make sincere and committed effort. In cooperative team learning there is a direct *return on personal investment*. We can't imagine any better strategy for supporting the development of an internal locus of control.

Accountability and Roles

While cooperative learning has enormous potential for making education a meaningful and rewarding experience for our at-risk students, as mentioned earlier, it also has the potential to put them at a greater disadvantage. Not infrequently, well meaning teachers implement cooperative learning in a manner that ironically serves to further alienate at-risk students rather than serving to enhance their feelings of membership, belonging, and usefulness. This occurs when insufficient attention is paid to individual and group accountability.

In a properly run cooperative team learning classroom, each child has a meaningful role to play and is a necessary factor in the success of their teammates. That is why we feel it is has such promise for building feelings of *usefulness*. However, if adequate attention is not paid to the principles of *effective* collaborative work we may find we are ending up with classrooms much like the ones we used to direct as novice teachers.

When we started teaching both of us enjoyed placing our students in groups, assigning them a joint project, and leaving them alone to complete it. While the assignments Dick provided his high school students were often quite complex, he rarely specified specific roles and responsibilities for each group member or provided the class with instruction in group process. The consequence of those omissions was what we call "sanctioned abandonment." The problem Dick found was that the most able students tended to do all the work. The at-risk students, often students without much self-confidence to begin with, simply allowed their more assertive classmates to carry the ball. Consequently, the weaker students would spend a full week or more without any meaningful engagement with their school work. Not only did sitting on the sidelines deprive them of valuable learning opportunities, it had to further reinforce their feelings of inadequacy.

This need not be the case if and when we pay appropriate attention to structuring individual accountability into our cooperative learning assignments. However, first we will have to teach our students some basic lessons regarding group process.

Students who have been schooled in the demands of conventional competitive instruction over the years have internalized a set of values and norms that are consistent with that form of classroom organization. However, to be successful in a cooperative environment they will need to learn some important lessons. Ann Shenkle (1989) pointed out that our successful, high-status students need to learn that:

♦ Each member must participate.

♦ Each person must listen to the others.

♦ Any question is a group question.

♦ No one is done until everyone is done. (Shenkle, 1989)

Likewise, she says, the at-risk student, the child with low academic status needs to be taught that:

♦ They can ask anybody in the group for help.

♦ Members of the group are required to help each other.

♦ Each contribution is of potential merit.

♦ Each member has responsibilities that must be accomplished in order for the group to turn out the best possible product (Shenkle, 1989).

At this point it would be helpful for you to try your hand at constructing a cooperative learning lesson that will work in a heterogeneous classroom and with significant potential for succeeding with your defeated and discouraged learners. The following Think and Do Exercise will help guide you through that process.

Think and Do Exercise—
Planning an Accountable Cooperative Learning Lesson

When developing a lesson or unit using the cooperative learning framework, it is useful to keep certain factors in mind. We've found answering the questions posed in the planning guide found in Figure 6.9 to be valuable in organizing our thoughts and ideas and then turning them into workable lesson plans.

Think of a lesson you want to teach in a cooperative format, then, using the planning guide provided, outline your lesson. Do you think the lesson that you've designed will reinforce your students' feelings of usefulness? Why or why not?

Figure 6.9. Cooperative Learning Planning Guide

1. Outcome desired: (Describe in product terms)

2. Rationale for using cooperative learning: (Why could this product not be produced as well and more efficiently individually?)

3. Role definitions: (For each role in the cooperative team specify the essential obligations/opportunities for this members contribution to the team)

4. Individual accountability: (How will each team member be held to account for his/her own contribution to the group project?)

When cooperative team learning has been properly implemented the consequences for students are remarkable. Not only have many studies documented improved levels of student academic performance when these structures are utilized (Slavin, 1995; Johnson, Johnson, and Holubec, 1990), but students report enjoying their education more. Perhaps most important for our purpose here is the finding that in classrooms using cooperative team learning, positive student attitudes towards students with learning challenges and students from other non-majority groups are enhanced. Any strategy that will cause all of the diverse students in a heterogeneous classroom to truly need and want to work with each other is a strategy that will make a significant difference in building students' feelings of *usefulness*.

Community Service

While cooperative learning offers us a structure for building our students' feelings of usefulness and making interdependence a natural part of the academic routine, it is not the only way that a school can telegraph a message to its students that they are contributing members of a social community. Increasingly, we are finding schools responding to the challenge posed by the late Ernest Boyer of the Carnegie Commission on Teaching. Boyer called for the institution of a new Carnegie Unit for high school graduation. He stated,

> "We conclude that during high school young people should be given opportunities to reach beyond themselves and feel more responsively engaged. They should be encouraged to participate in the communities of which they are a part. Therefore, we recommend that every high school student complete a service requirement—a new "Carnegie unit"—involving volunteer work in the community or at school."

> "The Carnegie unit, as historically defined, measures time spent in class—academic contact time. This new unit would put emphasis on

time in-service. The goal of the new Carnegie unit would be to help students see that they are not only autonomous individuals but also members of a larger community to which they are accountable. The program would tap an enormous source of unused talent and suggest to young people that they are needed. It would help break the isolation of the adolescent by bringing young people into contact with the elderly, the sick, the poor, and the homeless, as well as acquainting them with neighborhood and governmental issues (Boyer 1983, p.209)."

Service work is an opportunity for young persons to see and experience the impact of their efforts on the lives of other people. The two key words in the above statement are *impact* and *effort*. Historically, our schools have involved students in programs that serve charitable purposes. But these have asked for a rather passive involvement. While helping with canned food drives and collecting pennies for UNICEF certainly adds to the quality of life of those less fortunate, the lessons taught to participating students are often much less than we might hope for.

The giving that's involved in these "passive" activities consumes little energy from students. A contribution to the canned food drive is influenced more by what mom had in the cupboard than by a student's desire to help another human being. The collection of pennies has more relevance to one's stamina on Halloween night than one's commitment to feed the hungry. In addition, these activities are organized *for* the children not *by* them. Finally, they contribute to the view that those less fortunate are individuals to be pitied and looked after rather than capable people who may simply have a temporary need for a caring and helping hand.

A quality "service learning" program addresses each of the four principle needs (competence, belonging, usefulness, and potency) emphasized in this book. Service programs begin by fulfilling the students' powerful need to be needed or useful. This is because a good "service" program has the children working to provide a valuable service directly for persons in need. It involves the children in this work on an ongoing basis, so that they can feel a connection with the work and the client, and thereby develop a heightened sense of belonging. Finally the work involved must be important so that participation will produce feelings of competence, and because the work is important, its accomplishment should lead to an increased sense of personal potency.

While all children stand to benefit from participation in community service, the defeated/discouraged learners may stand the most to gain. As will be discussed at length in the next chapter, discouraged students may already have a tendency to view themselves as victims. Depending on the circumstances of his or her family, the child may have already begun to develop a negative view of self. Many at-risk students have no experiences that reinforce their self-image of being people who are capable of changing or controlling their lives, therefore, their helpless victim paradigm is accepted and internalized. By becoming service providers, at-risk children are able to begin internalizing the role of "actor" rather than "victim."

Service programs come in many shapes and sizes (McPherson, 1991). In some schools every class adopts a community agency (a nursing home, a recycling center, a homeless shelter) and then spends the equivalent of one day per month providing needed volunteer work for that organization. We recommend that students stay with the same agency and serve the same client group for at least a full school year so that they can experience both the impact of their work and feel a greater connection than could possibly be gained from the one shot "I gave at the office" syndrome.

At other schools the entire school adopts an organization and all the students are encouraged to find a way to contribute. Some may contribute to the clerical effort, others do maintenance work, and still others might read to clients. In this case the school as an institution develops a relationship with the other agency and as the agency prospers so does the collective consciousness of the school and the students who hold membership within the school.

In yet a third model, students select their own service project to which they are expected to provide a minimum amount of time per semester or year. Avenues for service can be within or outside of the school community. For example, students might tutor younger children or assist the school nurse in carrying out her duties. Other students might do volunteer work at the blood bank, YMCA, or at a local soup kitchen. Time logs and journals should be kept and shared, group discussions can be facilitated by teachers, where the lessons drawn from contributing to society are shared and processed.

A particularly innovative approach that involves students grades K–12 is the development of a scholarship foundation that will support the realization of career goals by all members of their class. These "Your Dream is Our Dream Foundations" are aimed at providing the same degree of "optimism" that Eugene Lang's "I Have A Dream" foundation (Levin, 2001) provided for the children of the elementary school he adopted in New York City. In this case, however, the resources of the foundation will be produced entirely from the labor of the students themselves.

Examples of fund raising activities could include kindergartners drawing pictures for the pages of calendars that are lettered by upper grade students and printed by the middle school students. Elementary school students could then sell the calendars door to door on Halloween night (instead of collecting candy) to raise funds for their class' foundation. Each child salesperson might explain that the proceeds of the sale will help classmates in financial need to realize their educational dreams.

Middle and high school students would be expected to give ten hours per semester of after school and weekend labor to the foundation. Community members could call a special phone number staffed by student volunteers to request help ranging from raking leaves to conducting spring cleaning. For example, when a community member had a ten-hour job to be done, the foundation would send five students for a two-hour period on a Saturday morning, and if the work was completed to the customer's satisfaction, the foundation would bill the customer for $5 per person hour for a total of $50 payable to the foundation. Private businesses and other donors would be asked to underwrite labor costs so the same service could be provided free of charge to senior citizens and low income residents.

Through this program, participating students can gain the deep emotional satisfaction that comes from doing hard work on valued meaningful real world tasks that provide a direct benefit for the community, all the while contributing to the realization of a precious dream of a classmate.

The "Your Dream is Our Dream" process culminates on graduation night with the awarding of scholarships. At this point everyone in the community is able to see that each member of the graduating class, regardless of level of affluence, was able to realize their dreams through the efforts of their classmates. While we are not aware of the full "Your Dream is Our Dream Foundation" being installed at any school, each of the parts are present and functioning in numerous locales. This "Your Dream is Our Dream" process simply puts all the pieces together in a manner that could truly reinforce belonging, usefulness, potency, and optimism for *all* students.

Whatever approach a school might choose to take with community service, the guidelines in Figure 6.10 will prove helpful.

Figure 6.10. Guidelines for Community Service

1. Will students be able to see the utility of their work?

2. Does the service require personal effort and sacrifice on the part of the student?

3. Does the school have a means to show its recognition and appreciation of student contributions?

4. Will the work be performed outside of classtime?

Concluding Comment

Our students see school as a social experience. It is here that they spend time with their friends and peers. For that reason it is the best environment to teach the skills of social responsibility. Unfortunately, when we organize classrooms competitively or individualistically, we miss out on that opportunity. By properly structuring meaningful interdependence into the student day and school experience, we will be able to provide students with a profound sense of their value to others. This is important and necessary for all children but can often prove to be a literal lifesaver for our once defeated learners.

References

American Association for the Advancement of Science (AAAS). (1993). *Benchmarks for science literacy.* New York: Oxford University Press.

Aronson, E. (1978). *The Jigsaw classroom.* Beverly Hills, CA: Sage.

Boyer, E. (1983). *High school: A report from the Carnegie Commission.* New York: Harper & Row.

Johnson, D., Johnson R., & Holubec, E. (1990). *Circles of learning: Cooperation in the classroom* (3rd ed.). Edina, MN: Interaction Book Co.

Johnson, D., Johnson R., & Holubec, E. (1994). *Cooperative learning in the classroom.* Alexandria, VA: Association for Supervision and Curriculum.

Kagan, S. (1985). Dimensions of cooperative classroom structures. In R. Slavin, S. Sharan, S. Kagan, R. Hertz-Lazarowitz, C. Webb, & R. Schmuck (Eds). *Learning to cooperate; Cooperate to learn.* New York: Plenum.

Kagan, Spencer. (1997). *Cooperative learning.* San Clemente, CA: Kagan Professional Development.

Levin, Carl. (2001, November). "In recognition of the Eugene M. Lang I Have A Dream Foundation." Congressional Record, 107th congress First Session.

McPherson, Kate. (1991). Project service leadership: Service projects in Washington State. *Phi Delta Kappan,* 27 N:10, p 750–753.

National Council of Teachers of Mathematics. (2000). *NCTM 2000 Principles and Standards for School Mathematics.* Reston VA: NCTM.

Ouchi, W. G. (1981). *Theory 2.* Reading, MA: Addison-Wesley.

Peters, T. J., & Waterman, R. H. Jr. (1982). *In search of excellence: Lessons from america's best run companies.* New York: Harper & Row.

Rapp, J. (1991). *The Effect of Cooperative Learning on Selected Student Variables.* Unpublished doctoral dissertation, Washington State University.

Sagor, R. (1986). Perhaps the nation is at-risk after all: Perceptions of a high school principal. *NASSP Bulletin,* May.

Senge, P. (1990). *The fifth discipline: The art & practice of the learning organization.* New York: Doubleday.

Sharan, S. (1990). *Cooperative learning: Theory and research.* New York: Prager Publishers.

Shenkle, A. (1989). *Reaching the student at risk.* Learning Institute, Springhouse, PA: Springhouse Corporation.

Slavin, Robert. (1986). *Using student team learning* (3rd ed.) Baltimore, MD: Center for Research on Elementary and Middle Schools, Johns Hopkins University.

Slavin, Robert. (1994). *Cooperative learning: Theory research and practice* (2nd ed.). Needham Heights, MA: Pearson Allyn& Bacon.

TIMSS 1995 http://timss.bc.edu/timss1995i/TIMSSNews.html.

7

DEVELOPING A SENSE OF PERSONAL POTENCY

Once we've provided our students with an opportunity to experience success (Chapters 3 and 4—*competence*), which should help build their self-esteem, and we've afforded them the chance to be accepted as unique individuals worthy of "membership" at school (Chapter 5—*belonging*), and we have given them opportunities to make meaningful contributions to their community (Chapter 6—*usefulness*); we have assisted our at-risk students in developing a strong foundation for resilience. This results in significant armament against alienation. However, there is one more basic need that must be nurtured if we are to become confident of their ability to ward off at-riskness. This is an attribute that too often is overlooked because on the surface, it appears socially unbecoming. This final leg of the "four horsemen of motivation" is a person's need for personal "power."

In contemporary society the pursuit of power is generally viewed as a base emotion. Politicians feel obliged to tell us that they aren't really covetous of power, but, rather find themselves so passionately committed to issues that they feel called to serve in elective office. As a society we've categorized humility, a positive attribute, as the polar opposite of *power seeking*. Consequently, we have grown to view individuals who admit to possessing a drive for power, whether it is over their own lives, others' lives, or over the larger society, as individuals of lesser moral fiber than the rest of us. That perspective is unfortunate because many thoughtful social scientists, William Glasser, chief among them (Glasser, 1990), make a compelling case that the need for power is as natural for human beings as eating and breathing.

While we all need to guard against ethical lapses, acts of inhumanity, and other abuses of trust, which have resulted too frequently from actions of the power-crazed, we must accept the fact that the desire to possess control over our own lives and the gaining of mastery over our environment is a natural drive for both children and adults. Ultimately, accepting the centrality of this need will prove crucial if our efforts to develop school programs that foster resiliency for youth are to succeed.

William Glasser, a child psychiatrist with particular interest in schooling and educational issues, has articulated a theory of human behavior called choice theory. Outlined in a book, *Choice Theory in the Classroom* (Glasser 1999). Here he explored a perspective on student motivation that is relevant for every educator who works with alienated youth or defeated/discouraged learners.

Choice Theory Explained

Choice theory is built on the premise that we humans are innately driven to maximize the satisfaction of a specific set of genetically ingrained needs. The five basic needs, according to Glasser are:

- survival,
- belonging and love,
- power,
- the drive to have fun, and
- freedom.

Glasser argues that these needs are an integral part of our genetic makeup, and therefore, from the time of conception cannot be denied. He contends that our entire lives are spent seeking out and enjoying "need satisfying" experiences. He contrasts his theory to the one offered by stimulus-response theorists, who, he points out, have dominated educational theory and practice for decades. Behaviorists argue that humans are naturally driven to achieve external rewards and/or to avoid extrinsic punishment. Glasser contends that this is a fraudulent perspective. By contrast he posits that human behavior is, in actuality, a continuing drive to seek out and repeat those experiences that we once found intrinsically satisfying. Specifically, this means returning to experiences that have, in the past, satisfied one or more of our five inbred needs.

Glasser metaphorically describes how this occurs. It begins with each of us developing a unique and personal "quality world." Glasser asserts that from our earliest moments, we experience events that are *need satisfying*. When experiencing such an event, we make a cognitive snapshot of that moment and that photograph becomes a picture in a photo album that represents our quality world. As a result, our quality world becomes a growing gallery of images and feelings that recall events that satisfied our six most basic human needs. Each choice we make during our lives, according to Glasser, is an effort to recreate and revisit the pleasurable experiences that live on in our quality world. For example, early in our lives most of us had our needs for love, belonging, and survival satisfied by our parents. That picture of unconditional familial love is carried with us throughout our lives. We then try to revisit and relive those quality world events through subsequent relationships and experiences.

This conception of a quality world helps explain some of the differences in behavior we see between successful and alienated students. In all likelihood our successful students have had more "need satisfying" life experiences than have their alienated peers. As a result they have many more pictures in their quality world photo album, to serve as referents for further investment of effort. Not surprisingly, with the successful student, many of these pictures relate to positive experiences that they have had, or may one day expect to have, at school. These snapshots may contain images of success, collaboration with teachers, or involvement with school tasks. Unfortunately, this has not been the case for the alienated students. For many of them, school has simply not proven need satisfying. They are unlikely to have felt much CBUPO at school, and consequently, they probably don't hold many images of school life in their quality world album.

The essence of choice theory is that we will continue to choose our behavior in accordance with an expectation that our choices will result in need satisfaction. Consequently, successful students will continue to choose to invest themselves in schooling, and unsuccessful students may choose to invest their time in other less productive pursuits. One can see how choice theory explains the difficulty that the defeated/discouraged learner has in developing the levels of "engagement" with school tasks that Welhage (1989) found to be so essential for success.

Ultimately, Glasser tells us that our choices in behavior are the single most significant way that we have to express our personal power. It is through these choices that we assert who we are and what we want to be known for.

The Concept of Total Behavior

Hardly anyone would disagree with the premise that we choose our behavior. Even Glasser's notion that we choose our behavior based on the expectation of receiving the satisfaction that those behaviors have provided us in the past seems self-evident. However, *Choice Theory* adds another wrinkle to the concept of the volitional aspect of behavior. Glasser stretches our present understandings by telling us that the behavior we choose must be understood in its totality and *total behaviors* have four inextricable parts:

1. the action,
2. the thoughts that coincide with the action,
3. the feeling associated with the action, and
4. the physiology that accompanies the behavior.

While most of us won't argue that we choose our *actions* and perhaps even the *thoughts* that go along with our actions, Glasser goes further, telling us that the *associated feelings* (anger, frustration, etc.) and *physiology* (a red face, indigestion, perspiration, etc.) are also part of that which we have consciously chosen. His key point here is that when we chose a particular behavior, we could just as easily have chosen an alternative. If the one we chose is not functional (leads to ulcers, academic failure, alienation, a poor self-concept), choice theory says that we had the option within us to choose otherwise. By accepting this view we see ourselves as choosing our indigestion, our self-concept, even our ulcers!

According to Glasser the problem with our understanding of total behavior is that we are reluctant to accept that we have control over particularly unpleasant consequences of our behavior. We find it easier to see ourselves as innocent victims who have little control over the circumstances that lead us to frustration, stress, or failure. It is that type of denial that leads to the problem of external attribution. As you recall from Chapter 1, at-risk youth generally have developed a belief system that explains what happens to them as a consequence of forces outside their control (an external locus of control). They see themselves as victims not actors. Therefore, they do not believe that they internally possess the power to satisfy the basic needs that Glasser tells us we are innately driven to have satisfied.

Understanding Attribution

To appreciate the consequence of misplaced attribution, it is helpful to explore the windows through which a young person views their personal efficacy. There are two dimensions for us to consider. The first is whether the student is inclined to attribute past experiences to luck (an external locus of control) or to personal action (an internal locus of control). The second dimension grows from an individual's pattern of experience, e.g., have experiences of success or failure been consistent or have they been varied (Alderman, 1990)?

Those two dimensions, internal/external, and stable/unstable can be displayed on a matrix as illustrated in Figure 7.1.

Figure 7.1. Locus of Control Matrix

Internal/Stable (1)	Internal/Unstable (2)
External/Stable (3)	External/Unstable (4)

It will be helpful to discuss the unique characteristics found in the four cells of this matrix, in particular regard to their implications for at-risk youth.

Quadrant 1—Internal/Stable

The young persons in this quadrant hold a belief that they are fundamentally in control of their school experience. Such individuals have experienced stability in terms of performance. The repetition of successful patterns of school behavior has led to high degrees of academic self-confidence. These children find themselves in the success-breeds-success mode, and, consequently, every positive outcome serves to reinforce preexisting feelings of personal empowerment.

On rare occasions we might encounter a child who posits internal attributions, yet consistently experiences failure. That profile is extremely problematic. Clearly, such children would be subject to serious self-esteem problems and could be prime candidates for clinical depression. Having internalized the responsibility for their shortcomings and not having learned alternative behaviors that lead to success, they have every reason to see themselves as "losers." Fortunately, such children make up only a small percentage of the youth we will see in our public school classrooms.

Quadrant 2—Internal/Unstable

These children believe that they are in control of their personal success or failure, and while they have not enjoyed universal success, they are disinclined to pass off the responsibility for their shortcomings to others. In most regards these children are well adjusted and they understand and accept personal responsibility for both their accomplishments and failures.

Quadrant 3—External/Stable

Here we find children who attribute their past and present performance to factors as outside of their immediate control. These children are believers in luck and conclude that lady luck has either been consistently smiling or frowning upon them. If these children are on a successful roll, they are likely to ascribe it to a streak of good fortune and will probably elect to keep rolling the die until or unless their luck takes a change for the worse. On the other hand, when and if these children experience a string of disappointments, it often leads to deep feelings of hopelessness. The children may logically conclude "what's the use in trying," and even worse, "what's the use in believing."

Quadrant 4—External/Unstable

These children are our classical gamblers. While they may fear that they lack personal control over the acquisition of desired outcomes, they have had positive experiences that lead the gambler in them to want to keep playing the game, because there is reason to believe that, over time, luck will improve.

Most of our defeated/discouraged learners can be found in quadrants 3 and 4. They are disproportionately externalizers who feel that success in school is beyond their control. Our task as teachers is to work with them to create dissonance around this belief. We need to teach them that they do indeed have control over the factors that influence achievement and consequently satisfaction of their basic needs.

To better understand this, let's put ourselves in the psychological position of an at-risk youth. Our needs have not been met at school, and the school process has not appeared to replicate many elements of our quality world. Furthermore, if our school experiences have been consistent over time, we would begin to lack faith in our ability to change the total behaviors that haven't been working satisfactorily for us.

The power of Glasser's Choice Theory is that it tells us that this pessimistic prognosis need not prevail. However, if we want to reverse this syndrome for at-risk youth it will require a substantial restructuring of the typical classroom and school. We have already looked at some of the pieces of that restructuring, e.g., quality assessment mastery expectations, problem-based constructivist learning, cooperative learning, learning style compatible classrooms, etc. These are good starting points. However, there are numerous other promising techniques that can assist us helping our at-risk students develop an internal locus of control.

Goal Setting/Achievement/Celebration Cycle

One of the most powerful techniques for the development and strengthening of an internal locus of control is the Goal Setting/Achievement/Celebration Cycle.

Affirmations

In recent years successful athletic coaches have found that structuring goal setting and then providing feedback on goal attainment can be a powerful motivator. It is not uncommon in high school and college locker rooms to see specific sets of individual and team goals prominently posted. They are spoken of and affirmed before each contest. In setting goals, players and their coaches discuss the needs of both the individual and the team, what they want to accomplish, and ultimately what they are willing to commit their energy toward achieving. Once those discussions have been held, teammates publicly state their commitment to a vigorous pursuit of both team and individual goals. Behavioral psychologists refer to these public pronouncements as the *affirmation* stage.

The act of affirmation is critically important. By publicly declaring our intentions to rigorously pursue particular courses of action, we place added pressure on ourselves to perform. Therefore, the act of affirmation itself enhances commitment. However, the affirmation stage only continues to have meaning if we anticipate a meaningful evaluation of our efforts. The athletes know that they can always look forward to the game or an upcoming contest as a test of commitment.

Unfortunately, many of us have not yet experienced this cycle with our work. Many teachers have had bad experiences with goal-based evaluation systems. In these systems, every academic year begins with a bureaucratic requirement to articulate goals and state them to a supervisor. Unfortunately, the process usually ends there. The teacher and supervisor are free to ignore the performance goals for the remainder of the year. It is no surprise that such cynical and incomplete approaches to the goal setting process have shown themselves to be useless as motivators.

On the contrary, in athletics, the contest or game provides a very direct and immediate form of feedback. If the athlete has declared an intent to rush for over 100 yards, complete 50 percent of his passes, serve five aces, or shut out the opponent, it will be clear and unambiguous whether or not the goal was achieved, exceeded, or went unmet.

On those teams where goal setting has become part of the routine, the locker room meeting following the game becomes a time to review affirmations, to take stock of shortcomings, and to celebrate successes. Not infrequently, tangible symbols of goal attainment are distributed: game balls, helmet stickers, or posters on the walls. Even when goals haven't been achieved, the process of affirmation and measurement serve to help refocus, recommit, and reaffirm individual and collective control over performance. These same cycles of goal setting, measurement, feedback, and celebration can be and are being applied in many schools and classrooms around the country.

Our goal should be to have our students set and achieve long-term goals that require significant planning and self-management. But, due to the history of failure that at-risk students bring with them into our classrooms, our initial goal setting efforts will work best if they begin with short-term targets that can be easily monitored and achieved with a modicum of focused and committed effort. The following four criteria are the ones that many of our teaching colleagues have found to be helpful in assisting students in framing goals.

- ◆ Is it desirable? Something you really want.

- ◆ Is it achievable? Something you can do.

- ◆ Is it believable? Something you think you can accomplish.

- ◆ Is it measurable? It describes where, when, and what will be accomplished.

The students need to answer all four of these questions affirmatively prior to receiving the teacher's endorsement and encouragement to pursue a goal. At the beginning of the year, it is wise to set daily goals in the primary grades and weekly goals in the upper grades. Even where the goal is a weekly one, it is still advisable (at the early stages) to monitor and measure achievement on a daily basis. At the end of the feedback period (day/week/etc.) it becomes the students' job to collect the evidence and report to the teacher or to their classmates on goal attainment. If the goal, which had been established, met the four criteria stated above; if the student put forward the requisite effort to achieve it; and if you, the teacher, provided adequate coaching; it is likely that the goal will be achieved. When that occurs it is time for high-fives and a congratulatory note or letter home. Should the effort have fallen short of goal attainment, then the children should be asked to reflect on what precisely went wrong and should develop a strategy to achieve the very same goal or a similar one, perhaps more realistically constructed, in the near future.

The faculty at Willamette Middle School in West Linn, Oregon developed a form that homeroom teachers used with their students to monitor goal attainment. That form (Figure 7.2, Quarterly Goals) was printed on four-part carbonless paper so that a copy could be sent home after each nine-week goal period. The cumulative sheet then served as a constant reminder of past performance. By using this written affirmation system and an advisory program (see Chapter 8) for coaching, the faculty at Willamette found that they could effectively help most students achieve their goals. In fact, the school counselor at Willamette found that consistent goal setting and follow-up produced an average increase of one full grade point (in a 4.0 system) with at-risk students in a mere nine-weeks time!

Figure 7.2. Quarterly Goals

Name: _____

A goal can help you achieve success if it is:

1. Desireable

    It is something you really want.

2. Achieveable

    It is possible—something you can do.

3. Believeable

    It is something you are confident you can accomplish.

4. Measurable

    It describes what, where, and when. At some point in time, you can say, "I did it."

1st Quarter Goal:

     I will _____

     Results _____

2nd Quarter Goal:

     I will _____

     Results _____

3rd Quarter Goal:

     I will _____

     Results _____

4th Quarter Goal:

     I will _____

     Results _____

Top Copy	Copy 2	Copy 3	Copy 4	Copy 5
Home-June	Home-April	Home-Jan.	Home-Nov.	Home-Sept.

Teacher as Coach/Student as Worker

The use of the goal setting/achievement/celebration model necessitates a particular type of student teacher relationship. It is a relationship best described as that of an *academic coach*. This is more than semantically different from our traditional understandings of *instructor*. As an academic coach, the teacher ceases to be the "supreme giver of grades" or the "great passer of judgments," instead, the teacher becomes a coworker, teaming with the student in a mutual effort to help the student succeed with tasks that both deem valuable.

A metaphor that we've found helpful is that of the Olympic diving or skating coach. When we watch these people coaching we see them engaged in true partnerships with the athlete. We see them consulting with their student, providing lots of feedback, and assisting the athlete in developing the necessary discipline to achieve a goal that is jointly valued. Not only does this type of relationship place the teacher in a new light (supporter or facilitator rather than boss), but it also transforms the student role into that of a worker. Increasingly, observers point out that in typical American classrooms, it is the teacher who is doing all the work, while many of the students just go along for the ride. Athletes who let their coaches do all the work would find it very hard to bring home a medal!

When we implement these new job descriptions, the student as the "knowledge worker" and the teacher as the "academic coach," it becomes very clear who is charged with which responsibility.

It is important to note that the current model, the teacher directed instruction approach to teaching, with the teacher doing most of the work, is relatively new to education. The basic assumption that justified the introduction of the teacher directed instruction model couldn't have been used in the era of the one room school house. And in most schools it can't be justified now! When one decrees that the teacher is to be the source of knowledge and the purveyor of information, it becomes desirable even imperative to have all the students at precisely the same cognitive place at the same time. If the students differ in readiness or level of understanding, the "direct instruction" teacher will be teaching over the heads of some and beneath the understandings of others. To expect a direct instruction teacher to do otherwise would require superhuman skills. But, even if it could be done, it would still be quite inefficient.

However, in a one room schoolhouse with the children spread across twelve grades, no one could reasonably expect the teacher to provide all that was needed through direct instruction. Neither time nor space nor energy permitted it. Rather, she was expected to be the manager of student learning. Her instructional job was to outline the tasks and then set the students to doing their own work under her guidance. It is a role that reformers now call the *guide on the side*, rather than the *sage on the stage*. It also looks surprisingly like the job of a foreman in a productive workplace. Foremen assist those under their supervision to do the best possible work. Then, when the work is accomplished, the entire team looks good.

There is another problem with the direct instruction model. In this model, the goals that are being pursued belong to the teacher alone. Students covetous of the affection of the teacher or driven to achieve a 4.0 GPA, perhaps will have a willingness to work hard in pursuit of another person's goal. But, if the children are not motivated by such things, which our at-risk students seldom are, then they can be expected to seek the easy way out, to negotiate a treaty (Powell, 1985), or disengage. None of those decisions should be expected to build an internal locus of control.

However, when we adjust our approach and become the *guide on the side*, we become a *facilitator*, a *coach*, or in corporate terms, a *manager*. In his book *The Quality School*, William Glasser (1990) describes in great detail the type of manager that is now considered most desirable in the corporate world. He does so by borrowing heavily from Edward Deming, the man who is considered by most to be the father of the "Japanese" approach to management. Deming and Glasser argue that schools and businesses no longer need the "boss manager" of the past, rather, they suggest that what we need are *lead managers*. A lead manager is someone who demonstrates the principles that Edward Deming taught the Japanese over 40-years ago and that later assisted that country in becoming one of the strongest economic forces in the post war world.

Four Essential Elements of Lead Management

Glasser (1998) states that there are four essential elements to the work of the lead manager. They are:

1. *The leader engages the workers in a discussion of the quality of the work to be done and the time needed to do it so that they have a chance to add their input. The leader makes a constant effort to fit the job to the skills and the needs of the workers* (p.31).

Traditionally, students work toward a single goal: the satisfaction of their teacher. While successful students may be willing to endure this, because they believe it will ultimately lead to desired ends, defeated/discouraged learners often see this as just another frustrating and alienating hoop to jump through. Those students will be inclined to see the "boss manager's" standards as way too arbitrary to motivate and sustain effort. However, when placed in a lead management situation, the students (workers) who have participated in establishing the standards of quality will be more likely to invest in their achievement.

2. *The leader (or a worker designated by the leader) shows or models the job so that the worker who is to perform the job can see exactly what the manager expects. At the same time, the workers are continually asked for their input as to what they believe may be a better way* (p.32).

In this way the teacher (lead manager) instructs the students (workers) on what is expected, but does not hold him/herself out as the ultimate expert. This posture both makes explicit and legitimizes the fact that the student could well have something of practical value to add to the work ahead. Considering the practical bent of many of our defeated/discouraged learners, inviting them into a discussion of the nature of the work to be performed could touch directly on one of their learning strengths. Just as it is hard to imagine an Olympic coach refusing to listen to input from the athletes, it is hard to imagine the lead managing teacher tuning out his/her students.

   3. *The leader asks the workers to inspect or evaluate their own work for quality, with the understanding that the leader accepts that they know a great deal about how to produce high-quality work and will therefore listen to what they say* (p.32).

In the traditional classroom the teacher is the sole quality control officer. While advantaged students will learn how to decipher the teacher's expectations, alienated students will probably find the teacher's expectations inscrutable. In either case, the students are taught only to work to the level of the boss' expectation and that the only goal is to meet this external standard. However, when the student is asked to help in setting the standard, then their quality world comes into the equation. Teachers who have employed this strategy often report that students will set and reach for higher self-imposed standards than their "boss-managing teachers" would have ever set.

   4. *The leader is a facilitator in that he shows the workers that he has done everything possible to provide them with the best tools and workplace as well as a non-coercive, non-adversarial atmosphere in which to do the job* (p.32).

In traditional classrooms where the teacher is both the prosecutor and judge, discouraged students sometimes are led to feel that their teacher has a vested interest in their failure. Student failure, it is presumed, lends proof to the claim that the work was difficult; it substantiates the bell curve, or might be seen as serving some other perverse need of the teacher. Yet, a lead managing teacher will be seen as wanting all of the students to succeed. As in the business world, the manager who presides over a high-performing team knows that he/she will be recognized and rewarded as a superior manager.

Although the lead management style of teaching is more fulfilling for educators, the students are the real beneficiaries of this approach. They work harder, they learn more, and they have an opportunity to take real pride in their efforts. It is that last factor, taking pride in their accomplishments, that is so needed by the discouraged learner. The boss managing teacher can't provide that pride, while the lead managing teacher can't keep students from bathing in it.

The following Think and Do Exercise: Lead Managing for Excellence, will give you an opportunity to try your hand at designing a unit of instruction that places you in the "lead manager" role.

Think and Do Exercise—
Lead Managing for Excellence

Assume that you want to change the traditional classroom roles. The students will become the workers and you will become the lead manager. Now keeping in mind one of your "defeated/discouraged learners" as well as one of your more advantaged students, consider how you might incorporate each of Glasser's four conditions:

1. The leader engages the workers in a discussion of the quality of the work to be done and the time needed to do it so that they have a chance to add their input.

2. The leader (or a worker designated by the leader) shows or models the job so that the worker who is to perform the job can see exactly what the manager expects.

3. The leader asks the workers to inspect or evaluate their own work for quality,

4. The leader is a facilitator in that he shows the workers that he has done everything possible to provide them with the best tools and workplace as well as a non-coercive, non-adversarial atmosphere in which to do the job.

Using the lesson plan worksheet provided in Figure 7.3, outline a potential lesson.

After completing the outline, ask yourself these questions:

♦ Do you think your plan will work?

♦ What will be the impact on your at-risk students?

♦ What will be the impact on your educationally advantaged students?

Figure 7.3. Lesson Plan Worksheet

Think of a skill or important piece of academic content that lends itself to the student as worker and the teacher as coach role definition.

1. Discuss how you might coordinate student work on that content in a manner that is likely to:

    a. meet basic student needs (survival, belonging and love, power, the drive to have fun, freedom.

    b. produce quality work

2. What will you do and what will the students be expected to do?

Before we leave the discussion of lead management and the new roles of "student as worker" and "teacher as academic coach" we think it would be worthwhile to review just how neatly this fits with the philosophy of constructivism.

Jacqueline and Martin Brooks' book *The Case for the Constructivist Classroom* (1999), provides a wonderful introduction to constructivist teaching. Among the ideas discussed in the book are the following five principles for good constructivist teaching.

- ◆ Teachers should seek and value students' points of view.
- ◆ Classroom activities should challenge student suppositions.
- ◆ Teachers should pose problems of emerging relevance.
- ◆ Teachers should build lessons around primary concepts and big ideas.
- ◆ Teachers should assess student learning in the context of daily learning.

Several good examples of instructional strategies based on these constructivist theory can be found in the book *Developing Logical Thinkers* by Dale Phillips (1999).

Phillips points out that there is an important link between constructivist methods and the development of student potency. In Chapter 5 we discussed the effect of using children's interests as a means of providing a sense of belonging to students. Similarly we can foster children's feelings of potency by allowing the children a degree of choice in the area to be studied. This can provide a real sense of control over the student's environment. By focusing on children's own ideas and then using those ideas as a base to build on, the children's sense of self importance and potency is enhanced.

Most of us have had the experience of figuring out something difficult by ourselves, informed only on our own ideas. Consider again the child in Chapter 4 who spent an entire weekend wiring an electric circuit and then excitedly reported, "I got it, Mr. Cox." This student derived a sense of competency from his work. Because he did this on his own, he could logically conclude that he would be able to reconstruct this understanding anytime he wished. Furthermore, this accomplishment led him to confidently predict that he would be able to construct other complex circuits. It is that confidence that informs us that this student does, in fact, feel potent!

Four Links to Success

In an article on motivating the at-risk student Kay Alderman (1990) raised four factors that she described as the *links to success* for at-risk students. Links to success refer to those factors that when adequately addressed by teachers, increased the likelihood of student success and the development of an internal locus of control. For that reason she felt these four factors ought to be regarded as the "route" to the internal locus of control. The four links are:

- Proximal goals,
- Learning strategies,
- Successful experience, and
- Attribution for success.

Alderman's point is that when goals are immediate and attainable, when the strategies employed are appropriate for the learner (neither too difficult nor too easy), and the classroom is organized for mastery, thereby making success predictable, then students will be likely to credit themselves for eventual success.

Alderman persuasively argues that continuous and deliberate attention to those four factors can help us to use classroom instruction to provide one more notch in the belt of the internal locus of control for our at-risk students.

To illustrate how attention to choice theory, the goal process, and the development of an internal locus of control can turn around the experience of an at-risk student, it would be good to consider one more case study. This one involves a student whom Dick encountered when working in an alternative school.

Brad: A Case Study

Brad was an alternative school student. Like his older sister he had dropped out of school, lived at home with his unemployed mother, and maintained only the most minimal involvement with school. During the previous academic year Brad and his sister failed to meet the attendance requirements at their school, but with their mother's intervention, they were allowed to stay enrolled, although they were receiving almost no academic credit for their efforts.

When the New Year began Brad made his annual "new year" resolutions but soon fell back to his old ways. While he appeared to like the new head teacher and he voluntarily signed up for all his classes, he and his mother had no difficulty inventing a myriad of excuses for his missing class. Hardly a day went by without a call from Mom, who needed an errand run right away. Trips to the grocery store or garage somehow always took precedence over school.

When the first quarter ended and students had to complete their self-assessment, Brad was visibly disappointed. Once again he had accumulated almost no credits, but worse, he had nothing to show for his interaction with the new head teacher whom he liked and identified with.

Mr. Cohen, the new head teacher, sat down for a conference with Brad to discuss his options. They discussed the situation reasonably. Without the acquisition of substantial credits during the next quarter, Brad would be dropped from the rolls. Over the objection of his mother and several of the other parents, the new head teacher had declared that the school would return to its old policy of dropping unengaged students and bringing in more committed students who were languishing on the waiting list.

Brad's mom told him that Mr. Cohen couldn't get away with it. But, in his heart Brad knew that Mr. Cohen was right. If other students wanted or needed the education more than he, they had a right to the limited spaces at the school.

Jointly a plan was drawn up and a contract written. Brad determined the number of classes he needed to attend weekly, the number of assignments he had to complete, and the independent study projects he had to fulfill in order to earn the necessary credits. He drew up a schedule with mid-term guideposts and asked Mr. Cohen to help him monitor his progress. They set an appointment for every Friday morning to review the work completed.

During the first week Brad's mother called him away for several "emergencies," so declared by his mother. While the end of that week showed progress over the first quarter, it was far from being on track with Brad's goal. He and Mr. Cohen talked about the situation and took a look at the work ahead. Brad reaffirmed his commitment. The question that went unspoken was, "Would Brad be strong enough to resist his mother's enabling behavior?"

On Wednesday of the following week, Brad was called out of Mr. Cohen's class for a phone call from his mother. Because this was a familiar pattern, Mr. Cohen didn't expect to see Brad again for the rest of the day. Therefore, the teacher could hardly suppress his grin when, five minutes later, Brad reentered the room, announcing to everyone, "I told her I just couldn't go! Gaining my credits is more important, and she could wait to get the laundry until after school!" Brad sat down, joined actively in the discussion, and had the look on his face of a man who had just won a major victory. He felt empowered to make things happen in his life. He had taken charge and it felt good.

Brad graduated at the end of the year, obtaining two year's worth of credit in less than a year's time. The next fall he entered the local community college. His mother led a short and unsuccessful rebellion against the head teacher, ultimately failing to get him to drop his "overemphasis" on academics.

The strength to break away from the pattern of victimization had to come from Brad himself. But he had some help. His personal relationship with Mr. Cohen helped him to feel supported. He now believed that he had a partner in the education enterprise. The mechanisms by which the school awarded credit (time spent, work produced, and mastery achieved) gave him clear targets to shoot for, and the development and affirmation of a plan and supportive monitoring by Mr. Cohen provided him with the structure he needed to take advantage of his pursuit of his own quality world.

Brad had all the necessary pictures of the quality world within his head; he simply needed the structure and encouragement of the school to show him how to satisfy his basic needs. Finally Mr. Cohen used his positive coaching relationship and friendship with Brad to create dissonance with his pattern of mother-supported self-destructive behavior. Ultimately the new pro-school behavior became more compelling than his old "school doesn't matter" attitude. Brad resolved the conflict by changing his attitude and then there was no stopping him!

A Final Note

In the previous chapter we talked about the value of community service for creating a sense of usefulness. There are few movements in education that have so much good going for them. Clearly, such programs promote social values that we wish all children to hold. Clearly, they do good for society, and they develop a sense of belonging and usefulness. But, more importantly for the thesis of this chapter, they provide our discouraged youth with an opportunity to see the "power" they can have on others. Earlier in this chapter we discussed the importance of learning that one can have an effect on the outcome of one's own life. Those feelings of personal potency are certainly important, however, when those feelings of control of one's own destiny are augmented with convincing evidence that one can make a difference in the lives of others and in the life of one's community, then the resulting feeling of power will be multiplied many fold.

References

Alderman, M. K. (1990). Motivation for at-risk students. *Educational Leadership*, 48, 27–30.

Brooks, & Brooks. (1999). *The case for constructivist classrooms.* Alexandria: ASCD.

Glasser, W. (1998). *The quality school* (3rd ed.). New York:Perennial.

Glasser, W. (1999). *Choice theory: A new psychology of personal freedom.* New York: Perennial.

Glasser, W. (2000). *Reality therapy in action.* New York: HarperCollins.

Phillips, D. (1999). *Developing logical thinkers.* Dubuque: Kendall/Hunt

Powell, A. G., Farrar, E., & Cohen, D. K. (1985). *The shopping mall high school: Winners and losers in the educational marketplace.* Boston: Houghton Mifflin, Co.

Wehlage, G. G., et al. (1989). *Reducing the risk: Schools as communities of support.* Philadelphia: Falmer Press.

8

CBUPO AND EFFECTIVE DISCIPLINE: THE TWO CAN GO TOGETHER

When members of a faculty start talking about the problems they are having with unsuccessful students, it rarely takes long before the discussion turns to classroom management. Intuitively we know that when students aren't experiencing success and aren't meaningfully engaged with their assigned work, they tend to become a handful for their teachers. This "fact of life" motivates many teachers to be on a constant search for the perfect discipline or classroom management system. What is often overlooked during this quest is the fact that the very techniques we utilize in managing our classrooms may further contribute to the alienation process. On the other hand, a good management system can help reduce at-riskness. A good classroom management system, like a good instructional strategy, will result in enhanced feelings of competence, belonging, usefulness, potency, and optimism (CBUPO) for all students.

Frequently, in the arena of classroom management the good intentions of well meaning teachers have added to the problems of discouraged youth. Efforts to assert authority in the classroom have all too often reinforced the discouraged student's external locus of control and resultant perception of self as victim.

For this reason, the starting point for our work with student discipline should be our understanding of the primary importance of developing a personal sense of potency (Chapter 7). Ideally, a comprehensive classroom management program will promote the feeling of CBUPO by all students. But at its least, a classroom management plan *must* reinforce the feelings of potency that grow from an internal locus of control.

In Chapter 1 we introduced the concept of cognitive dissonance. This theory helps us understand the inextricable link between behavior and attitude. It should be noted that cognitive dissonance theory is completely compatible with Glasser's Choice Theory (Chapter 6). Dissonance theory tells us that when indi-

173

viduals engage in behavior that conflicts with their attitudes or beliefs, they experience a heightened state of stress. Because humans naturally want to avoid stress, their instinctive reaction to a conflict between behavior and belief is to change whichever is easier. Once that shift is accomplished, consonance is achieved. As it is generally easier for people to alter their attitudes, we more often see children adjusting their attitudes toward school to bring them into alignment with their habitual classroom behaviors rather than the other way around. This occurs whether the prevailing behavior patterns are positive and productive or negative and self-destructive.

Once we understand this phenomenon, we can begin viewing our teaching selves as a type of *lead manager*; one who is attempting to create and facilitate opportunities for children to engage in productive behaviors that will be so rewarding that students will continue to *choose* involvement with them. The cognitive dissonance that this creates for defeated/discouraged learners should then be powerful enough to push their once negative attitudes into line with their new productive behaviors.

Our Primary Disciplinary Responsibilities

There are numerous reasons why we may want to create a well-managed classroom; chief among those should be to carry out three vital educational functions:

+ The maintenance of order,

+ The development of an internal locus of control, and

+ The promotion of pro-social behavior.

Those three purposes justify why we teachers should consider the management of classroom discipline as one of our most significant responsibilities.

Maintaining Order

First and foremost, it is imperative that our classrooms are places where students will feel safe, secure, and free to learn. Just as continuing disorder in the streets makes it impossible for citizens to feel secure when shopping in a downtown commercial district, so too, a disorderly and unfocused classroom makes achieving academic success an impossibility for many students. We have a paramount responsibility to provide order in our classrooms so that all our students can benefit from the instruction we provide.

Developing an Internal Locus of Control

Beyond our responsibility to provide classrooms in which learning can occur, we need to create classroom environments that reinforce our students' sense of personal efficacy. Whatever the disciplinary system, incidents of classroom misbehavior should trigger consequences for the offenders. Because research and common sense tell us that those consequences are disproportionately experienced by at-risk students, these are the kids who stand to learn the most significant lessons from our management system. Furthermore, they will likely be required to learn them over and over again! If an at-risk student regularly experiences responses to their behavior that they interpret as the outgrowth of their teacher's feelings, moods, and personal proclivities, it will serve to reinforce an external locus of control. This is the real, but hidden, cost of allowing students to believe that consequences occur based on our predilections. If, however, they perceive that the consequences they are experiencing are linked consistently and directly to their behavioral choices, then our management system will become a powerful tool for teaching students lessons about their own empowerment.

Promoting Appropriate Social Values

Most of us realize that our instructional obligations go well beyond teaching the basic academic disciplines. As teachers we want to help our students grow to be competent citizens, family members, and workers. As those of us who have tried to teach social studies know all too well, citizenship is not a subject that can be learned in the abstract. It is a discipline that is understood only through repeated experience. Our strategies for classroom management are our best vehicles for helping students develop "social cognition," or, in other words, learning how to live productively and constructively in society.

If we want our students to learn to be creative problem solvers, who avoid resorting to violence when in conflict, and if we want them to be contributors to the social groups of which they are a part, there is no better place to start than with our approach to discipline.

When we acknowledge the three primary educational purposes of classroom management, teaching self-discipline can be rightly viewed as part of the regular curriculum. This is a valuable perspective because it reminds us that we should no more resent spending time on teaching this content than we invest in teaching the skills of reading and math. In fact, Professor Forest Gathercoal (1990) of Oregon State University contends that we can, and should, use our disciplinary programs as vehicles for teaching constitutional law and the American legal system. His program, "Judicious Discipline," is based entirely on that premise.

Causes of Student Misbehavior

Every educator has their own list of suspected causes of student discipline problems, and a host of different psychological theories that purport to explain antisocial behavior. Yet, at their core, most of these explanations are based on the same principles. It would, therefore, be helpful to look at some of the leading theories and attempt to identify their significant points of agreement.

Motivations Influencing Misbehavior

Driekurs and Grey (1968) argued that most youthful misbehavior was an expression of two basic needs: the *need for attention* and *the need for power*. When these basic needs are frustrated, according to Driekurs and Grey, the child can be expected to engage in "attention getting" and "power/revenge" behaviors.

Attention Getting

Attention getting behavior is a logical manifestation of a child's need to be loved and to experience belonging. As upsetting and mean-spirited as a student's behavior may appear, when we look below the surface, we often see that the student's fundamental motivation was to simply garner more of our attention.

Power/Revenge

Closely aligned to attention getting is the motivation to control, or assert power over those in authority. As Glasser pointed out, human beings have innate needs for freedom as well as for power. Classroom misbehavior is one way children let us know of their need for control, retaliation, and/or power.

It is worth noting that Driekurs' and Grey's analysis of behavior motivation is completely compatible with the drive to satisfy the five basic human needs that Glasser articulated in choice theory (Chapter 7).

A Litmus Test for Assessing Discipline Programs

Curwin and Mendler (1999) in their book *Discipline With Dignity*, discuss a set of factors, which, although occurring outside of school, often exert a powerful influence on classroom behavior. Specifically, they suggest that the impact of things such as violence in the streets, violence in the media, and spreading moral decay have an impact that seeps into our classrooms. Unfortunately, there is not much we as teachers can do about those factors because they operate outside of our span of control. However, Curwin and Mendler also discuss several in-school factors that influence the amount and severity of student misbehavior (see Figure 8.1). These factors are worth discussing because they are brought about by the school itself.

Figure 8.1. In-school Causes of Discipline Problems

- Student Boredom
- Powerlessness
- Unclear Limits
- Lack of Acceptable Outlets For Feelings
- Attacks on Dignity

Adapted from Curwin and Mendler 1988

The first two items on Curwin and Mendler's list, *boredom* and *powerlessness*, can be addressed through the strategies we've already explored in Chapters 3, 4, 5, 6, and 7. Once our students are actively involved in their learning through participation in cooperative teams, once they have experienced high levels of success as a result of the use of a mastery orientation, and once our instruction has accommodated their unique learning styles, the likelihood that our students will experience boredom or alienation will be significantly reduced. Likewise, once we become skilled in applying choice theory and we make it clear to our students that they are in control of the degree to which their behavior proves need satisfying, it will be less likely that they will emerge feeling impotent or powerless.

The last three of the factors identified by Curwin and Mendler are: unclear limits, lack of acceptable outlets for feelings, and attacks on dignity. These are direct consequences of the approach we choose for classroom behavior management. Being clear about limits is essential, first, because young people want limits. Limits provide them with security as well as a sense that their elders genuinely care about them. When we say "Whatever you do is ok," the child infers, "We don't care what you do." But, perhaps more importantly, when our limits are unclear the child cannot easily develop a sense of personal potency because, if they are unable to predict the consequences of their behavior they are likely to explain the effects of their choices in terms of luck. We hear this in justifications like, "I must have caught my teacher on a bad day," or, "You just don't like me!"

Choice Theory teaches us that the concept of *total* behavior incorporates feelings. These emotional sensations are an essential ingredient of everything that we do. If children find themselves in environments in which their feelings cannot be adequately expressed, or worse, where they must be denied, the feelings don't just go away. More likely, the pressure to suppress feelings will simply cause the child to feel out of place, because it is impossible to deny something that is an inextricable part of their being. This is precisely the conflict that Michelle Fine and Nancy Zane (1985) observed in the low-income women dropouts whom they studied. A good behavior management plan allows children to express the feeling component of their total behavior. If, however, children find that expressing their feelings contributes to unpleasant or unproductive consequences, then we must help them to choose other, more satisfying, "total behaviors" or ways to express these feelings.

The last of the factors mentioned by Curwin and Mendler, attacks on dignity, is perhaps the most obvious but also the most frequently overlooked consequence of poor student management. At school the power relationship between adults and youth is clearly and inevitably unequal. While no one would argue that some aspects of this unequal power relationship are necessary for the proper fulfillment of our teaching and nurturing role, we still need to recognize that the existence of this power imbalance places the child in a vulnerable situation.

When a person in authority chooses to behave in what children take to be an arbitrary and condescending manner, it can, and often does, produce significant and long-lasting resentment. Conversely, when we respect our students' dignity, it doesn't imply leniency over strictness, rather, it implies our choice to express our caring and to place the child's needs first and foremost. Demonstrating caring and enforcing high expectations are not incompatible. While a child may not immediately appreciate strict discipline when it is administered by a caring parent, they do, nonetheless, know that what motivated the parent was a desire to help raise a responsible adult. However, when a child suspects that an adult was motivated by a desire to dominate, extract revenge, or for personal convenience, it will become a source of increased alienation from the adult world.

Curwin and Mendler's list gives us the beginning of a litmus test to assess approaches to classroom management. The list reminds us to consistently ask ourselves,

> "Will this approach enhance the student's academic needs for stimulation, their need for limits, understanding, and dignity, or will this system tend to increase their feelings of boredom, powerlessness, externalization, and alienation?"

Glasser provides us with another insight. Choice Theory tells us that misbehavior is more likely to happen when students doubt their needs will be met at school, and when the school they are attending doesn't resemble any of the pictures of the quality world that reside in their brains. For this reason we should add to our litmus test,

"Will this system help create a classroom approximating the 'quality world' sought by our at-risk students?"

Students' Academic Needs

Verne and Louise Jones (1990) in their book *Comprehensive Classroom Management*, point out that students come to class with academic needs, and that when those are not met, unwelcome disciplinary events are likely to increase (see Figure 8.2).

Figure 8.2. Student's Academic Needs

1. To understand the teacher's goals
2. To be actively involved in the learning process
3. To relate subject matter to their own lives
4. To follow their own interests
5. To receive realistic and immediate feedback
6. To experience success
7. To experience an appropriate amount of structure
8. To have time to integrate learning
9. To have positive contact with peers
10. To have instruction matched to their level of cognitive development and learning style

Adapted from Jones and Jones

If your approach to classroom management doesn't seem to be effective for your at-risk students, perhaps it is because some of their academic needs are not being met. The following Think and Do Exercise invites you to use the Jones and Jones list to assess your classroom.

Think and Do Exercise—
At-Risk Student Academic Needs Assessment

Choose 2 to 3 "at-risk" students that you currently work with. Using the form in Figure 8.3 "Academic Needs Assessment," ask yourself which of the student's academic needs are and which are not being currently satisfied in your classroom.

Figure 8.3. Academic Needs Assessment

Student Name: _____	Yes	No

1. Does the student understand my goals?

2. Is the student actively involved in the learning process?

3. Does the student relate subject matter to their own lives?

4. Does the student follow their own interests?

5. Does the student receive realistic and immediate feedback?

6. Does the student experience success?

7. Does the student experience an appropriate amount of structure?

8. Does the student have time to integrate learning?

9. Does the student have positive contact with peers?

10. Does the student receive instruction matched to their level of cognitive development and learning style?

Adapted from Jones and Jones

Schools Where Discipline Is Effective

Up until now we have concentrated on the classroom as a source of alienation or motivation. When we move to the issue of discipline it is appropriate to shift our attention to the school as a community, where the student is a member. School can, as a total and integrated organization, have a significant impact on the attendance, discipline, and social behavior of our students. It has always been clear that an individual teacher can convince students of her moral authority and the fact that she is working with the child's best interest at heart. Research has shown that the collective behavior of an entire school has a similar impact. In this chapter and in Chapter 9 we discuss schoolwide interventions in detail. However, when discussing discipline it is helpful to take notice of the characteristics of those schools that have consistently obtained low incidences of student misbehavior.

One of the more interesting and positive revelations from the body of research called *effective schooling* was the finding that in schools in which academic performance was universally high, attendance and behavior were also superior. This was first and most dramatically reported in the book *Fifteen Thousand Hours* (Rutter et al., 1979), which described effective high schools in inner city London.

Rutter et al. reported twelve characteristics of school environments where student academic performance, attendance, discipline, and even delinquency outside of school were lower than in socioeconomically similar schools. These factors were

1. Low levels of corporal punishment and minimal disciplinary interventions were associated with improved student behavior.

2. Praise for work in the classroom and frequent public praise for good work or behavior at general assemblies or other meetings was associated with better behavior.

3. Schools and classrooms that were well decorated with plants, posters, and pictures were associated with better student behavior.

4. The willingness to see children about problems at any time was associated with better student behavior.

5. Better behavior was noted in schools in which a high proportion of students had opportunities to hold some position of responsibility.

6. An interesting and perhaps unexpected finding was that schools with highest staff turnover often had the best behavior among students.

7. Most decisions were made at a senior level (administration) at schools with good outcomes, and staff members felt that their views were clearly represented in the decisions.

8. An agreed upon set of standards, consistently maintained, appeared more important in maintaining effective discipline than specific rules or a certain type of teaching approach.

9. Frequent homework and a check on staff members regarding administering homework was associated with better student achievement and behavior.

10. Very little class time (2 to 13 percent) spent in setting up equipment and materials was associated with better student behavior.

11. Starting the class on time, pacing throughout the lesson, and not ending early was associated with better student behavior.

12. A high proportion of topic time per lesson (65 to 85 percent) spent in interaction with the whole class rather than with individuals when using a formal class-based teaching approach was positively related to good student behavior. (Rutter et al., 1979)

Rutter's findings provide us with cause for optimism. The common theme running across all these elements was an expression of *caring* for the students' academic success, for the school environment, for the students' time, etc. And this was not an isolated study. Its publication was closely followed by another study by Edward Wynne. Wynne (1981) looked at elementary and secondary schools in Detroit and once again found that the values, norms, and cultural characteristics of the schools (as a whole) affected not only student academic performance, but also the degree of students' "pro-social" behavior. Findings from these studies as well as the work of many other effective schooling researchers such as Brookover and Lezotte (1979), and Ron Edmonds (1979) made a clear and compelling case that schools can, and do, make a difference in student behavior as well as achievement.

Principles and Processes for Effective Discipline

The question is, then, how should a school go about creating a positive approach to student management? Curwin and Mendler (1999) identified twelve processes that form the foundation of an effective discipline program. They contend that the foundation includes the following:

1. letting students know what you need,
2. providing instruction at levels that match the student's ability,
3. listening to what students are thinking and feeling,
4. using humor,
5. varying the style of presentation,
6. offering choices,
7. refusing to accept excuses,
8. legitimizing behavior you cannot stop,
9. using hugs and touching in communicating with kids,
10. being responsible for yourself and allowing kids to take responsibility for themselves,
11. realizing and accepting that you will not reach every kid, and
12. starting fresh every day.

In the book *Looking Into Classrooms* (2002), Tom Good and Jere Brophy offer four assumptions to guide effective classroom organization (Figure 8.4). These four features apply every bit as much to a school's overall approach to student management.

Figure 8.4. Assumptions for Effective Classroom Management

1. Students are likely to follow rules they understand and accept.

2. Discipline problems are minimized when students are regularly engaged in meaningful activities geared to their interests and attitudes.

3. Management should be approached with an eye toward maximizing the time students spend engaged in productive control of misbehavior.

4. The teacher's goal is to develop self-control in students, not merely to exert control over them.

Good and Brophy, 1991

One of the benefits of Good and Brophy's list is that it can be converted into a quick and effective needs assessment tool. The Think and Do Exercise below will give you an opportunity to explore your own assumptions about classroom management.

Think and Do Exercise—
Classroom Management Assumptions: A Needs Assessment

Using the *"Student Perception Survey"* (Figure 8.5), ask your students to report on their perception of your school's attention to three of the Good and Brophy assumptions for classroom management.

The fourth of Good and Brophy's assumptions speaks to the *effective use of class time.* They assert that classroom management should be approached with an eye toward maximizing the time students spend engaged in productive activities rather than from a negative viewpoint stressing the control of misbehavior. Use the Time Use Record shown in Figure 8.6 and a volunteer recorder (student or parent) to record classroom activity at five minute intervals over three typical days.

The data obtained from both the student interviews and from the Time Use Record will give you an indication of the attention you are giving to the four key assumptions of quality management.

Figure 8.5. Student Perception Survey

Name (optional): _____

Class: _____

1a. Do you feel that students in our school understand and accept the need for our school rules?

1	2	3	4	5
Not at all	Some do	About half do	Most do	Everyone does

1b. List the three rules that you feel are most important to people at our school and your understanding of the reason for each of the rules.

Rule: _____

Reason: _____

Rule: _____

Reason: _____

Rule: _____

Reason: _____

2a. To what degree do you find activities that interest and engage you at school?

1	2	3	4	5
Not at all	Rarely	Sometimes	Frequently	Always

2b. List three activities that particularly interest you at school?

     1. _____

     2. _____

     3. _____

3. Why do you think that the adults at our school pay attention to school rules, student discipline, and behavioral expectations?

Figure 8.6. Time Use Record

	Class:	*Date:*
Time:	**Assigned activity:**	**Percent on task:**
8:00		
8:05		
8:10		
8:15		
8:20		
8:25		
8:30		
2:25		
2:30		
2:35		
2:40		
2:45		
2:50		
2:55		
3:00		

Composite Report

Total minutes allocated to academic pursuits:

Total minutes allocated to management functions (set up, lunch tickets, getting coats, etc):

Total time allocated to non-classroom activities (lunch, assemblies, recess, etc):

Average time on task during academic/activity time:

A Variety of Systems

Generally, whenever and wherever discipline is discussed we find rabid debates over the core values that underpin the most popular approaches. Verne and Louise Jones (1990) analyzed this debate by offering a continuum of theories that classify the most popular classroom management systems.

All systems of classroom management can be seen as growing out of particular philosophical outlooks concerning the cause of student misbehavior. While many educators will get emotional over the philosophical underpinnings of these systems, we reserve our judgment and just ask one simple question, *"Is the program more or less likely to move a child out of his/her at-risk status?"* When the answer is "yes", we're satisfied. If the answer is "probably not," we should look for another system. At the end of this chapter, you will be given a set of questions to ask of a disciplinary program to determine if it supports the needs of at-risk youth. At this stage we simply want to alert you to the ideological godparents of each of the major approaches by adapting the Jones and Jones continuum (Figure 8.7).

On one extreme we see the approaches that emphasize elements of the instructional organization of the classroom. Here we find a range of systems, including the Instruction/Organization theories of Madeline Hunter, Caroline Evertson, and Jere Brophy. Fundamentally, these people are educators and theorists who believe that discipline problems arise out of the use of inappropriate instructional practices. They argue that when the instructional and organizational decisions of the teacher are correct, incidents of misbehavior will be low.

Next on the continuum we find the interactive/interpersonal theories of Carl Rogers, Thomas Gordon, and William Purkey. These authors believe that the heart of good classroom discipline lies in the relationship between the student and the teacher. They generally argue that if these relationships are warm, authentic, and built on the right values, misbehavior will be a rare event.

Further down the line is the problem solving approach promulgated by William Glasser, known as *Reality Therapy*. In this system problems are seen as arising out of the child's need for empowerment. Therefore, the recommended approach emphasizes teaching children how to analyze and systematically solve the problems that arose from their unproductive behavior.

On the more structured end of the continuum we find the behaviorist theories of B.F. Skinner and others. These approaches are based upon the pleasure/pain principle. Specifically, these theorists believe that students will be attracted to pleasurable experiences and will avoid aversive ones. Hence, the task for the teacher is to build in rewards for good behavior, while making engaging in misbehavior maximally unpleasant for the student. Because these approaches require the teacher to link behavioral choices to consequences, they are often called stimulus-response theories.

Figure 8.7. Continuum of Classroom Management Strategies

Interpersonal Relationships	Classroom Organization and Management	Instruction	Problem Solving	Behavioristic	Schoolwide Discipline
Jack Canfield	Jere Brophy	Walter Doyle	Rudolph Dreikurs	Wesley Becker	Lee Canter
Harold Wells	Edmond Emmer	Rita Dunn	William Glasser	Lee Canter	Daniel Duke
Thomas Gordon	Carolyn Evertson	Thomas Good	Thomas Gordon	Frank Hewett	William Glasser
William Purkey	Thomas Good	Madeline Hunter	Frank Maple	Daniel O'Leary	William Wayson
Richard & Patricia Schmuck	Madeline Hunter	David & Roger Johnson	Robert Spaulding	Hill Walker	
	Jacob Kounin	Bruce Joyce			
		Bernice McCarthy			
		Robert Slavin			
		Jane Stallings			

From: Vernon F. Jones & Louise F. Jones, *Comprehensive Classroom Management: Motivating and Managing Students,* 3rd ed. Copyright 1990 by Allyn and Bacon.

At the end of their scale Jones and Jones place the *Assertive Discipline* system of Lee Canter. They do so out of a belief that this system emphasizes punishment as the single deterrent against misbehavior. Although we have observed many classrooms in which this system has been applied that way, a careful reading of Canter's book and of his training programs reveals that this system, when properly implemented, utilizes rewards as well as punishment, and, in that way, operates much like the other stimulus-response programs.

To assess how well these various approaches to classroom management mesh with the needs of our defeated and discouraged learners, we will ignore the aesthetics of the system or the politics of its supporters and focus instead on whether or not it will likely lead to the development of an internal locus of control and the experience of significant feelings of CBUPO. To determine whether a system meets those tests we suggest the use of the CBUPO chart (Figure 8.8) to test classroom disciplinary systems. Instructions for the implementation of the Figure 8.8 chart follow in the Think and Do Exercise: Assessing the Management Program.

Figure 8.8. CBUP Chart

Name	Competence	Belonging	Usefulness	Potency

Think and Do Exercise—
Assessing the Management Program

Using the CBUP chart (Figure 8.8), check to see how well your approach to discipline is working for your discouraged learners. Under the column marked "name" list your most at-risk students. Then consider the approach that you are using to manage their behavior.

Consider the last time they misbehaved and how you handled the situation. Now ask yourself whether that event and its method of resolution have left the children with greater feelings of competence, belonging, usefulness, and potency?

If the answer is yes for all four feelings, then your system is just right for that child. If you find that you are writing *no* in many of the boxes it is time to consider another approach.

If the analysis of your discipline system with the CBUP chart shows it to be successful, then it doesn't matter how others use or view that system, because it is the right approach for you and your students.

Earlier in this chapter we argued that we implement a classroom management system for three reasons:

1. To maintain order,
2. To develop internal locus of control, and
3. To promote appropriate social values.

Social Responsibility

One way to determine whether a system is promoting appropriate social values is to examine whether it is what Curwin and Mendler call a *responsibility model* or an *obedience model*. See Figures 8.9 and 8.10.

Figure 8.9. The Obedience Model

Main Goal: Students follow orders.

Principle: Do what I (the teacher or administrator) want.

Intervention: Punishment is the primary intervention.

1. *external* locus of control
2. done *to* student

Examples:

1. threats
2. scoldings
3. writing "I will not _____ 500 times."
4. detentions
5. writing student's name on chalkboard

Student learns...

1. Don't get caught.
2. It's not my responsibility.

Figure 8.10. The Responsibility Model

Main Goal: To teach students to make responsible choices.

Principle: To learn from the outcomes of decisions.

Consequences:

1. *internal* locus of control
2. done *by* the student
3. logical or natural

Examples:

1. Developing a plan describing how you will behave without breaking the rule when you are in a similar situation.
2. Practicing appropriate behavior in a private meeting with the teacher.

Student learns...

1. I cause my own outcomes.
2. have more than one alternative behavior in any situation.
3. I have the power to choose the best alternative.

Logical Consequences

One of the earlier applications of the "responsibility model" was the work of Driekurs and Grey (1968) and their Logical Consequence approach.

Driekurs argued that punishment was an inappropriate response to student misbehavior. He felt that too often punishment fit right into the children's need for "attention" and then fed their motivation for "revenge." We have probably all had the child in class who needs our attention so badly that it doesn't seem to matter if it comes from our approval or disapproval.

Rather than relying on punishment, Driekurs and Grey suggest that teachers (and parents) rely on a system that allows the children to experience either the *natural consequence* or *logical consequence* of their behavioral choices. He contrasted logical and natural consequences with punishment in the following four ways:

- Logical and natural consequences express social realities.

  Punishment expresses power relationships.

- Logical and natural consequences must be directly related to the behavior.

  Punishment is not directly related to the behavior.

- With logical and natural consequences moralizing or moral judgments are avoided.

  Punishment inevitably involves some form of moral judgment

- Logical and natural consequences govern the here and now.

  Punishment deals with past history.

Contrasting Logical and Natural Consequences

An example of a *natural consequence* would be if the child failed to bring the proper materials to class, she *naturally* could not fully participate. However, when the other children went to recess then this child could borrow someone else's materials and complete her work. If, however, the teacher supplied the missing material during class time it would amount to "enabling" behavior. The child would learn that there was no natural consequence flowing from an irresponsible decision; therefore, she would be inclined to repeat it.

An example of a *logical consequence* is having the child who chose to write on his desk work along with the custodian after school as part of a cleanup detail. While helping the custodian may not be a natural result of this behavior choice, the student will easily see the logical connection. The act of vandalism (writing on the desk) created more work for the custodial crew, therefore, being made to help the custodian with his work is a logical consequence of this student's behavior choice.

We can see that this approach helps children make good choices by seeing that the social reality of their world triggers both the positive and negative consequences to their choices. The children are made to see that it is the social reality that governs the impact of personal choices rather than teacher's (or parent's) arbitrariness. Forms of punishment, be they hacks, swats, detention, or being made to stand facing the wall are all punitive responses to behavior that will be perceived by students as a result of the adult's superior power rather than with the child's choice. An unfortunate side effect of punishment is that it focuses the child's time, anger, and attention onto the punisher not onto the behavior that triggered the punishment. The Think and Do Exercise below gives you an opportunity to try your hand at crafting logical consequences to typical classroom behaviors.

Think and Do Exercise—Logical Consequences

Generate a list of ten nonproductive behaviors that your defeated/discouraged learners might engage in during your class.

List these on one column on a paper. Then come up with a set of choices (with consequences) that you could provide the student regarding those behaviors. Try to keep your consequences as logically connected to the behavior as possible.

If you decide to use the logical consequence model in your classroom, you will be wise to consider a set of implementation principles offered by Curwin and Mendler (Figure 8.11).

Figure 8.11. Implementation Principles

1. Always implement a consequence: Be consistent
2. Simply state the rule and consequence
3. Be physically close to the student when you implement a consequence
4. Make eye contact when you implement a consequence
5. Use a soft voice
6. Catch a student being good
7. Don't embarrass the student in front of peers
8. Be firm and angry free when giving your consequence
9. Do not accept excuses bargaining or whining

Adapted from Curwin and Mendler

Reality Therapy

One of William Glasser's first and most influential contributions to education was the development of an approach to student discipline called *Reality Therapy*. It was first explained in a book *Reality Therapy*, and later in a text titled *Schools Without Failure*. The essence of this approach is a seven-step problem solving process (Figure 8.12).

Figure 8.12. Seven-Step Problem-Solving Model

1. Be warm and personable and willing to become emotionally involved

2. Deal with the present behavior

3. Make a value judgement

4. Work out a plan

5. Make a commitment

6. Follow-up

7. No put downs and no acceptance of excuses

The seven steps of this process are handled in very brief one-to-one private conferences between student and teacher. Generally, these conferences last from thirty seconds to five minutes. Needless to say, Step 1, *being warm and personable*, must have been accomplished before any problematic behavior occurs.

Step 2, *dealing with the present behavior*, is absolutely essential. It does neither the child nor the teacher any good to dwell on the past. Our discouraged learners may have had such a negative history that if a discipline program leads them to feel that they have to atone for years of past misbehavior in order to get to first base, they may conclude that they are in a hole too deep to ever realistically climb out.

Occasionally, we find that students get stuck at Step 3, *making a value judgment*. This is a step that the student *absolutely must* make for him/herself as it is the key to the entire process. Reality therapy only works when, and if, the student has *decided* that their present behavior is problematic. When the student doesn't see any problem with, for example, name calling, vandalism, or the use of someone else's property without permission, it may be necessary to use the payoff matrix that was developed by Verne and Louise Jones (Figure 8.13). Generally, a short discussion with the student and having them use the payoff matrix will get him/her unstuck.

Figure 8.13. Payoff/Cost Model of Behavioral Counseling

	Short term	*Long term*
Payoffs		
Costs		

From: Vernon F. Jones. *Adolescents with behavior problems: Strategies for teaching, Counseling, and parent involvement,* p. 200. Copyright 1980 by Allyn and Bacon. Reprinted with permission.

The *plan of action*, as are all the steps in this model, is constructed by the student with the teacher serving simply as an active listener. The teacher's job is to help the student make wise choices but not to go so far as to actually make the choice for the student. The problem solving process only works when the student has complete ownership of the plan. The teacher, however, can and should be a key participant in the follow-up portion of the process. This is generally the toughest aspect of reality therapy for the teacher. Our natural tendency is to solve the students' problems for them. Often we find it hard to hold back good ideas from the student. But we've learned the more we interject ourselves at this stage, the more we deny students the responsibility they need to be taking for themselves.

The beauty of reality therapy is that it builds an internal locus of control. When a plan works, the students can take pleasure and pride in their successes. When the plan doesn't work as intended, the students should be helped to keep revising the plan until they are able to create a successful one. The best way to get a feel for reality therapy is to practice it. The Think and Do Exercise that follows invites you to experience reality therapy through a role play with a colleague.

Think and Do Exercise—Reality Therapy

Think of a particularly problematic behavior you recently encountered in class with a student. Find a colleague or friend and role play the seven-step problem solving process.

Reflect on how it felt to be the student and the teacher in this process.

Social Contracting

Closely related to the Reality Therapy approach is the concept of *social contracting*. As with logical consequences and reality therapy this procedure is inextricably tied to the social reality of the classroom and the school as a community. For this reason social contracting can enhance belonging as well as the development of social responsibility. There are two types of social contracts that we might want to consider using in our classrooms:

♦ Contracts between teacher and student, and

♦ Contracts between student and student.

Contracts Between Teacher and Student

The contract is a written agreement that the teacher and student negotiate to assist them in realizing a valued goal. What sets the social contract apart from the goal-setting process is that it involves commitments on the part of both student and teacher, while goal-setting (Chapter 7) involves commitment primarily from the student. Contracting can be particularly valuable with discouraged students who are lacking in self-confidence. When students have an external locus of control and feel that the total responsibility for accomplishing a difficult task has been placed on their shoulders, the fear of failure may be so discouraging that it will sink them. However, if the students believe that they have a partner in the effort, then persevering and maintaining self-confidence can become much easier.

There are several necessary elements for a successful social contract. The first is having a measurable and demonstrable goal. For example, *earning an A grade, making productive use of class time, completing all assignments*. Second, a statement of what it will take to achieve the goal is needed. These affirmative statements should be written as lists of commitments from both parties. For example, the students might agree to bring the appropriate materials to class, to be in their seats on time, and to refrain from visiting with friends. The teacher, on the other hand, might agree to start class promptly after the bell rings, to provide instructional activities that cover the entire period, and to make directions clear.

A good contract should also provide for feedback. These opportunities should be set at relatively frequent intervals so that if the plan isn't working out as well as expected, the contract can be re-negotiated so the parties can get back on track. The goal of any social contract is to have it fulfilled. It is only through the successful fulfillment of the agreement that an internal locus of control and optimism about future efforts can be reinforced.

Contracts Between Student and Student

There are many times when it is advantageous to have students resolve problems with their peers by negotiating a contract. Students who are inclined to scuffle on the playground or who have trouble collaborating in their cooperative learning groups are examples of learners who might be well served by a contractual approach to working out *their* problem.

While student/student contracts are used to foster social harmony, and while, in the long run, the fulfillment of such contracts should be their own reward, these intrinsic factors will probably not provide enough of an incentive at the outset. For this reason the teacher, working as a third party mediator, often solicits suggestions from the students for an extrinsic reward that will be desirable for both parties to be granted at the completion of the contract. A congratulatory letter home to parents, a trip to the local ice cream parlor, or something on that order is usually all that it takes to sweeten the deal for the students.

As with the *student to teacher* contract the *peer contract* must contain a demonstrable goal, a list of commitments, and a feedback/review plan. It also should contain a reference to the reward/benefit that will be obtained on successful completion.

The important thing about social contracting, as with reality therapy is that the teacher needs to participate in the process as an assister, not a director. The more ownership the students are able to feel about their contracts, the greater the empowerment they will obtain from it. Once teachers become comfortable with this process it becomes one of the best techniques for helping our discouraged learners develop an internal locus of control.

Conflict Resolution/Mediation Process

Many schools have found it beneficial to make use of a schoolwide conflict resolution process. When our interest is in helping students experience a sense of empowerment it can be helpful to utilize some form of mediation in assisting students to resolve their own disputes. The mediation process combines some of the best elements of social contracting with the problem solving features of reality therapy.

Most frequently the mediator is the teacher, who first establishes the fact that it will be the responsibility of the parties to settle their disagreement. The mediator's stated role is to assist the parties in understanding the issues and to help them search for common ground. The process begins with a reiteration of the rules for mediation:

♦ No name calling or interrupting is permitted.

♦ Disputants must tell the truth.

♦ Disputants must agree to resolve the conflict.

♦ All discussions are face to face.

The mediator then asks individual students in the dispute to tell their version of what happened as completely as they can by recalling the incident. The mediator takes verbatim notes and repeats back what is heard to verify the accuracy of the note taking. If the mediator writes something inaccurately, it is immediately corrected. Next the mediator repeats the process giving the other disputant an opportunity to recall the perceived and recalled facts.

If there are discrepancies between the two perceptions of what occurred, the mediator points it out and asks the disputants to reconcile the two versions. Once the facts are stipulated, the mediator asks the disputants for suggestions on how to solve the problem. The discussion continues until both parties agree to a resolution that they can abide by. The mediator then writes down what both parties have agreed to, and the settlement is signed by both parties. At that point the matter is considered settled.

Peer Mediation

In many parts of the country schools are training cadres of students, as early as in the elementary grades, to work as peer mediators (Roderick, 1988). Often the trained mediators are identified on the playground by distinctive t-shirts or other insignia. The training programs emphasize being nonjudgmental and the role of the mediator as an assister to others while solving their own problems. When a dispute begins either of the disputants can call for a mediator's help. The mediation session then occurs on the playground, in an office, or any other appropriate location. The process itself follows the same procedure as the adult-led mediation described above.

Peer mediation is particularly valuable for reinforcing feelings of potency on the part of the parties and creating feelings of usefulness on the part of the mediators.

The Resolving Conflict Creatively Project (RCCP) that was developed by the New York Chapter of Educators for Social Responsibility, in collaboration with the New York City Board of Education, has been training peer mediators in New York City for a number of years. In the 10 years since this project was initiated it has been replicated in literally hundreds of schools around the country. A third party evaluation of the NYC project revealed that the program was having a significant impact on all the students in the project schools. The list that follows includes a few of the findings obtained after only one year of implementation in five New York City elementary schools:

♦ there were 535 successful student mediations—an average of 107 per school;

- 85.4 percent of the teacher respondents agreed that students in their classes have been helped through their contact with mediators;

- 85.2 percent of the teacher respondents agreed that mediators' participation in the mediation component has contributed to increasing the mediators' self-esteem.

- 98.2 percent of the teacher respondents agreed that the mediation component has given children an important tool for dealing with the everyday conflicts that surface among students;

- 88.7 percent of the teacher respondents agreed that the mediation component has helped students take more responsibility for solving their own problems;

- 84.5 percent of the surveyed students who had used a mediator indicated that mediation was helpful to them;

- 83.8 percent of the surveyed student mediators agreed that being a mediator has helped them to understand people with different views; and

- 83.7 percent of the surveyed student mediators agreed that being a mediator has given them skills they can use their whole life. (Metis Associates, 1990)

The success of the RCCP project has been so great that the New York City Board of Education has encouraged adoption of the project throughout the city and has used it to diffuse tensions in some of its most racially charged and divided school environments. The evidence clearly suggests that when properly trained, student mediators may be best situated to solve even seemingly intractable social problems.

Assertive Discipline

At the far end of the Jones and Jones continuum (Figure 8.7) lies the *Assertive Discipline* program developed by Lee and Marlene Canter. While the Jones's classify this popular program as based primarily on punishment, that is not a fair characterization. When properly implemented teachers using *assertive discipline* make at least as much use of positive reinforcement as punishment. If used as developed, this program is more accurately categorized as based on the stimulus-response theories of Skinner and other behaviorist psychologists.

The Canters developed the initial Assertive Discipline program (they have since followed up with programs for paraprofessionals and parents) in the mid-1970s borrowing heavily from two popular movements of the time, assertiveness training and reinforcement theory.

Assertiveness training was an outgrowth of the feminist movement, based on the reasoning that among the contributing factors for women being denied access to opportunity was because they lacked the skills and confidence needed to assert themselves. Assertiveness training offered assistance, strategies, and support for people, thus allowing them to un-apologetically state and demand that they had needs that should be met and had wants that deserved being considered.

Reinforcement theory was the dominant idea in pedagogy in the 1970s. Grounded in the belief that the best way to elicit positive behavior from students was to reinforce desired behaviors with pleasurable extrinsic rewards. Behaviorists also instructed teachers wanting to discourage certain behavior to extinguish unwanted behavior by withholding reinforcement and/or delivering punishment.

Simply stated, assertive discipline was an approach to classroom management that told teachers they had the right to clearly, matter of factly, and unequivocally assert their expectations for positive classroom behavior. It gave them a system to back up that expectation with rewards for good behavior and punishments for infractions of classroom rules.

Assertive Discipline, is a four-step classroom process backed up by suggestions for gaining peer, parent, and administrator support. The four sequential steps to be followed by the teacher are:

- Setting limits

- Establishing consequences

- Applying consequences

- Applying group rewards

The first step, *setting limits*, is the process of establishing a set of classroom rules. The program guidelines suggest that these be limited so they can be learned, remembered, mastered, and understood. They should be clear and concise, and they should be prominently posted so that they can't be forgotten. Some teachers choose to involve students in the establishment of classroom rules, while others set up different lists of rules for different types of activities. For example, a teacher might have different expectations for the times when students are engaged with group work, teacher directed instruction, and/or seat work. Regardless of the "limit setting strategy" used, at the conclusion of this stage the students are expected to be clear about what constitutes compliance and what constitutes a violation of classroom rules.

The second step, *establishing consequences*, occurs by clearly delineating an escalating list of teacher responses to be utilized in case of infractions. The response hierarchy works as follows: The offending student automatically receives the first consequence on the first infraction during an instructional period/day. Each subsequent infraction a triggers another, and less desirable, consequence. While teachers are free to develop any set of consequences they deem best, most implement a set of responses like the following:

- name on board (warning)
- name plus one check mark (15 minutes detention)
- two check marks (30 minutes detention)
- three check marks (30 minutes detention and call home)
- four checkmarks (immediate trip to office, 30-minutes detention, and a call home)

Regardless of the consequences implemented by the teacher, assertive discipline always begins with a warning and culminates in removal from the room. The punitive consequences are established by the teacher and *must be* consistently applied on all occasions and to *all* students who elect to violate the behavior expectations. While teachers may choose consequences that work best for them, they must be ones that can be administered without interrupting the classroom routine, thereby thwarting a child's attention getting motivation. It is this desire to avoid reinforcing the *attention getting* motivation of the misbehaving child that makes the "name on the board" strategy so appealing to teachers. When that strategy is employed properly, instruction continues uninterrupted and the recalcitrant child becomes unable to sidetrack the teacher. If students are to consider this system fair, then the consequences of misbehavior must be taught and must be fully understood by all the students. For this reason consequences along with the rules are generally posted prominently in the classroom.

Similar strategies are used for granting *rewards* for good behavior. Because students need to learn that positive consequences will flow from regular and consistent decisions to behave in accordance with classroom rules, the provision of desirable rewards is essential. Typically, positive notes home, lunches with the teacher, or certificates from the principal are implemented as rewards in an *assertive discipline* classroom.

The last step in this process is the granting of *group rewards* for good behavior (it should be noted that while the assertive discipline program suggests group rewards it strongly discourages group punishment). The function of group rewards is to encourage peer reinforcement of the behavior modification process. The Canters offer several strategies by which an entire class or group can be rewarded for an individual student's decision to improve their behavior. One particularly popular approach is the use of the marble jar. The teacher informs the class that the empty marble jar on the teacher's desk will be filled with a marble whenever the teacher is particularly impressed by the positive behavior of a student in class. She tells them that whenever the entire jar becomes filled with marbles the entire class will enjoy a treat, perhaps a movie, popcorn party, etc. The teacher then uses the strategic dropping of marbles into the jar to reinforce improved behavior by individuals. What this often means is that the student who had created the most trouble in the past will be "caught behaving" by their teacher as frequently as possible. Other students may not understand why every good act by *Dick* is rewarded with a marble, but it is unlikely they will complain because *Dick's* good behavior is contributing toward a valued reward for the entire group. Rather than triggering negative peer pressure, this strategy places positive peer pressure behind *Dick's* new improved behavior.

When properly implemented, *assertive discipline* can help the discouraged child develop a greater internal locus of control. This happens because of the clear and consistent connection the program makes between the decision to choose a behavior and the application of a positive or negative consequence. In an assertive discipline classroom, children always know that the only thing that separates them from the positive or negative consequences is their personal choice of behavior. It is this clear relationship between cause and effect that supports the development of internal attribution.

Preventing Misbehavior

Regardless of the merits of any of these systems, it is clearly preferable to head off bad behavior habits before they begin. When it comes to student discipline "an ounce of prevention is always worth a pound of cure."

Proper Use of Praise

One of the best prevention techniques we can use is ample use of appropriate praise. Praise tells students both that they are competent and that they belong. Tom Good and Jere Brophy have done an excellent job of synthesizing the critical elements of quality praise (Figure 8.14).

Teachers have found that adherence to the components of quality praise and avoidance of the pitfalls of inappropriate praise have a dramatic effect on student attitudes about themselves, their classrooms, and their academic work.

Figure 8.14. Guidelines for Effective Praise

Effective praise	*Ineffective praise*
1. is delivered contingently	1. is delivered randomly or unsystematically
2. specifies the particulars of the accomplishment	2. is restricted to global positive reactions
3. shows spontaneity, variety, and other signs of credibility: suggests clear attention to the student's accomplishment	3. shows a bland uniformity that suggests a conditioned response made with minimal attention
4. rewards attainment of specified performance criteria (which can include effort criteria)	4. rewards mere participation without consideration of performance processes or outcomes
5. provides information to students about their competence or the value of their accomplishment	5. provides no information at all or gives students information about their status
6. orients students toward better appreciation of their own task-related behavior and thinking about problem solving	6. orients students toward comparing themselves with others and thinking about competing
7. uses student's own prior accomplishments as the context for describing present accomplishments	7. uses the accomplishments of peers as the context for describing student's present accomplishments
8. is given in recognition of noteworthy effort or success at difficult (for this student) tasks	8. is given without regard to the effort expended or the meaning of the accomplishment (for this student)
9. attritubes success to effort and ability, implying that similar successes can be expected in the future	9. attributes success to ability alone or to external factors such as luck or (easy) task difficulty
10. fosters endogenous attributions (students believe they expend effort on task because they enjoy it and/or want to develop task-relevant skills)	10. fosters exogenous attributions (students believe they expend effort on the task for external reasons-to please the teacher, win a competition or reward, etc.)
11. focuses students' attention on their own task-relevant behavior	11. focuses students' attention on the teacher as an external authority figure who is manipulating them
12. fosters appreciation of, and desirable attributions about, task-relevant behavior after the process is completed	12. intrudes into the ongoing process, distracting attention from task-relevant behavior

From: Jere E. Brophy, (1981) Teacher Praise: A Functional Analysis. *Review of Educational Research* 51: 32. Washington, D.C.: American Educational Research Association. Reprinted with permission.

Gaining Parental Support

One of the often neglected but extremely important strategies available to the classroom teacher is the enlistment of support from parents, and the enlistment of parents as allies and supporters of behavior management. When Dick began his work at a public alternative school he came face to face with a phenomenon he had heretofore only heard about. The parents of his students held profoundly negative attitudes toward the mainstream schools that their children had previously attended. When he probed to understand the genesis of these hostile attitudes he found that these feelings had their roots in the past experience of these parents' with school-to-home communication.

The parents had come to interpret any summons to the school as de facto criticism of their parenting skills. When their child acted out and they were called in they felt it was as if they were being called on the carpet. After repeated occurrences those feelings built resentment and anger. Parental resentment and anger (toward school authorities) will inevitably undermine a child's feelings about their teachers and the administrators they work with at school. By understanding and thereby avoiding the cycle of parental alienation we can remake the parent-school relationship into one of supportive allies rather than combatants.

We have found a six-step process for Gaining Parental Support (Figure 8.15) to be quite helpful whenever we're soliciting help from a parent who has a child that displays a behavioral or performance problem. These six steps were designed to be employed as part of a one-on-one conference (either by phone or in person). However, this process clearly works best when the teacher is sitting face to face with the parent(s) either at school or, preferably, in the child's home.

Figure 8.15. Steps for Gaining Parental Support

1. State your affection for the child
2. Express your concerns in terms of the consequence for the child
3. Solicit ideas
4. Agree to a plan
5. Develop a feedback loop
6. If it works, send a thank you note!

The first step, *stating your affection for the child*, is essential and must be done authentically. If you truly do not like the child then another approach (probably a transfer to another teacher) is in order. The reason why this step is so important is that there is nothing more dear to a parent than his or her own child.

When you tell a parent that you hold the thing most precious to them in high regard, then you have conveyed a powerful compliment. An honest statement such as, "I really love Dick's dramatic flair. He belongs on the stage! It is incredible how he can turn emotions on and off. Although, I will admit that on occasion that same attribute drives me a little crazy!" can go a long way to getting a parent conference off on the right foot. Typically a parent will respond with, "He is the same way at home and that drives his mom and me crazy also!"

Opening the conference with a discussion of the things you like and admire about a child establishes a rapport with the parents and demonstrates to the parents that you really do know something about their child.

Step two, *stating your concern in terms of the consequence for the child*, is critical. Frequently, we, as teachers, appeal to the parent in terms of the effect their child's misbehavior is having on us. "I can't teach with him talking all the time." or "It is impossible for me to control the class with that type of behavior going on." It isn't that those sentiments aren't true, but you may be complaining to the wrong audience for sympathy. Both Jonas and Dick have found that those are the types of statements that elicit sympathy from their own mothers, but unfortunately not from anyone else! You see, our mothers have a real vested interest in our happiness and professional fulfillment. However, the parents of our students shouldn't be expected to care if we are finding teaching easy or stressful.

On the other hand, what they do care about, and care a great deal about, is the educational prognosis for *their* child. It is for this reason that early in the conference we share clearly and concisely our concerns and we do so in terms of the educational consequence(s) for their student. An example might be:

> "I am worried about the impact that this pattern of behavior may have on Jill's future success. If she doesn't concentrate on her math now, she will have a tough time with the fourth grade work next year. Our experience has been that if students fall behind in fourth grade it is extremely difficult for them to catch up later."

Such a comment will catch the parents' attention because it speaks to a very real and very natural consequence that will likely happen to a person whom the parent truly cares about, their child!

Step three is easy to accomplish and is also often neglected. *Ask the parents for suggestions*. After all, the parents have been the child's primary teacher for years; they have lots of experience working with this child. In our experience such a request usually triggers one of two responses: a concrete suggestion or an expression of frustration. If the parent does offer a suggestion (and it's both legal and ethical), we do it! If it ultimately fails nothing has been lost, and if it works our alliance with the parent has been strengthened. If a parent expresses frustration it may sound like this:

"I don't know what to do! We've tried everything at home and she behaves the same way there. We hoped that you would have a suggestion; after all, you are the expert on young children."

Although we might have liked a concrete idea, an expression such as the one above can be valuable to receive. If the parent admits that they are also frustrated, we can begin collaborating without pretenses. When this happens we generally assert that while we don't have any magic answers, we do have some ideas that we could try together. The fact that we're' willing to try out a strategy that the parent would also like to see attempted, creates a strong bond between teacher and parent.

The next two stages of the process bear close resemblance to reality therapy. The parent and teacher need to agree to a plan of action and a process for sharing feedback. Perhaps the parent will agree to monitor homework on a nightly basis, and the teacher will agree to monitor on-task work in the classroom. Both parties might agree to report to the student daily on her progress, and then agree to talk each Friday afternoon at 3:30 for the next three weeks.

Perhaps the most important part of the six-part process is the last step, *if it works, send a thank you note.* Dick would always put a "tickler" note in his plan book for 6 weeks down the road. These notes served to remind him to check on how the plan was going. If it turned out that six weeks later the student, let's say Jill, had reformed from her earlier errant ways Dick would send her parents a thank-you note":

Dear Mr. and Mrs. Smith,

I am so delighted with the progress Jill is making in math. She appears to be enjoying it more and is doing a much better job at checking her own work and monitoring her behavior.

I know none of this would have been accomplished without your help and support.

Thank you so much.

> *Sincerely,*
>
> *Dick Sagor*

The value of the note, other than the courtesy it conveys, is how it reinforces the new positive relationship between home and school. As was mentioned earlier, in the homes of our discouraged learners the school has frequently been viewed as the enemy. Oftentimes, the parents of our at-risk students were themselves unsuccessful in school, likewise older siblings may be failing, and earlier interactions with the school may have been painful for the parent. These parents may not have a great many school pictures in their quality world photo album. An expression of appreciation and collegial respect will go a long way toward reversing that sad history.

Concluding Comment

Dealing with discipline is probably one of the most unpleasant things we are called on to do as teachers. It drives more of our colleagues out of the profession than anything else, but it is extremely important. When done properly it develops internal attribution, it fulfills children's need for power and can show them how to assert control over their lives, *and* it can strengthen home/school relationships.

The key to looking at classroom management in a positive way is to see it as a route to developing feelings of CBUPO and to see it as a separate discipline well worth teaching. Seeing management as a subject we are teaching makes sense, as the lessons it teach are essential lessons for our students to learn, especially our "at-risk" students. While there is a continuing debate over which is the best, or even what constitutes an appropriate approach to classroom management, it is clear that discouraged learners are well served by any system that meets the following guidelines:

System Guidelines

♦ Avoids anger

♦ Provides students with choices

♦ Deals with the present behavior

♦ Is consistent in application

♦ Is purposeful

♦ Builds feelings of potency

If your management system fits these guidelines then you are well on the way to helping your at-risk students to increase the feelings of potency they so desperately need.

References

Brookover, W. B., & Lezotte, L. W. (1979). *Changes in school characteristics coincident with changes in student achievement.* East Lansing, MI: Institute fo r Research on Teachig, College of Education, Michigan State University.

Canter, L., & M. (1976). *Assertive discipline: A take charge approach for today's educator.* Los Angeles: Canter and Associates.

Curwin, R. L., & Mendler, A. N. (1999). *Discipline with dignity,* revised ed. Alexandria, VA: Association for Supervision and Curriculum Development.

Driekurs, R., & Grey, L. (1968). *A new approach to discipline: Logical consequences.* Hawthorne, New York: Plume.

Edmonds, R. (1979). Effective schools for the urban poor. *Educational Leadership,* 37 (1), 24–27.

Fine, M., & Zane, N. (1985). Being wrapped too tight: When low income women drop out of high school." In L. Weis, E. Farrar, & H. G. Petrie (Eds.), *Dropouts from school: Issues, dilemmas and solutions,* (pp. 23–54). Albany, NY: SUNY Press.

Gathercoal, F. (1990). *Judicious Discipline.* Corvallis, OR: Caddo Gap Press.

Glasser, W. (1965). *Reality therapy: A new approach to psychiatry.* New York: Harper and Row.

Glasser, W. (1969). *Schools without failure.* New York: Harper and Row.

Good, T. L., & Brophy, J. E. (2002). *Looking in classrooms,* 9th ed. Boston: Addison-Wesley.

Jones, V. F., & Jones, L. S. (1990). *Comprehensive classroom management: Motivating and managing students,* 3rd ed. Boston: Allyn and Bacon.

Metis Associates, Inc., (1990). *The resolving conflict creatively program 1988–89: Summary of significant findings.* New York: Metis Associates.

Roderick, Tom. (1988). Johnny can learn to negotiate. *Educational Leadership,* January, 86–90.

Rutter, M., Maughn, B., Mortimore, P., Ouston, J., & Smith, A. (1979). *Fifteen thousand hours: Secondary schools and their effects on children.* Cambridge, MA: Harvard University Press.

Wynne, Edward A. (1981, January). "Looking at good schools." Phi Delta Kappan, pp. 377–388.

9

SCHOOLWIDE INITIATIVES THAT REDUCE AT-RISKNESS

Up until now we have been looking at programs and interventions that teachers could implement in their classrooms to prevent or moderate the impact of at-riskness. Clearly no factor, under our control, is more important to changing student attitudes towards school than the transformation of their daily classroom experience. After all, it is in our classrooms that they spend most of their structured time while at school.

However, if we confine our prevention efforts to the domain of the individual teacher and ignore a set of larger systemic organizational issues it can leave both students and teachers in a most frustrating situation. This isn't a new concern. Many years ago in a moving account of his own classroom *36 Children*, Herbert Kohl worried aloud about what would happen to his students when they left him and moved on to another teacher the following year. Regardless of the inventive and heroic efforts of any individual elementary school teacher, one can't ignore the fact that the children they nurture will move through a minimum of six more teachers before transitioning to a departmentalized middle school. If those experiences aren't successful in furthering the development of CBUPO and instead reinforce the very feelings of despair, alienation, and pessimism that put the child at-risk in the first place, then the resiliency building impact of one teacher's inspired teaching could be in vain.

The cost of neglecting system-wide issues will impact more than just the students. Teachers who find themselves, year after year, working alone in pursuit of an idiosyncratic vision, regardless its merit, are themselves at-risk. Teachers such as these are at-risk of burning out or perhaps worse, developing a deepening cynicism borne of the sheer loneliness of their struggle.

It is for these reasons that we now shift our attention to the impact that systematic methods of school organization can have on the experience of the defeated/discouraged learner. Just as organizational practices can teach unintended lessons through a *hidden curriculum* (see Chapter 5), creative and thoughtful schoolwide initiatives can make significant contributions towards making school meaningful for the at-risk student.

In the next two chapters we examine two types of schoolwide initiatives: those that can be easily introduced into a traditional school program and others that constitute significant departures from "business as usual" and, therefore, have been classified as *restructuring* initiatives.

When the first edition of this book was published the rationale for attending to early intervention was primarily a moral imperative. In the ensuing years most of the school systems in North America have been mandated to participate in a wave of standards-based reforms. In most cases reform legislation hasn't compelled specific changes in instructional delivery or even the introduction of specific educational programs. However, what most jurisdictions have started requiring is high-stakes testing of students to determine proficiency on a set of academic skills and background knowledge. Furthermore, those schools where students do not appear to be measuring up are subjected penalties as well as public ridicule. In numerous locales students who fail to demonstrate mastery are not being allowed to proceed with their education. Simply put at the dawn of the 21st century the costs of not addressing early school failure are greater for schools, students, and society than ever before.

Early Intervention

After examining the experience of at-risk students and the prognosis they face in "traditional" schools, Henry Levin of Stanford University asserted that we don't have dysfunctional kids, only dysfunctional schools. Levin is not alone in that view. Each year more and more thoughtful authors and educators have come to the same conclusion.

Take for example the experience of Elementary and Secondary Education Act (ESEA) Chapter 1 (formerly ESEA Title 1). ESEA Chapter 1 is the single biggest remediation effort ever undertaken in this country. First enacted during President Lyndon Johnson's administration as part of the nation's war on poverty, ESEA Title 1 was supposed to help equalize educational opportunity. Since 1965 the federal government has funneled billions of federal dollars into locally developed educational programs targeted at disadvantaged youth. Yet, according to many researchers and external evaluators, this compensatory education program hasn't worked for most of the children it was intended to serve. Lorin Anderson and Leonard Pellicer (1990), point out that the primary problem has been that, "expectations for students in compensatory and remedial programs are very low."

As a consequence of these persistent low expectations most ESEA Chapter 1 students become what Anderson and Pellicer labeled *lifers*. By this they mean that once placed in ESEA Chapter 1, the remedial student is unlikely to ever leave the compensatory curriculum. They contend that,

> "Compensatory and remedial programs should only be judged as successful when (and if) large numbers of their students return to and remain in the mainstream."

Using this standard they reluctantly concluded that this huge and well-intended federal program has largely been a failure.

As a result of the systemic problems with remedial programs Levin and his associates developed an approach called *accelerated schools*. This program grew out of an analysis on the rate of student progress in most pullout programs. Levin noted that the remedial student (by definition, a child who is already significantly behind) was being removed from their class, usually a class that was progressing at a normal pace, so they could be educated in a special environment that was moving at half that pace. After factoring in differences in homework expectations, and differences in allocated time and time on task (which is generally far less in compensatory classes) one sees that assignment to remediation means the student has been placed in a position that will result in their ending up farther behind their advantaged peers. No wonder this system creates lifers.

Levin's solution is to provide the remedial student with more than one year's growth in one year's time. The "accelerated school" philosophy is to move faster, not slower. Each school in the Stanford "accelerated schools" project is encouraged to go about this process in a manner that fits their local context and needs; however, what all accelerated schools have in common is a commitment to narrowing the gap between the at-risk learner and the successful student.

Research has established that the best strategy to overcome lifer status, while simultaneously decreasing the likelihood of early school leaving (dropping out), is to intensely focus on basic skill achievement (reading, language, and math) in grades K, 1, and 2. If our goal is provide these students with a successful long-term academic career, many have concluded that we make it our goal to bring the remedial student up to their peers by the end of third grade (Slavin, Karweit, & Madden, 2000, 2001).

"Success for All"

The project which was created at and is currently coordinated through Johns Hopkins University has succeeded in getting all students to grade level by the end of third grade in a number of schools beginning with a set of pilot sites in inner city Baltimore. Data now suggest that when properly implemented, entire student bodies (even at historically low performing inner city schools) can move to grade level or above (Slavin, Karweit, & Madden 2000, 2001). How were these remarkable turn-arounds achieved?

The effort began with a group of pioneers asking a set of questions:

- What would happen if we decided to provide children with all the programs and resources needed to ensure that each child would reach the fourth grade on time with adequate reading skills, no matter what?

- If we decided that no child would need to be assigned to special education for a learning problem unless they were seriously handicapped?

- If we decided that no child would need to be retained in grade or relegated to long-term remedial services?

- How could we design an urban elementary school that simply refused to accept the idea that even a single child will fail to learn to read? (Slavin et al. 1992)

In response to that challenge, the Johns Hopkins team, in collaboration with a set of pilot schools in Baltimore, Maryland began implementing a program with several essential elements, all of which were aimed at either prevention or immediate intensive intervention. The following features were incorporated into each pilot school:

Reading Tutors

Each "Success for All" school had a cadre of reading tutors who were themselves certified teachers. They worked in one-on-one tutoring sessions with students whose assessments showed them to be falling behind. These sessions employed the same materials and curricula as the reading program being experienced by the other children. The tutoring occurred at times other than the regularly scheduled 90-minute reading time. During the scheduled reading period the tutors worked as additional reading instructors, thus reducing class size for reading to approximately 15:1.

Joplin Plan Reading

In "Success for All" schools students are assigned to heterogeneous "home" classrooms. However, for reading instruction, these students are regrouped by performance level. By organizing instruction this way, the teachers can eliminate seat work and instead use the entire 90 minutes for skill development.

Eight Week Assessments

Every eight weeks each child is assessed by the reading teachers to determine who might be in need of tutoring, who no longer needs tutoring, and if someone appears to need other forms of assistance.

Preschool Program

Each "Success for All" school has half-day preschool and full-day kindergarten programs. While maintaining a playful atmosphere the kindergarten curriculum in these schools emphasized the development and use of language.

Family Support Team

Each school had a team made up of social workers, parent liaisons, and counselors to work with parents and provide parent education programs and "as needed" interventions when/if a family or home situation seemed to be interfering with the student's academic progress.

Program Facilitator

Each school had an individual in the position of program facilitator who worked along with the staff and the principal to oversee the successful implementation of the model. The program facilitator visited classrooms on a regular basis to help teachers with their instruction and provided support to individual children who were having difficulty. For example, the facilitator would often help with the development of the IAP (individual academic plan) for children who were presenting unusual instructional challenges. Incidentally, every child in the pilot schools was expected to have an IAP.

Special Education

In the pilot schools no students were referred to special education for problems with reading, because it was presumed that the regular education program would provide adequate support through the tutoring program.

The pilots demonstrated significant accomplishments in their first four years of operation. They succeeded in improving performance with the very poor, inner city, minority children that many schools complain are so difficult to teach. In the pilot schools almost all children ended up at or above grade level in reading, grade retention was reduced from 10 percent to near zero, and special education referrals for reading difficulties were eliminated. Because of the accomplishments at the pilot schools, "Success for All" has now been adopted by hundreds of schools in diverse settings across the country. Those sites that have paid attention to the seven essential elements cited above or have devised equally significant ways to provide the same service for their students have obtained similar results.

Significant improvement never happens easily. This near elimination of at-riskness at these schools has required a great deal of work and the model requires per pupil expenditures significantly higher than in other schools. At the pilot sites, additional resources were obtained by combining ESEA Chapter 1, Special Education, and other categorical funds and then using these resources to enrich the regular program. Many schools desiring to implement "Success for All" type programs may find it hard to acquire or justify the increased expense. This is unfortunate and generally reflects a short-term bias on the part of decision makers. Early school failure that is not effectively remediated carries with it tremendous long-term costs. Many states now require the retention of students below grade level. We need to remember that each year a child is retained will cost the taxpayers an additional year of schooling. The math is easy to figure. If a school retains just 13 children for one year, that action costs the same amount as taking another child from kindergarten through high school graduation. But the costs for additional years of schooling are just the beginning. The evidence suggests that students who leave their primary years lacking basic skills are much more likely to engage in drug abuse, delinquency, and become school behavior problems. Those problems cost the taxpayer dearly. Counselors, interventionists, alternative schools, probation officers, and juvenile facilities are all extremely expensive. But, those costs are nothing compared to the price that is paid if the failing student ends up in our criminal system. Over 90 percent of inmates at our penal institutions were seriously behind in basic skills when they left elementary school. Because the cost of a single year of incarceration is in excess of the cost of a 4-year college education at a private university, it is easy to see that using prison as an alternative to early intervention is far from cost effective. However, the greatest cost can't be measured in dollars. It is the cost in lost lives and unfulfilled dreams. Programs like "Success for All" aren't expensive if we consider the long-term costs of failing to invest early on. In the words of a commercial for preventative auto maintenance, "You can pay me now or pay me later!"

The "Success for All" program may not be the right model for every school. But, what it does demonstrate is the power of working from a new paradigm. Rather than focusing on how to deal with large remedial populations as though their existence was inevitable, the schools using this approach are committed to what Slavin and his colleagues have called *neverstreaming* or preventing failure before it even has a chance to become a syndrome.

Parental Involvement

One of the salient features of the "Success for All" model is the close working relationship between school and family. "Success for All" borrowed heavily on the parental involvement work of Yale Psychiatry Professor, James Comer. Comer had been working for several years with elementary schools in New Haven, Connecticut and Prince George's County, Maryland. Comer, a child psychiatrist developed an approach based on bringing teachers, parents, and students together as full partners in the educational process. The Comer schools do this by creating governance and management groups in each school. These groups assume responsibility for three things that Comer and his associates consider critical for school success:

♦ school atmosphere,

♦ the school's academic program, and

♦ the school's staff development program for teachers.

The Comer schools have shown us that when educators forge partnerships between home and school, dramatic academic progress can be produced.

The mutual mistrust and skepticism between parent and teacher that have hampered education for many minority youth is noticeably lacking in most of the schools in which Comer has worked. But in telling Comer's story there is also reason for concern. It is easy for people to misunderstand the true reasons for the academic successes achieved. The Comer schools are not the only ones that have sought to increase parental involvement. Over the past quarter century "parent involvement" has become a mantra chanted at nearly every public school. During this period we have seen little evidence that parental involvement alone will improve academic performance. In fact, we have some evidence that occasionally increased parental involvement correlates with declines in student performance.

In their landmark effective schooling study Wilbur Brookover and Larry Lezotte (1979) reported a fascinating finding. They had been investigating elementary schools throughout the state of Michigan. After dividing schools into three groups based on the direction of their standardized achievement scores (improving, declining, stable), they compared the three sets of schools. At first the researchers were surprised to find that the level of parental involvement was inversely related to the direction of student performance. In the sub-set of schools where achievement scores were declining the reported levels of parental involvement were actually higher then that reported at the improving schools. The only exception to this pattern was a sub-sample of schools that served exclusively minority populations. In those schools it appeared there was a slight positive correlation between parental involvement and school effectiveness.

While there are certainly other possible explanations for these findings there are two factors that merit some reflection before inaugurating a parent involvement program:

- the nature of the parental involvement, and
- the social organization of the school.

The Nature of the Parental Involvement

All parental involvement is not created equal. Many of the activities we invite parents to help with may actually draw attention and energy away from the school's essential academic mission. When this occurs we may inadvertently be depleting and misdirecting finite teacher and parent attention. While involving parents in the planning of a school carnival may appear, on the surface, to be a great idea and it may even generate considerable enthusiasm and even some needed external funding, it will also absorb valuable zero-sum time. The time invested in preparing decorations, setting up booths, arranging for prizes, recruiting volunteers, etc., all consume time that could be otherwise devoted to language acquisition, thinking skills development, or math problem solving. Because time is finite, schools that devote their energy to carnivals and similar activities will find that they have comparatively less time to devote to essential academic pursuits. When kids are being held accountable for their performance on state mandated achievement tests, this diversion of energy can have serious consequences.

Barbara Cervone and Kathleen O'Leary wrote an article back in 1982 that shed important light on this phenomenon. They offered a method of categorizing parental involvement by nature and type. They suggested that parent/school activities could be classified as either requiring active or passive involvement. For example, reporting to a parent on progress was classified as a passive activity, while tutoring was regarded as a high participation activity. In addition, the activities themselves could be conducted in a high or low participation fashion. For example, even with a low participation activity, such as reporting on progress, the teacher could accomplish this a number of ways, from simply sending a report card home, to asking for it to be returned with comments, to inviting the parents to attend an interactive student led conference. These dimensions of involvement could be charted on a graph such as that in Figure .9.1.

Figure 9.1. Parent Involvement Continuum

	Reporting	Special Events	Parent Education	Parents Teaching
Parents as Passive Participants	Good News Notes	Open House	Welcoming Committee	
	60-Second Phone Calls	Audiovisual Presentations	Parent Bulletin Board	
	Star of the Week	Potluck Supper	Information on Home and Weekend Activities	
	Newsletter	Father's/Mother's/Sibling's Day	Information on Community Resources	
		Spring Fling	Lending Library (Book, Toy, Record)	Make and Take Workshop
		End-of-the-Year Picnic	Classroom Observations	Teachable Moments
		The Gym Show	Workshops on Topics of Interest to Parents	Home Worksheets
	Call-in Times		A Course for Parents	Parent Teaching in the Classroom
	Parent-Teacher Conferences		Parent Objectives in the IEP	
Parents as Active Participants	Home-School Notebooks	Parent-to-Parent Meetings		
	(Parent Leaders)	(Parent Leaders)	(Parent Leaders)	(Parent Leaders)

Parents as Passive Participants → Parents as Active Participants

From: Cervone, Barbara Tucker, & O'Leary, Kathleen. Conceptual framework for parent involvement, *Educational Leadership* 40, 2: 49. Reprinted with permission of the Association for Supervision and Curriculum Development. Copyright 1982 by ASCD. All rights reserved.

Activities such as parent tutoring tend to fall in the lower right hand corner of the chart. We would expect that an activity occurring here would have a positive effect on student achievement, because it increases time on task, focus, and family involvement with priority academic goals. In all likelihood one of the reasons why parental involvement in the minority schools in the Michigan study correlated positively with improved student performance was because of the nature of that involvement. Poor, minority, and/or disadvantaged parents rarely have time for carnivals or mother/daughter teas. Yet, they do hold passionate feelings about their children's education. The programs they are likely to get involved with are the very ones that have a direct academic payoff for their children. This has been repeatedly demonstrated in the Comer schools. By involving parents and teachers in collaborative problem solving with the central issues of school atmosphere, academics, and staff development, Comer has intensified the academic focus of schools and families rather than diluting it.

Parent Support vs. Parent Involvement

One way we can gain positive results from our work with families is to reconsider the outcomes we are after. Parent knowledge regarding the school program and their enthusiastic support of the school's objectives has consistently shown positive correlations with student achievement. During the great wave of European immigration to the United States few immigrant parents had time to spend at their child's school. Frequently, the first time a parent entered the school building was to attend graduation, however, nothing was more important to these parents that to have their offspring succeed academically. All a parent needed in those days was a call from the teacher and the parent could get their child's attention.

Over the last 20 years minority (African American and Latino) parents have consistently reported in the Gallup Polls (Rose & Gallup, 2000, 2001) regarding attitudes towards education, a strong belief in the value of educational success to quality of life. Interestingly, minority parents have consistently rated the value of an education higher than do parents of European ancestry. Because of this we can count on these parents to "preach the gospel" of the school at home and reinforce what we are trying to accomplish. But, first they have to know what we are doing and why we are doing it this way. In addition, they need to believe that we truly have their family's needs at heart. Beginning with the Coleman report (Coleman, 1966), studies have consistently shown that poor minority children do better at private schools than at urban public schools. These results are even apparent when performance is contrasted with schools that serve equally disadvantaged populations and do so with equally or more limited budgets (usually Catholic schools). When researchers scratch under the surface they find that the parents do not do more at these private schools, but they understand the mission of the school better and feel that the school shares their family's values and dreams. Understanding and agreeing with the mission are crucial if we expect parents to reinforce that mission in their interaction with their children.

The lesson from the above should be clear. If we want children to prosper at school it is important that they get the same message on the value of schooling from *all* of the significant adults in their lives. For this reason we should be continually asking ourselves what can we do to make it more likely that parents will feel that they are in an ideological partnership with their child's school/teacher even when circumstances won't allow them to work together. The following Think and Do Exercise explores the development of parent support.

Think and Do Exercise—Increasing Parental Support

Using the chart in Figure 9.1 Parent Involvement Continuum, plot out all the parent involvement activities that have occurred in your school during the past semester. Ask yourself whether these activities are:

1. Helping teachers and parents speak with one voice on academic matters?

2. Helping focus more student time on academic learning tasks?

3. Helping the teacher/student accomplish academic objectives?

The Social Organization of Schools

In 1954 the United States Supreme Court, in *Brown v. Board of Education* held that "separate education is inherently unequal." That decision was not reached lightly. The record of the Brown case involved reams of sociological and psychological evidence that supported the educational value of heterogeneous grouping. The outgrowth of that ruling and the data that supported it was a national policy that not only fostered racial integration but was followed by other initiatives (Public Law 94–142) that mandated the mainstreaming of educationally challenged children. Mainstreaming, as a concept, was fostered by a host of studies. One of the more influential studies was conducted and published as early as 1968 by the president of the Council for Exceptional Children, Lloyd Dunn. Dunn found that educationally challenged youngsters in integrated settings, even without any special educational assistance, outperformed a control group that received education from trained special educators in self-contained classrooms.

Yet, in spite of all this data most schools continue to segregate students on the basis of their academic performance. This is done in three ways. Tracking (is discussed in greater length in the next chapter), special programs within

schools, and the proliferation of alternative schools developed for and popu-
lated almost exclusively by at-risk youth.

These grouping and sorting practices can lead to several critical problems, to
be discussed below, for our discouraged learners. Those problems are exacerbated by the workings of several "syndromes" that merit further examination.

Two Syndromes Affecting At-Risk Youth

Stigma

Programs, institutions, and subcultures tend to confer an identity on the individuals who are identified with them. For example, when we see a group of
girls dressed in Girl Scout uniforms walking down the street with boxes of
cookies, we make certain assumptions about them. Most folks would assume
that these girls are nice individuals who are about to participate in a wholesome
activity. Now suppose that instead we observed a trio of teenagers walking up
the steps of the courthouse with police officers on either side. Would we assume
that these were young people about to receive good citizens awards? We suspect not. More likely we would assume that these kids were in some sort of
trouble. The reason we make these judgments is that we are influenced by our
experience with both institutions: the courts and the Girl Scouts. Because we
identify the Girl Scouts with wholesomeness, we are willing to confer those
same attributes on the girls wearing the uniform. However, because we associate the courts and police with law breaking, we are equally inclined to confer
darker identities on the teens we see on the courthouse steps. There is nothing
sinister about this. It is only natural. The problem is that our schoolhouses are
also full of programs, institutions, and groupings that convey powerful
associations, both positive and negative.

The computer lab, the journalism room, the gifted education program, and
the drama room are all places we associate with positive activities. Upon seeing
youth enter or leave those venues we are inclined to think well of them. Other
programs convey decidedly different pictures. For many people in the school
community the special education classroom, the remedial reading lab, and the
vice-principal's office are places we associate with less than top scholars and citizens. Because of these associations, and regardless of our intentions, these programs and venues carry a *spoiled image*. This spoiled image of the program inevitably stains the children associated with them. This type of labeling even enters
the school vocabulary. We refer to John as a gifted student, Jill as learning disabled. Joe is an advanced placement student and Jim is a resource room kid. The
labels their peers bestow can be far less kind, for example, "Jim is a retard." The
unfortunate truth is that the more we treat children separately the more likely
they will be to take on the character of the programs they are assigned to. If the

program has a spoiled image the children associated with it end up carrying the same stigma.

Let us examine this phenomenon from the perspective of a program commonly used with at-risk youth, the alternative school. Several years ago Dick conducted a study at a public alternative school funded by ESEA Title 1 and organized to serve students who had already dropped out of the mainstream school (Sagor, 1974). The school was deemed successful by the district and ultimately became somewhat of a magnet for the youth of the community. There were numerous incidents of students who made the decision to drop out of their high school just to get a place on the waiting list for the alternative school. The alternative school students seemed happy, secure, and successful. Student morale was high and there was significant evidence to support those glowing appraisals.

For example, when asked to compare the quality of the education they were receiving at the alternative school to the district's mainstream schools almost two thirds of the students agreed with the statement, "Students can learn more at the alternative school," while less than 10 percent agreed with the statement, "Students can learn more in the regular high schools."

Based on these positive assertions the kids were asked if they would recommend the alternative school to a sibling who was doing OK in the mainstream. Surprisingly more than two out of three (69 percent) answered no!

A clue to why they would be reluctant to recommend such a "quality" program to a loved one was revealed by their response to another question, "Have you ever been put down for attending the alternative school?" Almost three quarters of the student body responded affirmatively.

But the problem wasn't only in the putdowns they received. The actual performance of the alternative school students was significantly below that of their peers in the mainstream. These students were earning academic credits 23 percent below the rate necessary to graduate from high school in four years. So, although they had thought they were doing well (compared to "normal progress), they were not. Absent the referent of successful students, they became content with a pace of performance that was well below the norm. This illustrates the problem that led the Supreme Court to determine that "separate education was inherently unequal."

Given those problems, how can we account for the continued positive feelings expressed by the alternative school students?

Rejecting the Rejecters

The sociologist Erving Goffman offered some insight into this in his landmark book *Stigma: Notes on the Management of Spoiled Image* (Goffman 1963). Succinctly put, an individuals feel stigma when they believe that others see them as somehow inadequate. Goffman spoke of an instinctual response of stigmatized individuals. He called this phenomenon *rejecting the rejecters*. He pointed out that once individuals internalize a stigma they are faced with two choices. The first choice, obviously, is accepting the verdict of the assessors as accurate. However, accepting the judgment of others that one's status as an "LD kid," "an alternative school student," or a "retard" justifies relegating one to second class citizenship. Acquiescing to that judgment comes with a heavy cost. Such acceptance is often devastating to one's self-esteem.

There is, however, another alternative. The individual who is being "put down" can simply brush off the stigma as unimportant. While having the label "delinquent," "defective," "handicapped," or "slow" is hard to ignore, it is easy to reject it as unimportant. In essence the "outsider" student can declare, "I wouldn't want to join your club anyway!" The "rejecting the rejecter" phenomenon helps explain why alienated students often choose to dress in a de facto uniform that announces their rejection of the prevailing social and cultural norms. The wearing of Goth clothing and body art may signal a clear rejection of the mainstream. We see our discouraged students skipping out on pep assemblies and declaring that these rituals are just "stupid wastes of time." If you listen you can often hear alternative school kids declaring that the mainstream school "sucks" while the alternative school they attend is really "rad." As educators we need to recognize that while those assertions may lack substance, they do serve a very useful purpose for the student. By making these claims the "rejected" student can salvage much needed self-esteem.

This phenomenon would not be so bad were it not for the fact that the act of rejecting the rejecter or rejecting the judgments of the mainstream can serve to further the alienation of the defeated learner. This is because once a label has been attached another phenomenon begins to take hold. We call this one, "If you've got the name, you might as well play the game."

If you've got the name you might as well play the game.

This syndrome helps explain the slippery slope to delinquency that many at-risk kids find themselves on. It also helps us understand why, regardless of how severe we make the penalties; recidivism rates remain so high among both juvenile and adult offenders.

To understand how this phenomenon works, consider the case of Joe, a young person who is picked up for shoplifting and is sent for two days to the local juvenile facility. The teenage telegraph system works beautifully, and in no time, it appears that everyone back at school knows exactly where Joe has been and why. Before he ever returns to school (even if this is his first offense) he is already known by his teachers and peers as a *delinquent*. Upon reentering school, he is looked at and treated differently. The critical decision that Joe now faces is how he should to respond to these expectations. Once again Joe will face two choices. He could return to school, declare that his experience with the law was the single worst experience of his life, and assert that the trauma he experienced was so great that he will never again stray from righteousness. Heck, he might even pledge to join the clergy. But this is unlikely. Such a posture would only affirm the negative judgments that others have already were made of him as a juvenile delinquent.

Joe's second choice is to swagger nonchalantly into school. To declare that the stuff he was subjected to was nothing and that the whole experience in the "juvie" was "cool." In essence when Joe takes this stance, he is telling the world, "If you want to see me as delinquent I will be the best and toughest damn delinquent you have ever seen!"

As educators, we should be constantly alert and concerned about putting students into this bind. In Chapter 1 we considered the power of cognitive dissonance. Clearly, the "If you've got the name, you might as well play the game" syndrome pushes our alienated students to deepen the consonance between their negative behavior patterns and antisocial attitudes. The more those attitudes and behaviors are allowed to reinforce each other, the harder it will become for the student to ever break out of this self-defeating cycle.

However, we shouldn't despair as there are a number of approaches that hold promise for avoiding the pitfalls described above.

In-School Diversion

The most intriguing of these is the in-school diversion program. Diversion is a concept borrowed from the criminal justice system. It is based on the assumption that a first-time offender is at a different place emotionally than the habitual criminal. The first-time violator may have just slipped over the line of acceptable behavior and could well be amenable to soft purposeful redirection. Therefore, the function of diversion is to "divert" the person away from the punitive and stigmatizing criminal justice system, with its institutions of negative identity, and instead channel the pliable "first offender" into alternative pursuits involving institutions of positive identity. The assumption is that more CBUPOs can be generated from having the individual involved with positive institutions than with negative ones.

The way diversion works in schools is as follows. A list is prepared of all the programs in the school that convey positive identity on participants. Examples might include athletics, clubs, drama, safety patrol, teacher assistants. The faculty then agrees to hold 15 percent of the spots in those programs for the purpose of diversion. This is a quiet agreement made among the staff and is best not publicized to the student body or to the community. Later, when a student comes to the attention of the Vice-Principal or disciplinarian as a result of a casual slip into negative behavior, the adult in authority is armed with a host of possibilities for diverting the student.

To illustrate how this might work we'll share an example from Dick's experience when he served as the principal at a large suburban high school.

Case Study: The Diversion of Jay

One day Mr. Taylor brought Jay down to the Principal's office. Mr. Taylor knew that Dr. Sagor, the Principal, was linked to the diversion program, and Jay's behavior in class, as well as the comments he wrote in his daily journal were leading Mr. Taylor to believe that if something wasn't done soon, Jay would inevitably find his way into trouble.

Jay was new to the school. In fact, he had attended three different schools during the past two years. He came to this community when his father was paroled from prison with the requirement that he relocate. Jay had shoulder length hair and had a preference for those tight fitting sleeveless T-shirts that showed off his well developed upper body as well as his tattoos. Mr. Taylor introduced Jay and told the Principal that Jay was unclear about the procedures for going out for sports. After that brief orientation Mr. Taylor left the office, giving Dick a discrete wink. That signal, and the prior agreements regarding diversion, was all Dick needed to start the process. He involved Jay in a discussion about athletics. Jay shared that he had been a wrestler and had achieved some degree of success at the junior high he last attended. But Jay had heard that it was too late to try out for wrestling at this school, because the deadline for sign-ups was the previous week.

Dick told Jay that this could be his lucky day. Dick shared that because the wrestling coach was a friend he would see if he could exert some pull on Jay's behalf. Dick asked, "Would he like me to give it a try?" When Jay said yes, that was all Dick needed. Without hesitation Dick walked with Jay into the locker room where the two of them approached Coach Nago. Knowing that the coach had reserved some spots on the team for just this purpose, Dick proceeded (with high confidence, knowing that things would go as he hoped) and appealed to the coach saying, "I know last week was the deadline for turning out, but my friend Jay is a new student who didn't understand our procedures. You see he assumed that because his hair was so long he wouldn't be allowed on the team." Dick then added, "Jay is a good kid who really wants to wrestle." Concluding with this plea, "Could you make an exception, just this one time, for my friend? I sure would appreciate it."

Coach Nago thought for a minute and asked Jay, "So you really want to wrestle? You look like you've been lifting some weights, have you?" Jay replied that he had been, and the coach said, "All right, this one time I'll make an exception!" He put his arm around Jay and led him off to check out the necessary gear. Jay was now hopefully on the way to a positive identity. Rather than being left to wallow in a negative identity as a "shiftless kid," Jay was now able to bathe in a socially sanctioned positive identity, that of an athlete, more importantly, "a wrestler," a position that carried real status in this school.

Why does diversion work? First it is built on programs that owe their existence to purposes other than rehabilitation. Wrestling wasn't created to serve at-risk kids. Rather, it was created to serve athletes. Even the best programs that are created for problem kids can't help but develop a spoiled image. One way we keep programs from developing a problematic identity is to keep the ratio of positive- to negative-appearing participants high. This is the justification for the 85 percent rule.

Another key to the success of diversion is the interpersonal element. In that short ten-minute interchange with Jay, three adults let him know that they cared about him and were willing to put themselves in his corner. First, Mr. Taylor intervened by bringing Jay to a person in authority who could help. The principal was then seen as a compassionate person willing to pull strings to help a kid out, and, finally, Coach Nago was willing to be flexible by helping this new kid on the block.

With a system like this Jay couldn't lose. If he stayed out for wrestling (which he did until his dad moved him again), he would benefit from the positive identity and status that was conferred by the wrestling program. But even if he had decided after a few days to drop the sport, he would have left knowing that he belonged at this school and that three important adults cared about him. Contrast those perceptions to how Jay might have felt if he had simply received a lecture from Mr. Taylor "to shape up or ship out!"

Diversion programs are most effective at the elementary level. This is because younger students will have a shorter history of association with a negative identity. In his book, *Ordinary Resurrections*, Jonathon Kozol recounts the stories of several young children he has come to know in the impoverished South Bronx. In explaining their optimism Kozol says, "They have yet to learn that the society they are growing and living in doesn't like them very much." While the harshness of Kozol's comment ought to serve as a call to action for all decent people, it also illustrates how the lack of a personal history with bias and defeat can make early redirection (diversion) an effective strategy for pointing our youngest youth in a productive direction.

But, no where is a focus on diversion more imperative than with our early adolescent, middle schoolers. Early adolescents have two psychological needs that they are innately driven to have satisfied: a need to be special, and a need to fit in.

While on the surface these two needs may seem to be in conflict, that isn't the case. The best way to understand how these needs fit together is to examine them in a social context.

As was discussed in Chapter 4, the need to belong is a basic human drive. As the middle school child goes through extraordinary maturational changes (hormonally and physically) having this need satisfied takes on increasing meaning. Mary Pipher has documented powerfully in her book *Reviving Ophelia* (1994), how middle school girls often adopt what they know to be self-destructive behavior because of how important they believe it is to be perceived as conforming to a feminine model. Teachers of 11- to 14-year old youth can easily spot the identities (both positive and negative) that are being attached to these children. During this period some youth become viewed by their peers (as well as adults) as "top students," or "jokers," or "outlaws," or "boy crazy," or "jocks," etc. Oftentimes, regardless of the particular label, having a special identity provides some short-term satisfaction for the young teenager. After all, being labeled by others means you are perceived as being special, being a somebody. For those fortunate students, those who have special identities that are socially acceptable, wearing their identity with pride and affiliating with a subculture (with the same identity: e.g., honor society, student government, band, etc.) will provide short-term psychological, as well as long term benefits.

However, for the middle schoolers whose special status comes from association with a negative identity, then satisfying their short-term psychological needs (being special and part of a group) comes at a high cost. These youth will certainly be engaged in the syndrome we discussed earlier "if you've got the name, you might as well play the game."

A most important time for educators to be sensitive to this phenomena is when student are transitioning from one school level (elementary to middle, middle to high, etc.) to another. If you look closely during these transitional periods you can see young people scanning the environment looking for an opening to carve out their special niche. If they look around at the positive roles and identities available to them, i.e., top scholars, student body leaders, athletes, and conclude that there is "no room at the inn," we often see them adopt (by default) other less productive roles. It is at this point that a well functioning diversion program can be a life saver!

To see how well diversion could work at your school take a stab at the Think and Do Exercise below.

Think and Do Exercise—Creating a Diversion Program

1. Examine the potential for diversion at your school. First, generate a list of all the programs that operate within the school that confer a positive identity on the participants.

2. Next, consider the people who could serve as the prime diverters (folks who are situated at the crossroads of students, faculty, and advisors, people such as counselors, deans, administrators, activity coordinators, etc.).

3. Finally, generate a set of protocols for how the diversion process would be triggered and implemented at your school.

Teacher Advisory Programs

One of the salient features of diversion programs is the caring relationship and the advocacy that adults deliver on behalf of at-risk youth. However, the isolated, idiosyncratic nature of those interventions is often not enough in itself to build resiliency, especially as the young person moves up through the grades. For this reason, many middle schools and high schools have institutionalized adult advocacy through the development of teacher advisory or *guide* programs.

Traditionally, in most American elementary schools each child was known by, cared about, and served by a single adult, their teacher, who demonstrated a special interest in the child's development. For many at-risk children, these classroom teachers often became the equivalent of surrogate parents. However, our schools have become steadily larger and more departmentalized, providing this type of nurturing "school family" for each child has become more and more difficult. As a result, each year many students logically conclude that no single adult cares, notices, or is taking any particular interest in them or their concerns.

In response to this trend school faculties have crafted programs that attempt to reinforce the feelings of belonging, connectedness, and intimacy for their students even if those students find themselves attending extremely large schools. One common feature of most efforts to make school more personal has been the development of teacher advisory or guide programs. The organizing principle behind these initiatives is to provide every student with at least one caring adult at the school who the student feels is sincerely interested in them, both as an individual and as a student. Schools have been successful in creatively crafting a wide variety of guide programs that fit the local context. As these programs differ in many ways there clearly is no one "best" model. There are, however, certain issues that every guide program should consider and address.

Issue 1: Assignment of Students

In some schools advisory group assignments are done randomly while in others, students are placed in accordance with a counselor's judgment of "best fit." Another approach allows the child the opportunity to choose their own guide teacher. Each of these approaches has both strong and weak points and a great deal can be gained through a faculty discussion of the pros and cons.

Among the advantages of randomized assignments is that they divide the workload evenly and they convey to students that the faculty is unified in its commitment to student assistance. On the negative side, random assignments provide no guarantee of a good fit.

The approach of having the adults make informed placements has been a successful approach when making student classroom assignments in child centered elementary schools. As with classroom assignments, placing this way requires that due consideration be given to the child's learning style, the advisor's strengths, and the fit of personalities. On the down side, this can be a very time consuming process and it doesn't allow the student the opportunity to exercise any power in choosing someone to be their special friend.

Allowing students to choose their own advisor is not only time efficient, but it places the student in the driver's seat. It can, however, exacerbate or bring to the surface faculty resentment, jealousy, and division. At the high school Jonas attended, an advisory program was introduced that granted the students the right to choose their own faculty advisor. The students were given three days to sign up with the teacher of their choice and a ground rule was set whereby no teacher was obligated to take on a load of more than twenty-five. As it turned out many popular soft-hearted teachers allowed significant over enrollments in their groups. We remember one very popular teacher/coach who accepted nearly 50 students into his advisory group. However, we also recall another teacher who was approached by only three students out of a student body of 800. When such disparities arise they open opportunities for some soul searching discussions for a faculty. However, it is worth keeping in mind that the culture of some schools simply cannot tolerate the tensions that this will produce.

Issue 2: Frequency of Meetings

Some schools provide a short period of time, sometimes as little as ten minutes per day for advisement. Others provide significantly more time (30 minutes or more) two or three times weekly, while a third approach is to provide a full class period or its equivalent once per week. Again, each of these approaches has both good and bad points. Whichever approach is utilized, quality advisory programs find it useful to structure opportunities for both one-on-one as well as group guidance.

In our review of guide programs from around the country there seems to be no limit to the creativity of faculties in designing programs or in structuring time. Clearly, the most common approach is the daily homeroom period. It is the easiest to schedule and fits nicely into the flow of the typical school day. Furthermore, it fosters daily contact between student and advisor. Another popular option is the use of a block of time that can serve different purposes on different days. For example, the half hour between 10:00 and 10:30 might be devoted to guide groups on Tuesdays and Thursdays, yet be devoted to assemblies on Fridays and club meetings on Mondays and Wednesdays.

At McClure North High School in Florissant, Missouri, the faculty fashioned a particularly creative program. Using a rotational schedule (Figure 9.2), each teacher was released from regular instructional duties once each week for two periods.

Figure 9.2. Advisement Conference Schedule

Monday—Team A: Smith, Dalton, Green, Williams, Edson, Reilly				
Date		*Periods*	*Date*	*Periods*
Sept.	15	1-2	Feb. 2 5–6	
	22	3–4	9	1–2
	29	5–6	16	3–4
Oct.	6	1–2	23	5–6
	13	3–4	Mar. 2	1–2
	20	5–6	9	3–4
	27	1–2	16	5–6
Nov.	3	3–4	23	1–2
	10	5–6	30	3–4
	17	1–2	Apr. 6	5–6
Dec.	1	3–4	20	1–2
	8	5–6	27	3–4
	15	1–2	May 4	5–6
	22	3–4	11	1–2
Jan.	5	5–6	18	3–4
	12	1–2	25	5–6
	19	3–4		

From: Hampton & Lauer. *Problems in secondary school administration: A human approach,* Copyright 1981 by Allyn and Bacon. Reprinted with permission.

This resulted in each class being canceled only once every five weeks. This hardly seems like much of a sacrifice of instructional time. With this schedule advisors had an option. They could always schedule individual appointments with the students they needed to see (if there was an emergent personal need, such as a recent flare-up in class, an unexplained absence, or necessary planning for post high school education). In those instances the advisor simply sent a guidance summons (just as counselors traditionally do; however, in this case the appointment was with the child's guide teacher), and the student would meet his guide in the advisement center. When and if the guide teacher felt that small group guidance was called for (for example: talking to five students who were all planning for apprenticeships or working with a particularly at-risk group), the advisor could call in just those students. On those rare occasions when it was deemed necessary for the entire student body to receive guidance (semester scheduling, etc.) the school just scheduled a guidance period for the entire student body.

At McClure North the efficiency of this model was enhanced by the existence of a roomy and warm student center and a terrific library. These facilities easily accommodated any students who are temporarily displaced from class. Even where one doesn't have that support, what the McClure program demonstrates is the degree of the flexibility that can be crafted by a committed faculty.

Issue 3: Cross-Age or Grade Level Groupings?

Some programs have chosen to foster a family feeling by having mixed age advisory groups, while others have felt that peer guidance is enhanced by keeping the groups as homogeneous as possible. New Trier High School in Winnetka, Illinois, which has successfully operated an advisory program for more than ninety years, even separates their groups by gender, further demonstrating that there is no one best model!

Issue 4: One Year or Multi-Year Assignments?

While some schools shift groups annually, it has generally been found that continuity in the guide relationship is preferable. Therefore, even when the groups are homogeneous, we recommend that the groups stay together with their guide teacher until graduation or promotion to the next level. Another virtue of the multi-year approach is that it provides variety for the teacher/advisor. While I might begin with a group of 6th graders, and find myself concentrating on their transitioning needs as they enter our middle school, three years later I would find myself helping these same advisees as they prepare for yet another transition, this time to high school.

Issue 5: Structured or Unstructured Meetings?

This issue comes up as part of the compromise that schools face when all teachers are expected to be advisors, yet some faculty are comfortable with the role while others are not. Providing schoolwide structured advising lessons (often dealing with career issues) gives the teacher who is lacking in confidence, a crutch. However, those teachers who find they take naturally to the advising role, may feel constrained by prepackaged lessons. A compromise is to expect each advisory group to develop its own unique project, while expecting every group to address certain common issues. Earlier we mentioned the coach with fifty students in his advisory group. One semester his group took on the project of creating and hosting a baby shower for a pregnant student in their group. While that project did raise some eyebrows, it certainly accomplished the goal of creating a family feeling within the guide group!

Issue 6: Total Faculty Involvement or Volunteers?

This issue is another way to get around many of the dilemmas mentioned earlier. When a school constructs their program using volunteers the average case load will become, by necessity, higher. However, so is the enthusiasm. One way around this dilemma is to offer advising as an option in lieu of other non-teaching duties (lunchroom and parking lot duty, etc.). This way those faculty members who are more comfortable with other types of student supervision can opt out of advisement, yet still carry their fair share of the workload.

Another, more expensive approach is the one used at New Trier High School. There, experienced and qualified teachers apply to be advisors. Those who are ultimately selected and serve do so in lieu of one of their other academic assignments. While this is expensive, providing advising for 125 students at New Trier costs as much as one full-time teacher, it also clearly establishes advisement as an important and top priority school project.

Child Assistance Teams (CAT)

This schoolwide intervention goes under various names in different locations (child study teams, teacher assistance teams, multidisciplinary teams, etc.). Whatever the name, these are all strategies that use in-school professional resources to provide consultative assistance to other teachers when planning interventions for students who appear to be at-risk. The usual format is to have a small standing committee made up of an administrator, a counselor, a special educator, and several volunteer classroom teachers. Typically, group meetings are open to any teacher with an interest or expertise in the student who has been referred.

Referral to the teacher assistance team is usually the first step in developing an intervention plan. When the referral process works correctly the team gets involved even before diagnostic testing. Not infrequently, requests for testing (should they occur) are an outgrowth of an initial team consultation. Generally, the process involves the team discussing the specific behaviors that concerned the teacher who made the referral and then suggesting a set of interventions for consideration. Occasionally, the group may request a special education referral. A key to the success of the child assistance team strategy is making sure that the process moves quickly enough to help the teacher before an instructional problem escalates into a disciplinary problem and begins careening out of control.

The one caution we would share regarding CAT is that faculty members need to see the purpose of the CAT as providing a problem-solving process to help teachers do a better job serving their own students. When care is not taken to articulate that purpose, the teams can be become mechanisms that inappropriately shift responsibility away from the classroom teacher and to the administration or special education department. When that happens the child assistance team (CAT) becomes another vehicle that labels students and moves them further out of the mainstream.

Push-In/Not Pullout Programs[1]

The historic separation of special and remedial education from the general education program presents many problems for at-risk students. As mentioned earlier these programs often convey a stigma, and by serving these students in separate settings, these programs tend to move at a slower pace and involve lower-level cognitive objectives (Oakes, 1985). On the other hand, one thing that has made special education and remedial education so popular is that they have forced those with authority to recognize that additional resources are necessary to provide appropriate services for students with special needs. Recently, a movement has been underway to continue targeting special resources to the special needs students (like with the "Success for All" Schools) but to do so inside the general education classroom. Some schools call this model *inclusion* while others dub it *integration*; still others call it *blended services*.

---

1   This discussion concerns serving special needs students in the regular classroom where otherwise traditional instructional approaches are utilized. *Inclusion* is discussed in length in Chapter 8. It is the perspective of the authors that "inclusive education" implies a radical departure from business as usual and is far more than merely providing educational service to special needs students in mainstream classes.

Whatever they are called, these approaches break down the barriers between special and regular education and hold great potential. However, as with anything else, they present their own dilemmas. The basic objectives of blended services and combining special and regular programs are:

- It keeps the classroom teacher as the primary manager of instruction,

- It keeps the child with their peers,

- It engages the child with the regular curriculum and its higher-level objectives,

- It supports the attainment of CBUPO for all, and

- It keeps the remedial student from falling further behind.

While those are powerful reasons to implement inclusion, there are some predictable problems that must be anticipated when implementing push-in programs. Many federal and state programs have regulations that require that specialists work only with "identified" students. Strictly enforcing these regulations as written can add to student stigma. However, most states and the federal government will now consider requests for waivers from these exclusivity regulations.

A Case in Point

You may recall that in Chapter 2 we shared the story of Dick's experience in implementing mastery learning" in his heterogeneous classroom. It was during that time that his school was undertaking a major initiative for the inclusion of special needs students. Therefore the only teaching carried out by the school's special education learning center, was additional assistance for special needs students as they worked on meeting the requirements of their regular education classes. Consequently, the staffing of special education was altered and started to emphasize the use of teacher aides who were assigned to work in required classes with the special needs students. Because Dick typically had between four and five students with IEPs in his required government class, an aide from the learning center was assigned to his class each day. Even when the class was viewing a film or engaging in teacher directed instruction, the aide was there to become familiar with the content that was being covered. Later, during the student's assigned time in the learning center, the aide was there to provide assistance in completing assignments, preparing for mastery tests, and, on occasion, orally administering a mastery test to students.

During the three years that Dick taught under that system the success of his special needs students equaled or exceeded the success of his mainstream students. Perhaps more importantly, the affective benefits for these once stigmatized students were enormous. Not only were they attending class in a regular classroom rather than being in a spoiled-image remedial room, they were being held to the same high standards (mastery expectations) as were the other non-disabled students. What was particularly gratifying was that Dick wasn't reducing the academic standards in his class. The only special allowance was the offer of additional assistance from the aide and more time to learn with the scheduled time period in the learning center.

Providing this type of support levels the playing field, while esteeming the learner. Special segregated classes, with special standards only serve to demean the slower or special learner. Upon reflection Dick realized that one of the best things about the system used in his school was the degree to which the presence of the aide and the availability of resource room support reduced teacher stress. Why? He put it this way,

> *"Whenever I saw Karen (the learning center aide) sitting in my room I knew that the ultimate success of these kids no longer rested on my fallible shoulders alone!"*

In blended elementary classrooms the special education aides can and often do provide an array of critical support services for the general classroom teacher. They can read to or orally instruct students who are intellectually capable but are temporarily behind in language. They can collect diagnostic data, observations, prepare time on task reports, conduct achievement testing, etc. Perhaps most importantly, their presence effectively reduces the adult to student ratio, thereby allowing the teacher to spend more concentrated quality time with each individual student.

One of the best approaches to blending services that we've seen is one that combines the benefits of the child assistance team (CAT) with "in-classroom support." Several schools have eliminated all their special pullout remedial programs and have reallocated the money saved to pay additional classroom aides and hire interventionist teachers. The "interventionists" are certificated teachers without a classroom of their own, whose sole job is to consult with and assist teaching colleagues with planning and teaching of at-risk students wherever and whenever necessary.

The common feature of all these initiatives is to keep at-risk students with their peers, to maintain high standards, while providing additional resources for the regular classroom. The benefits for *all* students can be enormous. A primary purpose of public education is preparation for democracy. There is no better preparation for a democratic citizen than to participate in a classroom community that reflects the wondrous diversity of our nation. But, it isn't only the students who receive the benefits, especially when blended services are provided properly. This type of teaching is far more satisfying for the "regular ed" classroom teacher. It is a great feeling being able to work with a wide range of students, while being confident that you have been given the necessary support to meet that challenge.

It is, however, important to insert a word of caution here. While it is exciting to see the emphasis on blended services and push-in programs, we need to be vigilant about the potential for these programs (and inclusion, which is discussed in the next chapter) to be used as Trojan horses by those reactionary forces that are bent on reducing appropriations and spending for students with special needs. In too many places, as old special categorical pullout programs are being dismantled, we are seeing classroom teachers inheriting larger loads, more problematic kids, and doing all this with less help. For this reason those of us who philosophically support mixed ability heterogeneous grouping must be diligent in demanding that the fiscal support necessary to assist special needs students be maintained and focused on meeting the needs of these at-risk children.

To help you think through the shift to push-in philosophy as opposed to a pullout approach find a teaching colleague and collaboratively do the following Think and Do Exercise.

Think and Do Exercise—Creating a Push-In Program

Inventory the resources available to construct a push-in program for your school. First, list all the special and remedial programs available to students in your school and the staff assigned to them. Then look at the schedules of students who are making use of those programs. If those students are accessing the special programs with time that could be better spent in academic classes, then they may benefit from a push-in program with more academic help.

Now ask some regular education teachers to describe the help they would need if they were to incorporate the special need students into their rooms.

Finally, compare the teachers' requests with the resources now being spent on the pullout programs and see if you could construct a financially viable push-in program for your school.

In the next chapter we will look at other schoolwide initiatives. Specifically, we will examine approaches that challenge some very basic prevailing assumptions about how schools are organized and that consequently may require radical restructuring of many of our current educational paradigms.

The following poem is one we enjoy because it provides us with a helpful reminder of the impact that the treatment of students has on their self-esteem and behavior.

Imitation

If a child lives with criticism, he learns to condemn.

If a child lives with hostility, he learns to fight.

If a child lives with abuse, he learns to hurt others.

If a child lives with encouragement, he learns to be confident.

If a child lives with fairness, he learns to be just.

If a child lives with tolerance, he learns to be patient.

If a child lives with approval, he learns to like himself.

If a child lives with love, he learns to find love in the world.

References

Anderson, L. W., & Pellicer, R. L. O. (1990). Synthesis of research on compensatory and remedial education. *Educational Leadership*. 48:10–16.

Brookover, W. B., & Lezotte, L. W. (1979). *Changes in school characteristics coincident with changes in student achievement.* East Lansing: Michigan State University, College of Urban Development.

Brown v. Board of Education 347 U.S. 483, 495 (1954), & 349 U.S. 294 (1955).

Cervone, B. T., & O'Leary, K. (1982). A conceptual framework for parent involvement." *Educational Leadership*, Nov.

Coleman, James S., et al. (1966). *Equality of educational opportunity.* Washington, DC: United States Department of Health, Education, and Welfare, Office of Education.

Comer, J. P. (1980). *School power: Implications on an intervention project.* New York: The Free Press.

Dunn, L. M. (1968). Special education for the mildly retarded—is much of it justifiable?" *Exceptional Children* 35:5–22.

Goffman, E. (1963). *Stigma: Notes on the management of spoiled identity.* Englewood Cliffs: Prentice Hall.

Kohl, H. (1967). *36 Children.* New York: World Publishing Company.

Kozol, J. (2002). *Ordinary resurrections.* New York: Random House.

Levin, H. (1987). Accelerated schools for disadvantaged students. *Educational Leadership*, 44:13–16.

Oakes, J. (1985). *Keeping track: How schools structure inequity,* New Haven: Yale University Press.

Mary Pipher. (1994). *Reviving Ophelia: Saving the selves of adolescent girls.* New York: Putnam.

Rose, Lowell C., & Gallup, Alec M. (2000). The 32nd Annual Phi Delta Kappa/Gallup Poll of the Public's Attitudes Toward the Public Schools. *Phi Delta Kappan* V82: N1, 41–57.

Rose, Lowell C., & Gallup, Alec M. (2001). The 33nd Annual Phi Delta Kappa/Gallup Poll of the Public's Attitudes Toward the Public Schools. *Phi Delta Kappan* V83: N1, 41–58.

Sagor, R. (1974). *The alternative school for dropouts, reform or retreat: A case study of a public alternative school.* Unpublished Ph.D. dissertation. University of Oregon.

Slavin, R. E., Karweit, N. L., & Madden, N. A. (2000). Research on achievement outcomes of success for all: A summary and response to critics, *Phi Delta Kappan,* 82 (1), 38–40, 59–66.

Slavin, R. E., Karweit, N. L., & Madden, N. A. (2001, April). *Reducing the gap: Success for all and the achievement of African-American and Latino students.* Paper presented at the annual meeting of the American Educational Research Association, Seattle, WA.

Slavin, R. E., Madden, N. A., Karweit, N. L., Dolan, L. K., & Wasik, B. A. (1992). *Success for all: A relentless approach to prevention and early intervention in elementary schools.* Arlington, VA: Edlucational Research Service.

10

MORE SCHOOLWIDE INITIATIVES AND A VISION OF RESTRUCTURING

In the Chapter 9, we discussed a variety of school improvement strategies with potential for helping schools reduce the rate of at-riskness. In the case of the "Accelerated Schools" and the "Success for All" programs, a collection of strategies has been assembled to make a whole school attack on this problem. These approaches have drawn the attention of policy makers and now several federal and state programs are requiring schools to implement whole school reform (WSR) models.

There are obvious advantages to taking a comprehensive approach. Oftentimes, however, political and other considerations may make it impossible to assemble a critical mass of supporters behind a proposal to significantly alter the status quo. Because of this it is worth noting that a number of the strategies discussed thus far could be instituted without causing much disruption to the current educational program. For example, child assistance teams or advisory programs are relatively easily introduced into traditional and/or conventional schools providing the faculty believes in them. In the preface we argued that as educators our first order of business should be to provide the necessary support for the students':

- ♦ Immediate or near term survival in the school's academic system.

- ♦ Immediate or near term success in the school/community's social structure.

While we might desire more major changes any intervention with promise to assist at-risk youth as they negotiate the existing academic system and school social structure more successfully is a step forward.

In this chapter we continue to look at the big picture. We do this by reviewing several additional schoolwide initiatives, a number of which go straight to the heart of the values and traditions that have evolved around public schooling.

Other than the few remaining one room schoolhouses, today's public schools are complex organizations. The root word for organization and organism are the same and as is the case with organisms, when one subsystem changes there are ramifications for the entire organism. This is why when schools introduce several significant changes at once it inevitably triggers a rethinking of every assumption that governs the school system. This explains why the more radical approaches to school improvement have been labeled *restructuring*. We begin this chapter by exploring a few of the prevailing values and traditions that need to be confronted if we want to improve the lot of our at-risk youth. This chapter concludes with a brief description of two current restructuring strategies (one elementary and one secondary) that offer significant promise for our at-risk students.

Value 1:
Expectations Should Fit the Individual

Ever since the Conant report (1967) the secondary schools of North America have been built on the assumption that students are best served by the offering of a *comprehensive* curriculum. This is grounded in a belief that young people come to us with different needs and, therefore, should be provided with the opportunity to study what is appropriate for them. As a consequence most high schools offer substantially different programs of study, each of which leads to a high school diploma. This system was put in place with the best of intentions. It was assumed that if a course of study served the students' long-range career interests it would keep them actively engaged in learning. Not surprisingly under this philosophy, schools created grouping practices (commonly called tracking systems) wherein students who were attending the same high school would be assigned to different tracks. These included general, vocational, or college preparatory streams where both the curriculum and expectations could be tailored to meet students' needs and aspirations. Convincing research now shows that these tracking processes didn't serve any portion of the school population well and placed our lower-track students at a particular disadvantage (Oakes, 1985; Slavin, 1990). While few schools use the tracking terminology anymore, the view that different kids need different programs with different expectations continues, only now they have new sanitized labels such as *career paths* or *school to work* programs.

In this chapter we will explore alternatives to tracking; we will reexamine the entire concept of the comprehensive school, and we will consider other types of restructuring that should cause us to fundamentally question the way at-risk students are now being served.

For years no one seemed to question the issue of school size. Fortunately policy makers are now beginning to take note of the research (Cotton, 2001; Wasley, 2000), which shows that large schools are neither more economical nor more effective. While large schools don't serve any child well, there are a number of factors that make large schools especially problematic for at-risk youth.

The Shopping Mall School

The most significant issue relating to school size is that large schools inevitably take on institutional characteristics. They become environments that require purposeful navigation rather than caring communities that emulate the qualities of family" Students desperately need the feeling of family if they are ever to develop and/or experience the power of membership. Arthur Powell (1985) pointed out in the book *The Shopping Mall High School*; the typical, comprehensive American high school is analogous to a shopping mall. The school's main goal is to have something for every taste, and it operates on the assumption that students' needs/desires differ radically from each other. The modern shopping mall, as an institution, doesn't attempt to adopt a common set of values and or styles. Instead it tries to please everyone by offering a diverse menu of specialty shops. While that may be a fruitful model for commerce, it is disastrous for schools.

The problem for at-risk students is that when their school chooses to avoid emphasizing one set of values over others, it begins to appear to the students that the adults in charge aren't personally committed to any core values. When such a school then attempts to assert particular behavioral or academic expectations upon the students, it is understandably interpreted as both arbitrary and unfair. This is a matter of critical importance because any interpretation of arbitrariness on the part of school authorities will undermine the at-risk student's ability to develop an internal locus of control. Furthermore, because at-risk students tend to have a practical orientation (see the discussion of learning styles in Chapter 5), they will often demand to know the purpose for an expectation before they are willing to invest in satisfying it. If school authorities appear unclear about the purpose served by the requirements, it is only reasonable to expect the most marginal students to perceive the school as a less than rational organization.

Curricular Diversity

At one time it was assumed that at-risk students would be best served at comprehensive schools with diverse curricula. It was felt that by having high schools with an array of offerings, ranging from Japanese to Home Economics, from Consumer Math to Physics, and Diversified Occupations to Shakespeare, every student would be able to find their own niche. In many schools it appeared that the single requirement imposed on the students was the requirement of seat time. Students were, in essence, told that they had to acquire 40 credits in four years, independent of the substance of those credits. This is analogous to telling a child at a buffet that the only expectation is to fill their plate with no regard to the nutritional differences between salads, desserts, meats, or vegetables.

Recent evidence has shown that this approach simply has not worked. A large scale study by Anthony Bryk and Yeow Thum (1989) demonstrated an inverse relationship between curricular diversity and the dropout rate. This meant that in the schools where students had fewer course options they were more likely to stay in school. Most importantly, these effects were demonstrated regardless of the student body's socioeconomic status. This finding may help explain the superior holding power of independent schools, which, because of fiscal limitations and size constraints, generally offer less diverse curricula.

Apparently, students infer that where a core curriculum exists, the school authorities have taken the time to consider what is truly important and consequently the students are more likely to feel that some coherent purpose lies behind their academic requirements. As an eight-year-old student in Marva Collins' West Side Preparatory school told a reporter from the CBS TV show, "Sixty Minutes," "Wow, when this teacher said you're gonna do your work here, I said this lady has really got her act together!"

Adult agreement on curricular goals inevitably implies to students that there is a set of priorities for the school community. School faculties that take this to heart are seen behaving in much the same manner as parents who strive to present a consistent set of family values to their children. The existence and articulation of shared values is one of the key components of the things we call family, community, or culture. The type of *membership* that at-risk students need to experience at school can only come from involvement with places that feel like communities and/or families, not like institutions or shopping malls!

One reason why our schools have had such a tendency to offer diverse curricula is because they have resisted the adoption of common mastery expectations for all students. The implicit fear was that certain categories of students would not be able to meet the resultant high expectations. Unless one holds a mastery learning philosophy (Chapter 3) it appears inhumane to demand adherence to a single difficult course of study.

The alternative that was followed in most communities (prior to the recent standards movement) was to offer programs that spanned a wide range of interests/difficulties so that everyone could, at least theoretically, feel successful. Unfortunately, it hasn't worked.

And it hasn't worked for one very simple reason: there is powerfully little self-image to be mined from modest achievements in low status remedial classes.

If you were persuaded to use a mastery approach for improving your students' feelings of competence (Chapter 3) we are asking you to consider the next step, achieving school-wide consensus on a core mastery curriculum. When 67 to 75 percent of our curriculum is the same for all students, it is reasonable to expect our program to appear to our students as coherent and planned. It is important to keep in mind, that when a faculty reaches agreement on a core curriculum it is still allocating 25 to 33 percent of the school program to the pursuit of unique student interests and passions. While it is difficult, and sometimes contentious to try to reach agreement on what belongs in the core, we think you will find, as more and more faculties have, that the investment of time in determining what matters" is worth the effort. The following Think and Do Exercise 10.1 should get you started with this process.

Think and Do Exercise—
Elements of Core Curriculum

Using the worksheet provided (Figure 10.1), have your colleagues list out the specific curricula, courses of study, or disciplines that they think should comprise 75 percent of the curriculum and which mastery expectations ought to apply to *all* students.

Then have them suggest the offerings or experiences that they would like to see made available as elective/selective experiences.

After you have filled out the forms see if you can reach consensus. If not, what were the issues and value disagreements that prevented consensus?

Finally consider what the impact will be on students when they experience those same value conflicts when negotiating their way through your school.

Figure 10.1. Core Curriculum Planning Sheet

School: _____

Grade Levels: _____

1. List the specific skills that students from your school will need to be successful at the next level of schooling or life experience (use additional paper as necessary):

_____

_____

_____

2. What academic training will each of your students need to experience to have a good chance of attaining the skills listed above?

_____

_____

_____

3. What specific content will your students need to be exposed to have the experiences and develop the skills listed above?

Required Content: _____ Time Allocated: _____

_____

_____

_____

Total Time allocated should equal 4 to 5 hours per day: _____

4. What educational experiences (course work) do you consider valuable but not necessary for all students to experience?

Elective/selectives Content: _____ Time Allocated: _____

_____

_____

_____

*Total Time allocated should equal 1 to 2 hours per day:*_____

Standards-Based Education

In recent years educational policy throughout North America has institutionalized mastery expectations for much of the academic program. This is not the first time this approach has been tried. Beginning in the 1970s an approach called *outcomes-based education* (OBE) became popular in many places. Many of the early experiments with OBE failed. Among the reasons for these early failures was that many of these efforts were far too prescriptive/limiting in terms of instruction. In the 70s and early 80s school reformers focused on finding the perfect technology for the delivery of a mastery program. At the same time very little attention was paid to the critical issues of philosophy and belief systems regarding diversity in learning and learners.

Currently, educators have no choice but to embrace mastery expectations. Because in most locales students are required to meet state proficiency standards to graduate and because we want every student to receive a diploma, we have no choice but to expect mastery from everyone (at least on the standards).

At the last school where Dick served as Principal, West Linn High School, the faculty decided to implement mastery expectations for all the required courses. Because many members of the faculty had previous experience with initiatives that had called themselves "mastery learning" (many of them didn't trigger happy memories), the teachers decided to call their program HERTIO (this acronym stood for *High Expectations Reinforced Through Instructional Organization*). The HERTIO program was built on a set of principles that applied across all subject areas.

- There would be certain essential objectives that had to be met by all students.

- No student would be permitted to fail simply because of their learning rate or other issues of aptitude.

- Each department would establish a "scholastic safety net" to ensure that students with motivation would and could achieve mastery.

- The format/process employed by each department could be different to accommodate both the requirements of the discipline and the professional creativity of the teachers.

The first year of implementation involved only those required classes taken by ninth graders, and each year an additional grade level was added. The teachers met for a special conference two days before school began, during which presentations were made by each department on their specific mastery expectations. The first week of school had all the ninth grade students attending a special before-school study skills class that was taught by the ninth grade teachers. Then, during the first days of classes, each teacher made a point of knowledgeably referring to what was occurring during the rest of the students' day. Of course, the students accused their teachers of *conspiring* against them! However, they also realized the fact that our talking together meant we cared about their success.

It was exciting to see the variety of approaches implemented in different departments. Some examples of the way the HERTIO process was implemented and the *safety nets* that were developed included the following:

Language Arts

All major papers had to be written until a specified level of proficiency was achieved. Scoring rubrics were distributed in advance and were used to evaluate each paper. Major papers could be rewritten until the mastery level (4, on a 5-point scale) was reached.

Science

To be considered mastered, each unit test had to be passed at the 80 percent criteria level. The same test could be retaken, but the criteria level went up with each retake (85 percent for the first retake, 90 percent the second and 95 percent the third). The science teachers believed that this would encourage students to try harder the first time around.

Math

Students were informed that they would be kept from going on to the next level (of math) if they failed to achieve a grade above a "C." However, the safety net that the math department built was strong enough to save any student who was willing to try. The math teachers staffed a help room after school each day and each morning before school for forty-five minutes. Whenever a student was dissatisfied with the score they posted on a unit test they could retake the test, provided they had all their homework in and they had attended a help session. If those conditions were met then the student was free to retake the test as often as necessary.

The math department's approach illustrates one of the best things about the mastery process for at-risk students. Their regulations reflected the social reality. Teachers are busy people; however, they were willing to give extra time to help students who were willing to meet their part of the bargain (doing the homework). Requiring a "C" grade for advancement made sense because one would not likely succeed in a sequential curriculum without mastery of the prerequisite skills. However, every student could proceed with confidence that they would hit the criterion level if they simply did their work and took advantage of the safety net. In the three years Dick worked with that program not a single student (who took advantage of the "safety net") failed to achieve the grade of their choice.

No discussion of the HERTIO program would be complete without a reference to the faculty's line of chocolate bars. To raise funds for a scholarship that the faculty awarded to a student who best exemplified the values of HERTIO (hard work producing mastery), they created their own line of chocolate bars. These were called HERTIO bars, with apologies to the Hershey Chocolate Company, and were said to contain milk chocolate and academia nuts. The chocolate bars (Figure 10.2) emphasized the playful aspect of the process.

Figure 10.2. Chocolate Bar

The school's symbol (Figure 10.3) emphasized the reason for our high expectations. We cared.

Figure 10.3. West Linn High School

Where the Teachers Care Enough to Expect Your Very Best? (Tom Ogan)

Any standards-based initiative needs to begin with a clear picture of the outcomes or targets that are desired or needed. One of our favorite elementary schools has developed an annual ritual. Once per year the second grade teachers spend a day visiting at the early childhood center that feeds their school. A few days later the fifth grade teachers spend a day visiting the middle school where these children will ultimately matriculate. These visits are followed by extensive faculty discussions about the terrain that must be covered for these children to be successful. At this school the discussions always proved fruitful. As a consequence of this process the teachers continually are asking themselves,

"How can we get every one of these kids to the level where they need to be in the allotted time?"

In the years we've watched this faculty they have become quite successful at hitting their target for every student who has with them for at least two years.

If you are considering such a schoolwide effort, keep in mind that whenever a mastery approach or for that matter, any other instructional method, is allowed to become too rigid and/or too dogmatic, good creative teaching may be frightened away.

Necessary Ingredients for Standards-Based Education

The appearance and structure of any mastery learning program must vary according to the local context, but the necessary ingredients for standards-based education should always be present (see Figure 10.4).

Figure 10.4. Necessary Ingredients for Standards-Based Education

1. A common belief system which includes a sense that "all students can and do want to learn."

2. Agreement on the essential elements of the curriculum that are to be mastered by every student.

3. A management system that provides for differences in learning rates.

4. An assessment system that does justice to the mastery objectives.

5. An instructional delivery system that demands mastery, while allowing for teacher creativity.

Faculties that have instituted standards-based education have found items 1, 2, and 4 to provide the greatest challenge.

The Belief System

It is time consuming to reach agreement on a belief system, but attempts to implement schoolwide or district-wide standards without prior agreement on the nature of learners and the essentials of the learning environment will doom a project to failure.

The Time Dilemma

Finding ways around the time dilemma is tough but not impossible. Schools have utilized strategies from homework hotlines, telephone lines manned by teachers in the evenings, to summer school programs, to six week "credit recovery" mini-terms following each of two 15-week semesters. There is no one correct approach, but standards won't lead to educational equity unless it is understood that some students require more time and assistance if they are to attain mastery of high standards.

Failure to acknowledge this reality will result in an unacceptable amount of student failure or disengagement. Furthermore, we know it will be the at-risk students who will disproportionately experience this failure. The Think and Do Exercise below, "The Scholastic Safety Net," will give you an opportunity to explore some components of a scholastic safety net for your school.

Think and Do Exercise—
The Scholastic Safety Net

Assume that you were going to implement a mastery expectation plan to go along with the core curriculum that you developed in the Think and Do Exercise: Elements of Core Curriculum (p. 243). Also assume that the students in your school learn material at different rates. What will be the attributes of the scholastic safety net you will put in place?

Keep in mind:

- ♦ You want to build an internal locus of control (don't be an enabler!)
- ♦ You want to keep standards high.
- ♦ You don't want to penalize students for factors out of their control.

Schoolwide Behavioral Expectations

Just as having common curricular goals implies a consensus on values by the educational community, so does having common behavioral expectations. In fact, practically every effective schooling study has concurred in the finding that, in schools where all children perform well academically, the faculty held a consistent, high, and common set of behavioral expectations (see, for example, Edmonds, 1979; Rutter, 1979).

To understand the critical importance of creating a school-as-community for at-risk students, one only needs to consider the consequence of its absence. When two students walk down the hall of their school during class time, talking loudly and peppering their conversation with obscenities, and they pass by several open classroom doors before finally a teacher emerges and castigates them for their rudeness, what will they conclude? It wouldn't be surprising for them to dismiss the reprimand they receive as a tirade coming from "someone who must have a *thing* about being quiet." That is a reasonable conclusion from the student's perspective. After all, they possess evidence that the same behavior didn't bother at least four other teachers at the same school!

Another example is the student who consistently visits loudly with his neighbor during class time. What if his behavior didn't seem to offend anyone until sixth period, when a teacher finally expressed a concern that this behavior was keeping other students from learning. Will that explanation be accepted by the student as sincere? And if it is, what does it say about the stance of the student's other five teachers? These two examples illustrate the problem created by inconsistent and unshared expectations. Perhaps, more importantly, when our expectations are inconsistent the student being reprimanded /disciplined is reinforced in their victimization. To an at-risk students with an external locus of control, adult inconsistency, will cause them to feel even more like victims of arbitrary and unfair treatment. Those feelings and experiences are precisely the things that reinforce an external locus of control.

While it is impossible for a large faculty to forge the same tight common values on behavior that a married couple might adopt for child rearing, it is still possible for a faculty to agree on a common set of key behavioral expectations that they feel are of value and will be productive for their learning community. Although there may be classroom specific expectations, commonly held schoolwide expectations will reinforce for students the reality that the behavior of the adults in their school is guided by a common set of values. Figure 10.5 provides a set of guidelines that you and your colleagues should consider when developing schoolwide behavioral expectations.

Figure 10.5. Guidelines for Schoolwide Expectations

1. *Make them few.*

   Long lists of expectations take on the appearance of law books. Children will view them as rules for rules sake. A few meaningful and global expectations are all that's needed. After all, ten commandments were all that God required to outline his expectations!

2. *State them positively.*

   They should alert students to how they are expected to behave, rather than direct their attention toward misbehavior.

3. *Require 100% support.*

   Only place on the schoolwide list those expectations that every adult in the school is prepared to backup consistently. Once adopted the expectations will comprise a social compact between the adults in the school. Each staff member must realize that they are pledging to each other to consistently respond to any violation of these expectations.

4. *There is clarity on what is expected.*

   Students and staff need to be clear about what constitutes meeting and what constitutes violating an expectation.

5. *Consistent response.*

   It is not as important how we respond to violations, as it is that no infringement goes unaddressed. It can often be enough to simply say "We don't talk that way here." or "At this school we don't use other people's belongings without permission."

Figure 10.6 (CO-OP) is a sign reflecting the common behavioral expectations of a high school in Oregon. This sign was displayed in each classroom and prominently around the school. The four expectations:

- Respect for Class Time,
- Respect for Ourselves,
- Respect for Others, and
- Respect for Property

created the acronym CO-OP.

Figure 10.6. CO-OP

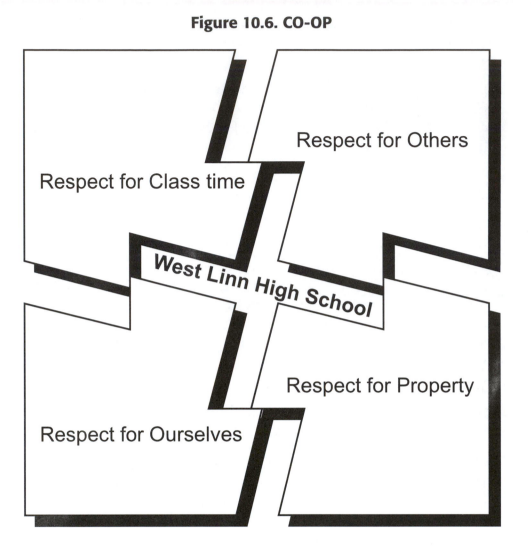

The statements found in Figure 10.7 are the specific behaviors that this faculty determined constituted a violation of the CO-OP expectations.

Figure 10.7. Behavioral Expectations

1. Students will demonstrate respect for the importance of class time by being in class regularly, on time, and with the appropriate materials.

   Specific Behaviors to be Addressed:

   1.1 Irregular attendance

   1.2 Tardiness

   1.3 Unpreparedness (books, paper, pens, at start of class)

   1.4 Loitering in halls

2. Students will demonstrate respect for other people by demonstrating consideration and good manners by not interrupting speakers, using appropriate language in public, and refraining from behavior that might disturb classes, assemblies, or individuals.

    Specific Behaviors to be Addressed:

    2.1   Interrupting classmates or teachers

    2.2   Disrespectful audience

    2.3   Profanity

    2.4   Excessive volume (voices, radios, etc.)

    2.5   Intimate behavior (beyond hand-holding)

3. Students will demonstrate respect for the property of others by only using personal or school property with the owner's and/or responsible person's permission.

    Specific Behaviors to be Addressed:

    3.1   Vandalism (graffiti, destruction)

    3.2   Theft

    3.3   Lack of consideration/care for borrowed property

4. Students will demonstrate respect for themselves by putting forward their best effort, showing pride in their accomplishments, and accepting personal responsibility for their level of preparation.

    Specific Behaviors to be Addressed:

    4.1   Off task

    4.2   Incomplete assignments

    4.3   Sloppy work

    4.4   Cheating

The following Think and Do Exercise is an opportunity for you to try your hand at crafting a set of behavioral expectations for your entire school.

Think and Do Exercise—
Behavioral Expectations

Generate a list of the behavioral expectations that you feel your faculty could agree to. Consider the five guidelines for effective schoolwide expectations when you construct your list. Ask several students what they would conclude from a faculty wide commitment to this set of expectations.

Academic Standards and Authentic Testing

Thusfar we have talked about courses of study and behavioral standards. While these are important, they don't define what school is and why we require students to attend. That is the role for content standards. Content standards (or clear statements regarding what we expect students to know and be able to do) are what gives education its form.

Traditionally, we have assessed the attainment of academic objectives through paper and pencil examinations. However, this form of assessment often appeared to our students to be more like *mystical* choice than multiple choice.

Frequently students have not seen a clear relationship between our requirements and the world they see outside of school. This is another example of where a lack of coherence is particularly problematic for the at-risk student. The defeated/discouraged learner needs to see purpose in his work, and correctly filling in a bubble sheet usually doesn't satisfy as an adequate explanation of purpose.

Because of the perceived irrelevance of school objectives to the challenges of the real world, terms are used, like *schoolwork* to distinguish what one does in school from real work. Schoolwork is done for a teacher and is rewarded with a grade, while real work is done for a discriminating consumer, has social utility, and is worth something to someone other than the producer him/herself.

Traditionally, when students appear unwilling to do schoolwork, educators have employed coercive and punitive measures to gain that commitment. The most popular of these approaches have been grades and graduation requirements. In addition we now have grade level benchmarks (with failure in many states meaning retention) and proficiency testing for graduation.

In this era of proficiency-based promotion and graduation the consequences of failure have been accentuated. Entry into the military, the job market, and higher education is now controlled by the successful completion of standardized examinations. While these tests could, theoretically, provide motivation for students, they could also be seen by our defeated and discouraged learners as just one more irrelevant and alienating feature of the schooling process. Recent increases in drop out rates (Greene, 2002) are evidence that this is already occurring in many locales.

Perceived irrelevance is not the only issue created by the dichotomy between schoolwork and real world work. If one is unsuccessful with schoolwork, it is easy to place the blame on someone else's shoulders. Discouraged students often tell their teachers that the reason for their low performance lies with the evaluator (the teacher) or the nature of the test (it is irrelevant, too difficult, or boring). After a while those negative attributions become attached to everything related to the organization (after all school is the only place where I'm asked to do these stupid and boring things).

Those attitudes simply add more fuel to the fire of alienation already burning inside the discouraged learner. This doesn't need to be the case. One doesn't see the separation of schoolwork and real work everywhere in the schoolhouse. Unfortunately though, where we do see it is in the academic classrooms. In vocational education, for example, students are evaluated on the products they produce, whether it is the quality of the furniture they manufactured or the welds they made in the metal shop. In our fine arts classes, students produce artwork or music that is assessed by an audience's ears as melodious or not, and in athletics student performance is either good enough or not good enough to prevail over the opponent.

Those types of standards, what we now call authentic standards (because their authentic value is understood in the value system of the real world) are perceived by students as meaningful targets to shoot for. Likewise, when one hits an authentic target, it provides concrete irrefutable evidence of competence. In schools authentic standards are generally demonstrated through some form of public or semipublic exhibition, and there is only one acceptable criterion for achievement—mastery.

There are many examples of authentic assessment in schools. For example, the articles in the school paper, storybooks written and illustrated by and for younger children, the public performance of the band and choir, and the production of saleable items in shop. With creative planning there are infinite possibilities for this type of public real world application of school learning. For example, a fifth grade class in Lake Oswego, Oregon, studied the recreational needs of their community and then designed an architectural plan for a waterfront park development. When they finished their work, they presented their plan complete with a written narrative and architectural charts to a packed city council meeting.

A group of high school students from Centennial High School in Gresham, Oregon, spent several weeks studying the management of Columbia River Salmon and the requirements for successful recovery of this endangered specie. They grappled with the competing social and economic needs for hydroelectric power, recreation, and commercial fishing. Their project was evaluated through a public presentation of the student's Salmon management plan before a panel of teachers and fish biologists from the Bonneville Power Administration. Not only was the student work regarded as relevant and well done, but the fish biologist decided to incorporate some of the students' suggestions into their own Salmon recovery plan.

The fifth grade park designers and the high school conservationists concluded their projects with an exhibition. Rather than being required to take an exam they prepared a summary of their work to a recognized panel of experts.

There are many analogies in the real world. When seeking employment artists submit portfolios of their work. Architects produce plans and lawyers argue cases. It is the quality of these producibles that we use to determine the competence of the practitioner. As teachers we can set up the same types of assessment systems in our classrooms; however, when we use exhibitions and other types of authentic assessment in school we will need to focus on three critical planning issues:

- The clarity of our learning targets
- The performance(s) that will be used for the assessment
- The criteria for evaluation.

The Clarity of Our Learning Targets

Whenever artists prepare for a performance, they begin with a clear picture in their mind's eye about the product they intend to produce. Sports psychologists call this *visualization*. If one watches an Olympic high jumper prepare for the event, you will generally see them close their eyes and mentally go through a complete and successful jump. Not only does this exercise give the athlete a clear picture of what is expected, but sport psychologists tell us it even improves their level of performance. Nothing is more frustrating for at-risk students than to be in an environment where what they are expected to do is unclear. These same students don't experience a similar lack of clarity in the expectations placed on them in music or vocational education. The teachers of those subjects tell their students, with some degree of precision, how a well-tuned car will operate, or how a well-played concerto will sound. If we, as academic teachers, are to ask our students to prepare a piece of authentic work for assessment we must become just as explicit with our expectations of what constitutes excellent work.

The Performance That Will Be Used for the Assessment

Here the issue before us is how will the students demonstrate their knowledge or skill.

- Will the student be asked to orally report on how to tune a car? or,
- Will the student be asked to tune an actual car in class? or
- Will you observe the student teaching a classmate how to tune a car motor?
- Will you ask the student to write a report on a political issue? or
- Will you expect the student to give testimony to the city council? Or

- Will you expect the student to answer an essay question on an exam, or

- Would you ask the student to submit an original opinion piece to the school paper?

All of the options mentioned above would require an authentic demonstration of skill and knowledge. They differ only in the degree of real world application.

Determining Criteria for Evaluation

This last aspect of planning asks us to consider how the knowledge/skill will be assessed. If we are teaching music, we might observe a performance or listen to a tape of the student's music. If we were teaching auto-shop, we might test drive the car or rate the motor's performance on a shop computer. But, how shall we determine if a piece of writing, a science experiment, or a history project hit the target?

The most popular technique is to construct a scoring rubric that can be shared with the students (and any other interested party) in advance. A good rubric reflects a range of potential performance from poor to excellent. Figure 10.8 is an example of a scoring guide used in Oregon for the assessment of writing proficiency (Spandel & Stiggins 1990).

Figure 10.8. Scoring Guide Example

Analytical Scoring Guide
The Six Traits

Ideas and Content

Score of 5. This paper is clear, focused, and interesting. It holds the reader's attention. Relevant anecdotes and details enrich the central theme or story line.

The writer seems to be writing from experience and shows insight: a good sense of how events unfold, how people respond to life and to each other, and how ideas relate.

Supporting, relevant, telling details give the reader important information that he or she could not personally bring to the text. This writer seems to notice what others might overlook.

The writing has balance: Main ideas stand out; secondary ideas do not usurp too much attention.

The writer seems in control and orchestrates development of the topic in an enlightening, entertaining way.

The writer works with and shapes ideas, making connections and sharing insights that reflect his or her own thinking.

Score of 3. The paper is clear and focused, even though the overall result may not be especially captivating. Support is attempted, but it may be limited or obvious, insubstantial, too general, or out of balance with the main ideas.

The writer may or may not be writing from experience but, either way, has difficulty going from general observations to specific points or useful insights.

The writer seems to have considered ideas but only superficially and in a way that enables the reader readily to second-guess the plot or the main points of the text.

Ideas, though reasonably clear, often tend toward the mundane; the reader is not sorry to see the paper end.

Conclusions or main points seem to echo observations heard elsewhere; only o occasion do they seem to reflect the writer's own thinking.

Supporting details tend to be skimpy, general, or predictable.

Control is sporadic; the writer is beginning to define the topic but isn't there yet.

Score of 1. The paper lacks a central idea or purpose, or forces the reader to make inferences based on very sketchy details.

Information is very limited or simply unclear.

Details do not ring true; they evolve from clichés, platitudes, or stereotypes and not from the writer's own thinking or experience.

Attempts at development may be minimal or may clutter up the text with random thoughts from which not central theme emerges.

The writer has not begun to define the topic in any meaningful or personal way.

Organization

Score of 5. The organization enhances and showcases the central idea or theme. The order, structure, or presentations is compelling and moves the reader through the text.

Details seem to fit where they're placed.

An inviting introduction draws the reader in, and a satisfying conclusion leavest he reader with a sense of resolution.

Transitions are smooth and weave the separate threads of meaning into one cohesive whole.

Organization flows so smoothly that the reader may not be conscious of organizational patterns or structures unless looking for them.

Score of 3. The reader can readily follow what's being said, but the overall organization may sometimes be ineffective or too obvious.

The introduction and conclusion are recognizable, though not so well crafted or well connected to the central theme as the reader might wish.

Placement or relevance of some details leaves the reader occasionally confused or impatient.

The paper sometimes moves along at a good pace but at other times bogs down in trivia or speeds along too rapidly.

Transitions sometimes work well; at other times, the connections between ideas seem forced, inappropriate, or too easily anticipated.

Despite problems, the organization does not seriously get in the way of the main point or the story line.

Score of 1. Organization is haphazard and disjointed. The writing lacks direction, with ideas, details, or events strung together helter-skelter.

There is no clearly identifiable introduction or conclusion.

Transitions are very weak, leaving connections between ideas fuzzy, incomplete, or bewildering.

Details often serve only to confuse the reader to fill space; they do not contribute to the central theme or the purpose of the text.

Noticeable gaps in information confuse and confound the reader.

Pacing is consistently awkward, so that the reader feels either mired down in irrelevant trivia or rushed along at a breathless pace.

Lack of organization ultimately obscures or distorts the main point or the purpose of the text.

Voice

Score of 5. The writer speaks directly to the reader in a way that is individualistic, expressive, and engaging. Clearly, the writer is involved in the text and is writing to be read.

The paper is honest and written from the heart. It has the ring of conviction.

The language is natural yet provocative; it brings the topic to life.

The reader feels a strong sense of interaction with the writer and senses the person behind the words.

The projected tone and voice clarify and give flavor ro the writer's message.

Score of 3. The writer seems sincere but not full involved in the topic. The result is pleasant, acceptable, sometimes even personable, but not compelling.

The writer seems to weigh words carefully, to keep a safe distance between writer and reader, to avoid risk, and to write what he or she thinks the reader wants.

The writing tends to hide rather than reveal the writer.

The writing communicates in an earnest but fairly routine manner, and only occasionally amuses; surprises, delights. or moves the reader.

Voice may emerge strongly on occasion, only to shift or to disappear a line or two later behind a facade of general, vague, or abstract language.

Score of 1. The writer seems wholly indifferent, uninvolved, or dispassionate. As a result, the writing is flat, lifeless, stiff, or mechanical. It may be (depending on the topic) overly technical or jargonistic.

The reader has no sense of the writer behind the words and no sense of a real desire on the part of the writer to communicate.

The writer seems to speak in a kind of monotone that flattens all potential highs or lows of the message.

The writing communicates on a functional level, at best, without moving or involving the reader at all.

Delivery is so consistently flat that the reader may find it hard to focus on the message even when the wording seems reasonably clear and correct.

Word Choice

Score of 5. Words convey the intended message in an interesting, precise, and natural way. The writing is full and rich, yet concise.

Words are specific and accurate; they seem just right.

Imagery is strong.

Powerful verbs give the writing energy.

Vocabulary may be striking, but it's natural, and never overdone.

Expression is fresh and appealing; slang is used sparingly.

Score of 3. The language is quite ordinary, but it does convey the message: It's functional, even if it lacks punch. Often, the writer settles for what's easy or handy, producing a sort of "generic paper" stuffed with familiar words and phrases.

The language communicates but rarely captures the reader's imagination. While the overall meaning is quite clear, some words may lack precision.

The writer rarely experiments with language often seem overdone and calculated to impress the reader.

Images lack detail and often depend on the reader's own knowledge of the topic.

Clichés, redundancies, and hackneyed phrases are common.

A few key verbs may liven things up, but equally often, abstract, general, or flat language robs the text of power.

Score of 1. The writer struggles with a limited vocabulary, groping for words to convey meaning. Often the language is so vague and abstract or so redundant and devoid of detail that only the broadest, most general sort of message comes through.

Words are consistently dull, colorless, or abstract. There is little for the reader to grasp.

Monotonous repetition or overwhelming reliance on worn, threadbare expressions repeatedly clouds or smothers the message.

Often words simply do not fit the text: They seem imprecise, inadequate, or just plain wrong.

Imagery is very fuzzy or absent altogether; the text is "peopled" only with generalities.

Verbs are weak and few in number; *is, are, was, were* dominate.

Sentence Fluency

Score of 5. The writing has an easy flow and rhythm when read aloud. Sentences are well built, with consistently strong and varied structure that makes expressive oral reading easy and enjoyable.

Sentence structure reflects logic and sense, helping to show how ideas relate.

The writing sounds natural and fluent; it glides along with effective phrasing, one sentence flowing effortlessly into the next.

Writing is appropriately concise, yet not terse. Sentences display an effective combination of power and grace.

Sentences vary in structure and length, adding interest to the text.

Fragments, if used at all, work well.

Dialogue, if used, sound natural.

Score of 3. Sentences tend to be mechanical rather than fluid. The text hums along efficiently for the most part, though it may lack a certain rhythm or grace, tending to be more pleasant than musical. Occasional awkward constructions force the reader to slow down or reread.

Sentence structure sometimes clearly conveys relationships between ideas, and sometimes not. Connections between phrases or sentences may be less fluid than desired.

The writer show good control with simple sentence structure but variable control over complex syntax.

Sentences sometimes vary in length or structure, but, for the most part, the writer falls into a pattern and sticks with it.

Fragments, if used, sometimes work but sometimes seem the result of oversight.

Dialogue, if used, sometimes rings true but sometimes sounds forced or contrived.

Sentences, though functional, often lack energy.

Some parts of the text invite expressive oral reading; others may be a bit stiff.

Score of 1. The paper is difficult to follow or to read aloud. Sentences tend to be choppy, incomplete, rambling, irregular, or just very awkward.

Nonstandard English syntax is common. Word patterns are often jarring and irregular, and far removed from the way people usually write or speak.

Sentence structure does not generally enhance meaning, In fact, it may obscure meaning.

Most sentences seem disjointed, awkward, confused, or nonsensical. They may begin one way and then go off in another direction altogether.

Word patterns often subject the reader to relentlessly monotonous rhythms (e.g., subject-verb-object).

Conventions

Score of 5. The writer demonstrates a good grasp of standard writing conventions (e.g., grammar, capitalization, punctuation, usage, spelling, paragraphing) and uses them effectively to enhance readability. Errors tend to be so few and so minor that the reader can easily skim right over them unless specifically searching for them.

Paragraphing tends to be sound and to reinforce the organizational structure.

Grammar and usage are correct and contribute to clarity and style.

Punctuation is smooth and guides the reader through the text.

Spelling is generally correct, even on more difficult words.

The writer may manipulate conventions—particularly grammar—for stylistic effect.

The writing is sufficiently long and complex to allow the writer to show skill in using a wide range of conventions.

The writing is sufficiently long and complex to allow the writer to show skill in using a wide range of conventions. Only light editing would be required to polish the text for publication.

Score of 3. Errors in writing conventions, while not overwhelming, begin to impair readability. While errors do not block meaning, they tend to be distracting.

Paraphrasing may be inconsistent. Paragraphs sometimes run together or begin in the wrong places.

Terminal (end-of-sentence) punctuation is almost always correct; internal punctuation, however, may be incorrect or missing altogether.

Spelling is usually correct, or reasonably phonetic, on common words.

Problems with usage are not severe enough to distort meaning.

The writer may show reasonable control over a very limited range of conventions, but the text may be too simple or too short to reflect real mastery of conventions.

Errors in all areas tend to show some consistency, for example, a writer may misspell a word the same way throughout the text.

Moderate (more than light but less than extensive) editing would be required to polish the text for publication.

Some errors are minor and seem to reflect hasty editing.

Score of 1. Numerous errors in usage, sentence structure, spelling, or punctuation repeatedly distract the reader and make the text difficult to read. In fact, the severity and the frequency of errors tend to be so overwhelming that the reader finds it very difficult to gocus on the message and must reread for meaning.

Te writer shows very limited skill in using conventions.

Basic punctuation (including terminal punctuation) tends to be omitted, haphazard, or incorrect.

Spelling errors are frequent, even on common words, and are not always phonetic.

Paragraphing may be highly irregular, absent altogether, or so frequent (every sentence) that it bears no relation to the organizational structure of the text.

Extensive (e.g., more than moderate) editing would be required to polish the text for publication.

Using a tool like this, enables the students to assess their own work and judge with some precision how well their performance approximates the expectation. By using rubrics or scoring guides, students know what they are shooting for and how far they still have to go. When, at first, they miss the target they are able to see what improvement is needed if they are ultimately to achieve mastery.

Discouraged students often respond enthusiastically to this type of teaching/assessment. What they have seen as arbitrary in traditional teaching/assessment only added to their frustration and alienation. Grades, percentiles, and grade level equivalents cannot be expected to have much meaning for these students. But clear evidence on their success hitting and/or missing explicit targets has clarity to it that these students will instinctively respond to.

Simulations

Some skills that can be authentically assessed, for practical reasons, must be done as simulations. Simulations can still capture students' imagination, but, this depends on how well they approximate the real world. For example, when Dick taught high school social studies, his students annually competed in a metropolitan area mock-trial competition. The students argued their cases in the county court house before judges who were members of the bar. With attention paid to all the trappings found in a real trial, these students found this to be a most authentic way to learn about the American judicial system.

Fifth grade students in Kansas City, Kansas, spend several weeks studying their communities in preparation for spending an entire day working in a simulated city at the "Learning Exchange." During their day in "Exchange City" students hold jobs as bankers, policemen, city councilors, shopkeepers, news reporters, etc. During the day at the "exchange" they carry out commerce, conduct civic affairs, and manage their personal finances. By the end of the day they have a host of simulated experiences that they can process with their teachers at a "town meeting."

Each of these simulations engaged students meaningfully in work that approximates tasks done by professionals in the real work world. As a consequence they contain more motivational value than schoolwork, per se. The following Think and Do Exercise invites you to consider ways that your students could exhibit their attainment of mastery with a piece of academic content.

Think and Do Exercise—
Demonstrating Competence Through Exhibitions

This exercise will help you explore the use of the exhibition as a form of authentic assessment. Think of one of the disciplines that you normally teach and a unit of study that you have assessed in a traditional (schoolwork) fashion.

Now plan for an "authentic assessment" using the three key planning issues.

1. Be clear about the learning targets

    What do you want the students to be skilled at after working through this piece of academic content? Be able to express the skill clearly enough that students have no confusion over what you are expecting.

2. Choose the performance

    How do you want the students to demonstrate their skill or knowledge with this content—a visual performance, a written work, or another form of exhibition? Be sure that the demonstration is such that you (or other observers) can get a clear picture of what the student can and cannot do.

3. Assess the performance

    How do you plan to determine the degree of mastery demonstrated by the student? Construct a 3- to 5-point scale with examples of poor, fair, good, and excellent products that you can compare the student's work against.

School Restructuring

Up until now we looked at some themes and issues that challenge some of our traditional assumptions regarding public schooling. For example, in the last chapter we talked about adding the role of advisor to the teacher's job description. We introduced the notion of prevention rather than remediation and the idea of eliminating tracking and replacing it with "never streaming." We explored moving away from the comprehensive school and adopting a core curriculum with common academic and behavioral expectations that could be assessed authentically.

All of these features have one thing in common. They seek to create the school as a singular cohesive community. These changes push us to see the school as "family" instead of as an impersonal institution. Taken together these changes can make attaining a sense of membership much more likely for *all* students, particularly those currently most at risk.

We now turn our attention to a few comprehensive school change models that incorporate many of these features simultaneously. When educators attempt such wholesale changes what inevitably results are school structures that look fundamentally different from what many of us have become accustomed to.

Elementary Schools: Multi-Aged Grouping and the Non-Graded School

Increasingly, many elementary school faculties have seen the benefits that can be derived from reconfiguring their schools for maximum heterogeneity. These schools group students who would normally be in different grade levels, consequently, in the literature they are often described as "non-graded" (Goodlad & Anderson, 1987; Anderson & Pavan, 1993). In non-graded schools, teachers work with the same cohort of students for several consecutive years. When considering the needs of the at-risk student, one can see much to commend this approach to restructuring.

Unfortunately, the basic organizational theme of most schools is time, not mastery. At the end of a course, semester, or year a decision needs to be made either to pass the student on or to hold the student back. As we know the consequences of holding a child back can be devastating. Statistically students held back have a far greater chance of dropping out of school. However, advancing students who have not yet demonstrated mastery presents other problems for the student. If the student goes ahead without reason to feel competent and/or belonging, especially if the curriculum is sequential, the student will surely be set up for failure.

Another problem with organizing schools around time is that it can adversely affects the student-teacher relationship. At home a parent knows that the child they have this year will be the same one they will have responsibility for next year. Child rearing is thereby understood to be a long term project. What we don't accomplish today as parents we can still come back to tomorrow, next month, or next year. But at school the adult-child relationship is often far too transitory. By March teachers realize that the end of the year is rapidly approaching. After June the student becomes someone else's concern. Teachers know that what they put off today, they can't pick up again next year. Our role becomes one of getting the student ready for the next teacher, not ready for life!

All of that is avoided in the multi-age, multi-year assignment. If, as the teacher, I know that I will have the same students for two years, it keeps me from panicking if their reading readiness is lagging behind their math readiness. I know that I have the freedom to emphasize reading now and wait to work on math later. I know that what we haven't finished in June, we can come back to in the Fall. In a very real sense these become "my" students because our relationship extends beyond the boundaries of the school calendar. Furthermore, there is added efficiency. Time is not lost at the beginning and end of the school year with students having to become oriented to a new classroom with different expectations and new routines. Perhaps more important, is the fact that the classroom becomes more like a "family," with older students assisting younger students, both socially and academically.

There are a number of alternative organizational structures for elementary schools currently being experimented with around the country to accomplish these same goals. The most common are

- ◆ *Two-grade splits*. Each teacher has two grades in the classroom: 1 and 2, 3 and 4, 5 and 6. The students then stay with the same teacher for 2 years with 50 percent of the class entering a new room each year.

- ◆ *Teacher teaming*. A group of teachers has responsibility for a group of same-age children for several years. The team then can divide up the students and time as it sees fit. Generally the same children will work with the same team for three to four years.

- ◆ *Teacher rotation/looping*. Teachers plan the curriculum in two grade teams 1 and 2, 3 and 4, 5 and 6. However, each teacher works with one group of same-age students for two years. For example, one teacher would take a group of 28 third graders and work with them for two years. The following year she would pick up another group of third graders and keep them for two years. This frequently is called "looping."

What all these approaches have in common is the opportunity to break the log jam of time. By doing so these structures provide at-risk students (and others) a greater opportunity to be part of a classroom community and develop a sense of belonging; they give the student a greater chance to achieve skill mastery along with the consequent feelings of competence, and where the structures provide for cross-age tutoring students are even able to gain feelings of usefulness from the "family style" organization.

Coalition of Essential Schools:
A Secondary Restructuring Program

In 1984, Theodore Sizer presented one of the most influential books in modern secondary education, *Horace's Compromise*. In that book he detailed the failings of the modern comprehensive high school despite the dedicated efforts of thousands of deeply committed teachers. He argued that the structure and organizing principles of our comprehensive secondary schools made compromising quality education inevitable.

The book gave rise to a movement called the *Coalition of Essential Schools* (Sizer, 1992) that was originally directed by Sizer and now is managed by Brown University. Currently there are hundreds of schools in the coalition and while each school is different, they all share a common set of commitments. Each Coalition school has pledged to guide their restructuring efforts in accord with the following nine essential principles.

1. The school should focus on helping adolescents learn to use their minds well. Schools should not attempt to be "comprehensive" if such a claim is made at the expense of the school's central intellectual purpose.

2. The school's goals should be simple. Each student should master a number of essential skills and be competent in certain areas of knowledge. Although these skills and areas, to varying degrees, reflect the traditional academic disciplines, the programs' design should be shaped by the intellectual and imaginative powers and competencies that students need, rather than by conventional subjects. The aphorism "less is more" should dominate: Curricular decisions are to be directed toward the students' attempt to gain mastery rather than by the teachers' effort to cover content.

3. The school's goals should apply to all students, but the means to these goals will vary as these students themselves vary. School practice should be tailor-made to meet the needs of every group of adolescents.

4. Teaching and learning should be personalized to the maximum feasible extent. No teacher should have direct responsibility for more than eighty students; decisions about the course of study, the use of students' and teachers' time, and the choice of teaching materials and specific pedagogies must be placed in the hands of the principal and staff.

5. The governing metaphor of the school should be student as worker, rather than the more familiar metaphor of teacher as deliverer of instructional services. Accordingly, the prominent pedagogy should be coaching to provoke students to learn how to learn and thus to teach themselves.

6. Students embarking on secondary school studies are those who show competence in language and elementary mathematics. Students of traditional high school age who do not yet have appropriate levels of competence to start secondary school studies are to be

provided with intensive remedial work so that they can quickly meet those standards. The diploma should be awarded on successful final demonstration of mastery for graduation—an Exhibition. This Exhibition by the students present the individual's grasp of the central skills and knowledge of the school's program, and may be jointly administered by the faculty and higher authorities. Because the diploma is awarded when earned, the school's program proceeds with no strict age grading and with no system of credits earned by time spent in class. The emphasis is on the students' demonstration that they can do important things.

7. The tone of the school should explicitly and self-consciously stress the values of anxious expectation ("I won't threaten you, but I expect much of you"), of trust (unless it is abused), and of decency (the values of fairness, generosity, and tolerance). Incentives appropriate to the school's students and teachers should be emphasized, and parents should be treated as essential collaborators.

8. The principal and teachers should perceive of themselves first as generalists (teachers and scholars in general education) and next as specialists (experts in a particular discipline). Staff should expect multiple obligations (teacher/counselor/manager) and a sense of commitment to the entire school.

9. Administrative and budget targets should include substantial time for collective planning by teachers, competitive salaries for staff, and an ultimate per-pupil cost not more than 10 percent higher than that at traditional schools. Administrative plans may have to show the phased reduction or elimination of some services now provided for students in many traditional comprehensive secondary schools.

How do essential schools go about accomplishing this? The key is accepting the premise that "less can be more." The essential schools have broken away from needing the large catalogue of classes and separate subjects and instead embrace a core mastery curriculum.

By accepting the notion of teacher as generalist they have been able to create more student–teacher interaction through reduced teacher loads (if not class size). They reason that it is better to teach 60 students in a multidisciplinary format and meet with them for two hours at a time than to split up a teacher's attention and focus across 120 to 150 different students each day.

By eliminating tracking and moving to mastery expectations for all students and demanding demonstrations of competence through exhibitions and authentic testing, they have been able to build a structure that supports the development of the new roles of teacher-as-coach and student-as-worker. By incorporating the role of counselor into the teaching role they have enhanced each student's feeling of belonging and membership.

Because of these structural changes the essential school has great promise for structuring feelings of CBUPO into the daily lives of most students. It is still too early to have conclusive evaluation results from the coalition schools, but the qualitative evidence is overwhelming. Dropout rates are down, college admissions are up, and formerly at-risk students now seem deeply engaged with their schoolwork (Muncey & McQuillan, 1996). One thing is clear, the coalition experiment is one that is spreading rapidly and certainly bears watching.

Concluding Comment

These new school structures being experimented with in both elementary and secondary schools around the country offer great promise for at-risk youth. The elimination of tracking and the presence of common mastery expectations support the students' need to feel competent. The creation of more intimate family-like structures at school can only enhance a student's feeling of belonging. The emphasis on student as worker and multi-age grouping create new opportunities for interdependence and the generation of feelings of usefulness, and efforts to assist students in the creation of authentic demonstrations of competence will assist them in developing feelings of personal potency.

However, the real beauty of all these initiatives is that they are good for all students, both the able and the disadvantaged. If initiatives like these become widespread, we won't need special "spoiled image programs" to serve at-risk youth very much longer.

The words of two great educators are worth considering here:

First, from John Dewey:

"What the best and wisest parent wants for his own child, that must the community want for all of its children."

And, from James Comer:

"Schools are going to have to modify the way they work to make it possible for low income kids to be successful in school. If not, the rest of us are going to be victimized by people who are frustrated, disappointed, and angry: people who have seen others on television who are actually no brighter than they are but who have had different experiences. And they're simply not going to tolerate it. That's why I say there's probably no more important mission in our society today than educating low-income and minority children."

References

Anderson, R.H., & B.N. Pavan. (1993). *Nongradedness: Helping it to happen*. Lancaster, PA: Technomic Press.

Bryk, A. S., & Thum, Y. M. (1989, February). The effects of high school organization on dropping out: An exploratory investigation. Madison, WI: Consortium for Policy Research in Education Research Report Series RR-012.

Conant, James B. (1967). *The comprehensive high school: A second report to interested citizens*. New York: McGraw-Hill.

Cotton, K. (2001). *New small learning communities: Findings from recent literature*. Portland, OR: Northwest Regional Educational Laboratory.

Edmonds, R. (1979). Effective schools for the urban poor. *Educational Leadership*, October, 15–24.

Goodlad, John I., & Anderson, Robert H. (1987). *The nongraded elementary school*. New York: Teachers College Press.

Greene, Jay P. (2002). *High School graduation rates in the united states*, New York: Center for Civic Innovation, April.

Muncey, D. E., & McQuillan, P. J. (1996*). Reform and resistance in schools and classrooms: An ethnographic view of the Coalition of Essential Schools*. New Haven: Yale University Press.

Oakes, J. (1985). *Keeping track: How schools structure inequity*, New Haven: Yale University Press.

Powell, A. G., Farrar, E., & Cohen, D. K. (1985). *The shopping mall high school: Winners and losers in the educational marketplace*. Boston: Houghton Mifflin Co.

Rutter, M., Maughn, B., Mortimore, P., Ouston, J., & Smith, A. (1979). *Fifteen thousand hours: Secondary schools and their effects on children*. Cambridge, MA: Harvard University Press.

Sizer, T.R. (1984). *Horace's compromise: The dilemma of the American high school*. Boston: Houghton Mifflin Co.

Sizer, T. R. (1992). *Horace's school: Redesigning the American high school*. Boston: Houghton Mifflin.

Slavin, R. E. (1990). Achievement effects of ability grouping in secondary schools: A best-evidence synthesis. *Review of Educational Research* 60(3): 471–499.

Spandel, V., & Stiggins, R. (1990). *Creating writers: Linking assessment and writing instruction*. White Plains: Longman.

Wasley, P.A., Fine, M., Gladden, M., et al. (2000). *Small schools: Great strides*, Bank Street College, New York.

11

EVALUATION OF AT-RISK PREVENTION PROGRAMS

Several years ago Dick attended a meeting of the regional coordinating committee for a neighboring state's "Student Retention Initiative." Arriving a little late, he discretely took a seat in the back of the room and listened carefully so he could become attuned to the context of the deliberations. Soon he realized that what was being shared were status reports on recent activities under the umbrella of this comprehensive effort for increasing the state's graduation rate.

One speaker discussed the importance of establishing a referral agency to aid youth who were on the streets, another spoke eloquently about the health problems encountered by homeless teenagers, he was followed by a speaker reporting on the difficulties involved in raising funds for a community teen center. The final report was on the status of ongoing work to provide prenatal care for pregnant teens. All of these important issues tugged at Dick's heartstrings, but the totality of the report left him to wonder, "What would an alien anthropologist have inferred when observing such a meeting?" If asked to guess what this group was working on, based on this discussion, most reasonable folks would never have guessed, "reducing the dropout rate."

Unless, of course, one believed that the cause of at-riskness in our high schools and the high dropout rate was the direct result of teen homelessness, the shortage of teen centers, and/or the absence of adequate prenatal care for pregnant teenagers. Those explanations hardly seemed logical to Dick, as these issues usually arise only after youth have already disengaged from school.

This experience lead Dick to suspect that the "Student Retention Initiative," which ultimately failed in its goal of reducing the state's dropout rate, was unsuccessful largely because of a problem that plagues many prevention programs designed for at-risk youth. These problems don't result from the level of energy or commitment of the people involved. No one could find people who cared more than the people involved in this statewide effort. Rather, two spe-

273

cific systemic problems with the "Student Retention Initiative" foreshadowed its eventual failure:

- ♦ First, program developers didn't engage themselves and others in a rigorous focus on theory when the program was planned, and

- ♦ Second, by focusing exclusively on large-scale mega-trends (the drop-out rate) it became difficult for the program managers to see "the forest from the trees."

A Timely and Rigorous Focus on Theory

When planning and developing at-risk prevention programs we are well served to follow a time honored methodology of our medical counterparts practicing in the field of epidemiology. This shouldn't be much of a stretch, because in the opinion of most educators, at-riskness is reaching epidemic proportions (i.e., we are seeing more and more at-risk students each year).

When public health officials become aware of a syndrome that is continuing to spread, the first thing they do is search for insight(s) into the cause(s). Before doctors could effectively eradicate smallpox, polio, or malaria they first needed to identify the cause(s) of these diseases.

The same applies to those of us working with the problem of at-riskness. All programs aimed at drop-out prevention, school safety, or other issues relating to youthful alienation should be grounded in reasonable theory(s) regarding the causes of alienation. If not, the likelihood that these programs will veer off course and become ineffective is great.

The reason prevention initiatives must grow out of a theory on causation is because these efforts will not succeed unless they address the root of the problem. Additionally, the theory we hold should provide the supportive rationale for employing a particular intervention(s) as opposed to an infinite number of alternatives. When we are unclear on the rationale for using a specific intervention, it results in program managers focusing more on *process monitoring* rather than true *program assessment*.

During our careers in schools we have seen numerous evaluations of programs that were deemed to be successful. Usually these reports contain statistics on the number of clients served, rather than the number of clients served *successfully*. Evaluations of these programs often contained anecdotal testimony on how happy students were with the program they participated in. But, when one carefully reviewed these evaluative reports it was often impossible to find data on the achievement or acquisition of concrete outcomes by the participants. Whenever we encounter this type of reliance on process monitoring (at the exclusion of outcome assessment) it ought to alert us to ask for clarification on the "true" purpose of the project. Was it *prevention* or was the actual goal *pacification* (see Chapter 1)?

Three Distinct Program Purposes (From Chapter 1)

Because prevention and pacification have fundamentally different goals, their assessment should employ different criteria. For example, when we find ourselves reacting positively to reports of quality special education and/or alternative school programs due to data showing that the students are content and happy and because a significant number of students were served and retained over time, it ought to indicate to us that the program's true goal was, in reality, pacification not prevention. This is because, if the "true" goal was prevention, treatment, or remediation, we would expect to see data on "cure rate" instead of number of clients served.

We suspect that the fact that program evaluators and administrators continue to evaluate their programs using irrelevant criteria is not a factor of evil intent or incompetence, rather we think it is the result of an act of omission committed by otherwise sincere and committed professionals. This chapter will discuss a six-step process that weaves assessment into the work of program development. Furthermore, as this book is focused primarily on "prevention," our discussion will focus on the assessment of programs designed to stem the production of at-riskness.

A Six-Step Process[1]

The six sequential steps of this integrated program planning and assessment process are:

- ◆ Step 1. Stating a clear target. In the case of at-risk prevention this means drawing a clear picture of what we would expect students on a trajectory for success to look like.

- ◆ Step 2. Articulating a theory on the causes of "at-riskness"

   Specifically this means offering a clear and logical rationale for why we believe some students aren't currently hitting the targets outlined in step 1 above.

---

1   This six step process makes use of the techniques and strategies of action research. A detailed treatment on the use of action research for program improvement can be found in the book, *Guiding School Improvement with Action Research*, Richard Sagor, ASCD 2000.

◆ Step 3. Selecting specific interventions

The choice of interventions must be based on the likelihood of these interventions to address the root causes of the problems identified in step 2, and their potential for assisting students in realizing the targets outlined in step 1.

◆ Step 4. Selecting benchmarks

These are used for continuous assessment of the success of the interventions selected for implementation in step 3.

◆ Step 5. Continually monitoring progress with the benchmarks

This involves collecting data via the continuous monitoring of the benchmarks developed in step 4. This data will then be used to adjust interventions as needed.

◆ Step 6. Conducting a final evaluation

The final evaluation should focus on the attainment of the ultimate objective of the project (in this case the eradication or amelioration of at-riskness).

Figure 11.1 shows the relationship of the six steps of this model.

Figure 11.1. Six-Step Program Evaluation Process

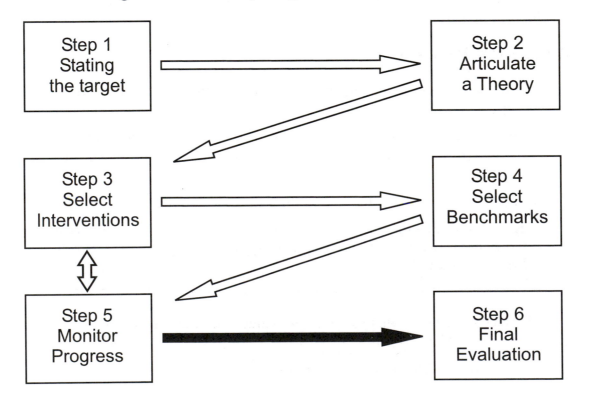

Step 1. Setting a Clear Target

One of the more overused and least understood buzzwords in education is *vision*. Simply put, vision enables us to see clearly in our mind's eye what precisely we are endeavoring to achieve. Data from fields as diverse as athletics and manufacturing have demonstrated convincingly that when people are clear and focused on a set of specific outcomes, achieving those outcomes becomes much easier. The following Think and Do Exercise is a strategy we have found helpful for producing a shared vision along with program targets that provide focus for an at-risk prevention program.

Think and Do Exercise—
Developing a Vision of Success

At a meeting of stakeholders (for example a faculty meeting or parent advisory meeting) ask the participants to close their eyes and imagine the following scene:

You are visiting a school and have noticed a student who appears to be doing quite well. You observe the child for a while and the more you watch the more confident you become that this child is receiving a CBUPO-rich experience at school. Consequently, you engage the child in a conversation. You share your positive perceptions with the student and the student tells you that your assessment was right on target. This child provides you with ample evidence that he not only loves attending school but is prospering academically, socially, and emotionally.

Now, employing as much detail as possible, write out specifically what you observed this student doing and write out what you heard this student saying that made you so confident of his eventual success.

Have the participants share the scenarios they have written.

Create a composite picture of a student headed for success. The composite picture becomes the overall vision for your program.

Once an overall vision has been produced, the group should review the vision asking this question:

What specific attributes were demonstrated by the student (in our vision) and what specific attributes were present in the program this child was experiencing?

List the answers to that question on a piece of chart paper.

The resulting list should contain two sets of "outcome targets;" the first being *student performance targets* and the second *program targets*.

Step 2. Theory Articulation

Theory articulation focuses our attention on what we understand to be the chief factors contributing to the increase of the at-risk population. As educational epidemiologists, if we are going to successfully design treatments for a problem, or even more importantly, to prevent its occurrence, we will need to invest some significant time figuring out what exactly it is we should be working on.

This phase, theory articulation, is where we must satisfactorily answer two critical questions, otherwise we won't succeed in reducing the incidence of at-riskness. Specifically we must ask,

- Do we (the faculty and staff) believe at-riskness has identifiable causes, or do we believe it is the result of random events?

- If we believe that it is the result of specific discrete causes, then do we believe that those causes are amenable to remediation?

If the answer to either of those questions is no, then our time is being wasted on dropout prevention. Instead, our efforts should be better aimed at what Jerry Conrath calls *rescue and relief* or some other form of *pacification* with the potential to help these poor unfortunate kids whose destiny has put them and will unfortunately, keep them from experiencing success in our classrooms.

However, this entire book has been devoted to assisting those of you who would answer *yes* to the above questions. From the start our premise has been that at-riskness does have a set of causes and those causes are subject to mediation. That being the case, our feeling has been that we *can* design programs and interventions with significant potential for success. We must concurrently, develop assessment techniques with potential for helping us document program performance and provide us with on-going guidance as we go about our work. The six-part evaluation process is a strategy designed to accomplish just that.

As mentioned above, when developing assessments for at-risk prevention programs we must first ask:

"What do we understand about the causes of at-riskness?"

The Student Retention Initiative group, which Dick visited, in all likelihood, began their work asking the wrong questions. We suspect they asked, "What are the needs of teenagers at-risk and other young people living on the street?" The interventions that resulted were clearly grounded in answers to those questions. Furthermore, if rigorously pursued, those interventions might well have helped to alleviate the pain and suffering of those disempowered and disengaged young people. However, it simply isn't logical to expect those same interventions to arrest the rising tide of dropouts. This is because those interventions weren't developed or chosen based on a coherent theory on the cause(s) of the drop-out phenomenon.

As discussed in Chapter 1, there are three dominant and separate theories on at-riskness. Although they grew out of different theory bases, these approaches aren't discrete and frequently overlap. One theory holds that at-riskness is the result of *clinical pathology*, another posits at-riskness as a direct consequence of *environmental deficits*, while the third maintains that at-riskness is created by imperfections in our organizational structures, or, in other words, *institutional pathology*.

Depending on which of these theories one holds, the interventions pursued will be different. Holders of the clinical pathology orientation likely want to provide therapeutic interventions for afflicted youth, while those who hold the environmental deficit theory want to organize developmentally appropriate remedial/acceleration programs to backfill the missing experiences, and those who adhere to the institutional pathology explanation try to make changes in organizational/institutional practices.

We'll illustrate with some examples. Suppose our theory on at-riskness is grounded in an institutional pathology perspective. Furthermore, let's say that we see a causal link between the development of low self-esteem and the likelihood of dropping out. We should then be asking ourselves, where and how does a student acquire high or low self-esteem? Because, generally, it is assumed that self-esteem is the cumulative by-product of one's interactions with others, then making appropriate changes in the interactions that occur at school could have the potential of altering the self-esteem building function of the school. Such an analysis would justify creating a program aimed at reducing at-riskness by implementing practices such as eliminating tracking and other stigmatizing procedures (see Chapter 7).

If, however, our sense of the causes had their genesis in a environmental deficit theory, and for example, if we concluded that at-riskness was based on missing certain experiences, we should initiate an accelerated, mastery-based, remedial program, aimed at teaching the missing skills or attributes.

Finally, if our perspective on at-riskness was grounded in a clinical pathology perspective, then we ought to be attracted to a treatment model. At least for the purpose of assessment this would be an efficient theory to hold, as treatment programs are relatively easy to evaluate. Because the justification for treatment programs comes from the medical paradigm, so do the models for their assessment. In spite of the fact that clinical evaluation is easy to accomplish, we often resist properly assessing these programs.

Treatment programs are based on a belief that the at-risk student suffers from an identifiable condition. For this reason it is irresponsible for educators to promote interventions/treatments (grounded in a theory of clinical pathology) unless they have confidence in their ability to conduct a reliable diagnosis. If, however, we assume that we can accurately and confidently identify the presence of a condition, then we ought to be equally confident of our ability to validate its absence. Such skills make evaluation quite straightforward.

Our clinical programs, such as counseling, outside referrals, and residential treatment schools, should be expected to demonstrate that after treatment, the student subjects are either cured or are in remission (the same criteria used in medical research). However, if the success of treatment cannot be documented, then allowing those interventions to continue indefinitely is tantamount to educational voodoo.

We don't know why the evaluation of these programs is so rare, but it is certainly tragic that tens of thousands of youngsters are being regularly subjected to clinical interventions at school with little or no evidence as to their effectiveness. That having been said, let's return to the assessment of prevention programs.

Step 3. Selecting Interventions

Step three, *selecting interventions*, flows out of the intellectual work we engaged in during step two. At this point we are searching for a logical alignment between the perceived causes of a problem (at-riskness) and the strategies that we intend to employ to counteract those causes. When medicine wants to prevent a virus, it develops a vaccine. For example: to prevent and treat genetic diseases, medical researchers are now looking to gene therapy. The solution to any problem needs to have a logical connection to the cause of the problem.

Disaggregation

Disaggregation refers to breaking a large sample into its constituent parts. Disagreggation is important in this context because it allows us to assess the impact of a project's interventions on a specific target group (i.e., the at-risk students). To accomplish this it will be necessary to compare two groups of students, those who are at-risk and those who aren't. The easiest way to accomplish this is by making a list of the factors that the school has identified as correlates with at-riskness. Typically, these include such things as consistent achievement below grade level, poor attendance habits, low grades, transiency, etc. Consequently, those students who are identified as at-risk (because of the presence of a number of these correlates) are classified as such (for purposes of program evaluation only). Other students, those who do not manifest those characteristics, can then be classified as the comparison group.

Choice of Interventions

Decisions on proposed interventions should be governed by two questions:

- ◆ Is the proposed strategy consistent with our theory of at-riskness?
- ◆ Is there empirical evidence to support our belief that these interventions will work in this setting?

While focusing on those two questions may seem obvious, they are often overlooked. Not infrequently, educators truly believe that their schools or their flawed organizational practices are significant contributors to at-riskness, yet they develop pacification programs (such as alternative schools) to take care of the students rather than changing the mainstream school or fixing the identified flawed practices. This is like trying to cut off the flow of a river at midstream. It rarely works. It is far easier to divert a body of water at its source. Rigorous attention to the connection between the chosen interventions and our underlying beliefs can do a lot to prevent later frustration when we encounter disappointing results.

On other occasions, a strategy might connect quite well with our theoretical orientation yet be impractical or inappropriate for our school or community. Again, it is far more efficient to visit this issue early on when there is still time to pursue alternatives rather than to wait and discover incompatibility after a great deal of time, money, and energy has been expended.

Once those questions have been answered and interventions selected it is time to shift the focus to the selection of interim indicators.

Step 4. Selecting and Developing Benchmarks.

We defined at-riskness in this book as follows,

Any student who is unlikely to graduate on time along with their agemates and with the self-esteem and skills necessary for success at the next stage of life is at-risk.

If one accepts this definition, then it will mean the ultimate success of our efforts can't possibly be known until after the student's class graduates. That is an awfully long time to wait for data on program effectiveness. So how should we proceed to assess our work in the short run?

Recently NASA sent a probe to Jupiter. It will take several years for that probe to reach its target. Once the launch was accomplished did the NASA engineers just go home and say lets get together again in a few years to see if we hit our target? No way! On the contrary, they immediately began using telemetry to track the probe and when their data called for it, they made mid-course corrections. This is why benchmarks (or signposts along the intended route) are so important. During step one when we set the vision, we defined our ultimate outcome(s), now in step four we will articulate those signposts (benchmarks) that we expect the student to encounter at various and specific stages along the way. Figure 11.2 is a form that a school team can use when developing rubrics, which display your benchmarks in the sequence that they should be passed.

In the six-stage model, these anticipated observable changes in student attitudes and behavior are called *performance benchmarks*.

Figure 11.2. Developing Benchmarks to Track Progress

1. List each student performance, attribute, characteristic that you want your program to strengthen (i.e., enhance feelings of competence, belonging, usefulness, potency and optimism)

2. For each performance, attribute, characteristic listed in item 1 above, determine what is the most minimal observable demonstration of that performance, attribute, characteristic (i.e., enhanced feelings of competence—student occasionally concurs with positive external assessment of her work). Label these as "beginning benchmarks."

3. For each performance, attribute, characteristic listed in item 1, determine what would constitute a moderate demonstration of that performance, attribute, characteristic (i.e., enhanced feelings of competence—without prompting the student identifies areas where he consistently produces quality work). Label these as "developing benchmarks."

4. For each performance, attribute, characteristic listed in item 1, determine what would constitute a complete demonstration of that performance, attribute, characteristic (i.e., enhanced feelings of competence—in arenas that the student values, the student expresses pride in their success, can identify with specifically what qualifies this work as high quality, and can articulate what was done to achieve success). Label these as "strong benchmarks."

5. For each performance, attribute, characteristic listed in item 1, list in sequence, every discrete and unambiguous demonstration of the performance, attribute, characteristic that could be observed falling between the behaviors described in items 2—beginning and 3—developing, and between items 3—developing and 4—strong.

6. Create a table with as many columns as necessary to accommodate each separate, discrete, unambiguous demonstration of behavior for each performance, attribute, characteristic (see example below). Write in observable behavior identified above.

Enhanced Feelings of Competence

Beginning	Developing	Strong
The student will occasionally concur with a positive external assessment of their work.	Without prompting the student identifies areas where they consistently produce quality work.	In areas that the student values, the student will express pride in their success, can identify with specifically what qualifies this work as high quality, and can articulate what was done to achieve success

7. Review each table carefully asking the following questions:

   a. Are the behaviors listed clear and unambiguous?

   b. Are the behaviors listed in each easily distinguished from those on each side?

   c. Is every behavior listed a demonstration of the performance, attribute, characteristic?

   d. Are there efficient ways we can collect data on student status on these behaviors?

8. When you can answer each of the questions posed above for each performance, attribute, characteristic then you have developed benchmarks and rubrics that will help you track your progress toward your ultimate goal.

Performance benchmarks help us to make midterm predictions on whether the ultimate outcome, the graduation of skilled and emotionally secure students, is likely to occur. They also can serve as "early warning systems," alerting us to which interventions are not being successfully carried out.

Most institutional theories hold that at-riskness results from attitudes that students develop about themselves in relationship to the school. Likewise, most environmental deficit theories hold that at-riskness is a result of the expereinces/skills students missed out on or behaviors they didn't engage in. Therefore, accurately measuring changes in student attitudes and behavior becomes essential for evaluation of programs based on these theories.

The best window into the attitudes held by students are their self-reports and the best window into their behavior is by direct observation. This is fortunate because that data is so easy to collect. If students are feeling successful, welcome, needed, and empowered they should be able to tell us. Likewise, if they are feeling incompetent, alienated, and disempowered, they are quite adept at reporting it. Frequently, schools evaluate the adequacy of their programs using only data and perceptions held by teachers but not by students. Teacher reports on changes in student attitudes can be unreliable due to the influence of conscious and unconscious bias. For this reason, evaluators of at-risk prevention programs should consider student self-reports as *one* important "primary source" of material. If the data from student surveys or interviews is at odds with data obtained from the faculty, it is not the accuracy of the student data that should be brought into question, but, rather the reason for the existence of these differing perceptions.

Ultimately the success or failure of the identified students, in passing our predetermined sign-posts, should inform us if mid-course corrections are called for.

There is another set of benchmarks we need to monitor at this stage. These are *implementation benchmarks*. The purpose of establishing these benchmarks is to help us monitor the implementation or faithful enactment of program interventions. After all, if the interventions aren't carried out according to plan, why should we expect them to succeed? The Think and Do Exercise below offers a method that can help you design a process for assessing progress on implementation benchmarks.

Think and Do Exercise—Assessing Implementation

♦ List each activity that should be occurring if the program is being properly implemented.

♦ Next to each item listed include the time frame and or occurrence. For example: by October first or every other Friday.

♦ Decide how you can efficiently and consistently collect data on the scheduled implementation of each activity.

♦ Commit to collect the data and schedule regular meetings to discuss the results.

Step 5. Monitoring Success

At this stage our focus becomes data, specifically data on whether the interventions are in fact producing the intended changes in performance with the targeted students. The purpose of this data is formative. We need to keep in mind that data on performance doesn't reflect on us. It doesn't say anything about how good we are, how bad we are, or how committed we are. Rather, what it tells us is how effective the implementation of our interventions has been in producing changes on our indicators (which, as you recall, were our correlates of at-riskness). The sole purpose of this data is to help us to refine our work on the interventions. It is at this point that we begin to draw tentative conclusions about both the appropriateness of the theory(s) informing our work and the interventions we've attempted.

Discrepant Data

The questions raised by discrepant data are particularly important when working on programs based on institutional theories. This is because these approaches alert us to the potential presence and influence of a hidden curriculum. Sometimes the only way to find out if a hidden curriculum is in operation is by discovering that students are, in fact, experiencing the program in a different manner than the way we, the adults, had expected or intended.

Because of the value of these different perceptions, the six step evaluation model recommends, whenever possible, collecting three different sets of data for each indicator. Researchers call this procedure *triangulation*. Triangulation, or using multiple windows on the same phenomena, gives much greater validity to the conclusions drawn.

Let's say that we want to determine the degree to which our students are feeling successful at school. We might choose to survey or interview a cohort of students, in addition we might gather data on how teachers are observing those same students experiencing school, and finally we might collect data on the grades and credits earned by those students. If all three sets of these data concur, that's fine. But suppose the grades are high and the teachers think the students are feeling successful, yet the students are still reporting a lack of self-confidence. We should then ask what might explain this? Does it mean that our standards had been lowered in a well meaning, yet patronizing fashion? Or is there another explanation? Such an event might have gone unnoticed without the use of multiple independent data sources.

If we are following an environmental theory of at-riskness, it means we are positing the existence of a defined set of experiences, skills, or attributes that need to be achieved by an individual if that person is to exit the ranks of the at-risk. Therefore, the indicators we want to use to assess program performance should focus on the presence or absence of those same skills or attributes. This is another situation when it is advisable for evaluators to use three independent data sources for each indicator. For example, if the theory we hold is that young people with poor skills in social cognition are more inclined to be more at-risk than students who have strong social cognition skills, then we might want to observe the identified students in classroom settings and later collect data through student interviews as well as with interviews of their teachers.

As was the case with evaluations of programs based on institutional theories, discrepant data will always provide valuable insights.

Figure 11.3 is a sample of a data collection plan taken from the implementation of the CBUPO theory.

Figure 11.3. Data Collection Plan

Data to be collected from every student each December and May and disaggregated by at-risk status, gender, and ethnicity.

Attribute	Data Source 1	Data Source 2	Data Source 3
Enhanced feelings of *Competence*	Direction of Grades/Tests	Student Survey	Teacher Survey
Enhanced feelings of *Belonging*	Participation in Activities	Student Survey	Teacher Survey
Enhanced feelings of *Usefulness*	Participation in Community Service	Student Survey	Teacher Survey
Enhanced feelings of *Potency*	Parent Survey	Student Survey	Teacher Survey
Enhanced feelings of *Optimism*	Parent Survey	Student Survey	Analysis of student long-range plans

Step 6. Determining Outcomes

Often we are unable to determine the success of programs with at-risk youth because most traditional indicators of school success (graduation rates, dropout rates, college admissions rates, etc.) only include those students who happen to be left in the class when it graduates. However, in many schools the population that graduates isn't representative of the entire population that experienced the school's programs. Particularly in schools with high rates of transiency, this type of snapshot data, taken at graduation time, reveals very little, if anything, about what successes or failures could fairly be attributed to the at-risk prevention program implemented over a thirteen year period.

For this reason, the six-stage assessment model recommends that program evaluation occur by cohort. Earlier in step five you were advised to disaggregate the sample into a set of "at-risk students" and "non at-risk students." After assigning students to these cohorts they should be continually tracked and compared throughout their school careers.

Throughout the course of the at-risk prevention project, it is necessary to monitor and report on the at-risk cohort and a random sample of the non at-risk group, across all the performance benchmarks. When the two cohorts reach graduation (or any other equally critical transition) the performance of the two cohorts should be compared and contrasted. One technique that we've found particularly helpful is the *academic post mortem*, a process whereby a longitudinal post hoc examination is made of the school careers of the two cohorts.

Among the outcome indicators, which shed light on the success of a prevention program and have been incorporated into this type of an academic post mortem, are:

- Direction of performance

  Were the grades and achievement scores for each of the two cohorts rising, falling, or plateaued?

- Involvement in activities

  Did the at-risk students participate as much as their counterparts, for how long, and when did disengagement occur?

- Attendance

  Was there a history of truancy among the at-risk cohort, and did truancy rates increase, decrease, or plateau during the project?

- Post-high school aspirations

  Are the declared post-high school aspirations of the at-risk group consistent with their high school performance, and how do they differ from other students? Did aspirations change during their school careers? If so, in what direction?

These and other outcome indicators can form the structure of the post hoc review. By contrasting the performance of the at-risk cohort with their classmates as well as with at-risk cohorts from other schools, preliminary judgments can then be made about both the validity of the underlying theories (which initially gave rise to the program) as well as the viability of the specific interventions attempted. Lastly, a truly comprehensive academic post mortem will serve as a richly descriptive needs assessment to guide future work.

Figures 11.4 and 11.5 were taken from an academic post mortem conducted at a suburban high school.

Figures 11.4. Academic Program Experienced

Because slightly over one third of the courses open to selection by West Linn students are elective in nature and, considering that many of our requirements can be satisfied through selectives, it seemed valuable to look at the difference in how our four achievement cohorts choose their course work. The table below shows academic credits earned based on achievement cohort. For the purposes of this analysis *academic courses* were defined as language arts, math, science, social studies, and foreign language.

Average Academic Credits Earned

CAT quartile	0–25	26–50	51–75	76–100
Mean	15.8	21.54	26.877	31.20
Median	16.5	21	27	32

CAT = Child Assistance Teams

It is clear from this table that the students with greater ability take more course work in the academic disciplines. This is ironic, because the students who are weakest in academic performance apparently spend the least time studying academic course work.

Another indication of this phenomena is displayed in the chart below that reveals the average number of credits earned in mathematics.

Average Credits in Math

CAT quartile	0–25	26–50	51–75	76–100
Mean	2.86	4.45	5.506	6.47
Median	2	5	6	6

Here we see that the students whose achievement is above grade level, average approximately three full years of mathematics, where our lowest achieving students are taking barely over one year.

The patterns of enrollment in vocational education and fine arts are harder to understand. This information base appears in the following charts.

Average Vocational Credits Earned

CAT quartile	0–25	26–50	51–75	76–100
Mean	4.4	6.64	6.013	4.53
Median	6	6	6	4

Figures 11.5. Discipline

The Disciplinary Vice Principal was presented a list of the class of 1986 and asked to indicate which individuals represented significant or somewhat significant disciplinary problems. The list that he worked with did not indicate the achievement levels for these students. For that reason it surprised us to note that of the twenty-six students, the Vice Principal identified only two of these as students whose achievement test scores fell below grade level. The other twenty-four students were above the national average in academic achievement. (An interesting side point is that he identified nine students who were not in our sample because they were not four-year members of our student body.) If the trend from this data is accurate, a likely conclusion from these findings is that the overwhelming majority of our discipline problems are presented by our more able students. We found this to be one of the true surprises in this retrospective look on the class of '86.

Discipline Problems

CAT quartile	0–25	26–50	51–75	76–100	Total Sample
Number	1	1	12	14	26
% of Cohort	14%	4%	16%	12%	10%
% of Total	4%	4%	46%	54%	

CAT = Child Assistance Teams

Post High School Experience

As illustrated in the chart below 90 percent of the students who were with us at West Linn for four full years graduated on time with their class. We are not certain what significance to place on the corollary finding that a slightly higher percentage of third-quartile students completed graduation requirements than did their higher-achieving classmates from the fourth quartile. Otherwise, the graduation rates seemed to offer little surprise.

Graduation

CAT quartile	0–25	26–50	51–75	76–100	Total Sample
Number	5	24	73	107	209
% of Cohort	71%	86%	95%	90%	90%
No. in Cohort	7	28	77	119	231

The Six-Stage Process in Action

To better understand how the six-stage program assessment process works, we now trace it from vision setting to theory articulation through final program evaluation. We'll use a middle school as our example.

Imagine that Cougar Junior High School (a hypothetical school) has committed itself to a major effort to both reduce and prevent at-riskness. Their work is grounded in a theory that holds that at-riskness is created by and exacerbated through involvement with dysfunctional institutional structures. Therefore, their approach combines features from both the developmental deficit and institutional pathology perspectives. Figure 11.6 is a concise statement of the Cougar vision.

Figure 11.6. Cougar Middle School Theory

At-riskness declines when young people:

♦ Are competent and feel successful at school

♦ Feel a sense of belonging and affiliation at school

♦ Feel a sense of usefulness

♦ Have an internal "locus of control"

After much deliberation, the Cougar staff adopted a theory holding that when young people feel a sense of competence and are experiencing success in school, when they feel a sense of belonging and affiliation within their school community, when they feel a sense of social usefulness at school, and when they feel a sense of personal potency as a result of building an internal locus of control, they won't continue to be at-risk. They then agreed to the flow-chart shown in Figure 11.7: Cougar Middle School Theory, as their theory. This theory was posted in the faculty room and was prominently featured in all their materials.

Figure 11.7. Reducing At-Riskness with CBUPO

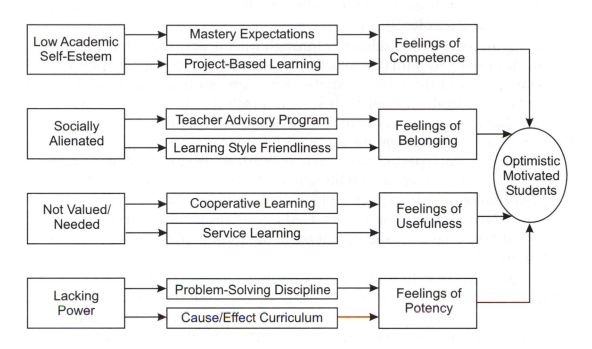

Feeling secure with their theory, the Cougar staff proceeded to develop a comprehensive at-risk prevention effort. This began by identifying at-risk students in a manner that was consistent with their perspective. They compiled a list of students who:

- Weren't experiencing success in school (as evidenced by consistently poor grades or low achievement scores), and

- Who were having affiliation difficulties (as evidenced by teacher, parent, and counselor referral).

This identification process produced a cohort that represented approximately 20 percent of their student body. This group, while not singled out for special treatment, was the group that was to be monitored so the impact of the prevention program could be ascertained.

The Cougar Middle School prevention program was predicated on the assumption that by strategically altering organizational behavior, the school would influence the degree to which students derived feelings of competence, belonging, usefulness, potency, and optimism.

Student needs for competence were to be addressed by the introduction of the mastery expectations (Chapter 3) and authentic learning (Chapter 6) throughout the curriculum , by eliminating the "C," "D," and "F" grades, by replacing all remedial pullout programs with before- and after-school acceleration classes (see Chapter 9), and by providing additional in-class support for students whose skill levels qualified them for ESEA Chapter 1 or special education assistance (Chapter 9).

Belonging was to be addressed through the introduction of a "homebase" teacher advisory program (Chapter 9), elimination of tracking (Chapter 10), and the strategic use of the school activities program. All teams and clubs were to have an open enrollment policy as well as a recruitment program. The faculty decided that the organizing theme for the school would be "We are family," and therefore, each activity would have SOPs (standard operating procedures) that delineated how each participant was to be made to feel like a valuable member of the *family*. SOPs covered such things as playing time, rotation of officers, and the presentation of individual achievement awards. The homebase advisory program placed each student in a mixed-age advisement group with an adult who would become their significant adult other for at least their three years at the school.

Usefulness was to be addressed through the use of cooperative learning in classrooms and the organization of a community service program (Chapter 6), wherein each student donated five hours of service work per week to be devoted to an area of their choosing, which would provide useful service to others (cross-age tutoring, recycling, helping in a local retirement home, Natural Helpers, etc.).

The development of an internal locus of control was to be addressed by the use of Reality Therapy and Choice Theory in all classroom management practices and in the schoolwide behavior management program (Chapters 7 and 8). All accountability systems in the school were organized around goal setting and placing an emphasis on the logical connection between cause and effect (Chapter 8). Likewise, curricula in Science, Social Studies, and Language Arts were revised to emphasize cause and effect relationships. Testing practices were changed and began to emphasize student exhibitions (Chapter 10).

The assumption guiding all these program changes was that, taken together, they would increase the likelihood of students deriving feelings of competence, belonging, usefulness, and potency throughout their school experience that would lead to optimism, thereby *preventing* at-riskness.

Having articulated this theory and selected a set of interventions grounded in the theory, the Cougar Junior High School staff was left with the task of establishing performance indicators. Remember, the long-range goal of their project was for all students to maintain continuous good-standing enrollment, culminating in high school graduation with their peers. If, and when, that goal was achieved (for all Cougar Junior High School students) then the project could declare itself a success and declare its underlying theory validated. However, the staff was not comfortable waiting six years to determine if they were on the right track. Hence, they set about developing a set of benchmarks. It was understood that these benchmarks needed to grow from the adopted theory on at-riskness.

To find appropriate benchmarks, the project team asked themselves these questions:

- How will we be able to tell if our students are feeling *competent* and successful?

- How will we be able to tell if our students are feeling a sense of *belonging* and affiliation with the school?

- How will we be able to tell if our students are feeling needed and *useful*?

- How will we be able to tell if our students have an *internal locus of control*?

The project team quickly agreed that one source of information would be the kids themselves, another could be the observations of significant adult others in the students lives, and the third should come from objective independent measures. Furthermore, they agreed to periodically conduct a "process audit" to verify if all project activities were, in fact, being implemented as planned.

The staff felt confident in their theory, truly believed that if the interventions were faithfully carried out, and if data on the benchmarks demonstrated that the correlates of at-riskness (feelings of failure, alienation, uselessness, and impotence) were in decline, then they would be justified in their expectation of reaching success with their long-range goal.

When the first group of Cougar Junior High School students moved up to Mountain Lion High School arrangements were made to annually monitor and report back on the performance of the at-risk cohort as well as on the performance of a comparable sample of non at-risk students. These reports were to be reviewed annually by the Cougar planning team. The planning team also visited the High School once each year to conduct interviews with former Cougar students. In these interviews the students were asked to reflect on their experience at the high school and the preparation that they had received cognitively and affectively at Cougar. An annual report combining these two sets of data was shared each Fall with the Cougar Junior High School staff so changes and adjustments could be made.

Finally, the Cougar Middle School faculty developed an outline of the data they needed to review for a final report on their effort, an "academic post mortem" on the class of 2008. The high school registrar and the school administration agreed to supervise the collection of this data. Figure 11.8, Academic Post Mortem, lists the data the Cougar staff asked to be collected from the files at Mountain Lion High School. This data would inform their conclusions on the success of the project. Note that all of this data would already exist in the files and archives at the high school and required no further data collection.

Figure 11.8. Academic Post Mortem

- ◆ Grades achieved/direction
- ◆ Achievement level/direction
- ◆ Academic courses taken
- ◆ Activities pursued
- ◆ Attendance/discipline
- ◆ Post high school placement
- ◆ Rank in class
- ◆ Electives taken

The Cougar faculty is pleased with their process for several reasons. First, they believe that their program interventions were sound. Second, they had confidence in the appropriateness of both the benchmarks and outcome indicators that they committed to use. Finally, they felt empowered by the assessment process itself, because they would be the ones to determine success rather than an external evaluator.

Summary

It is imperative that the goals of programs dealing with the at-risk phenomena be made clear. If the goals are treatment oriented or custodial in nature, then the outcome expectations should not include such things as a reduction in the rate of at-riskness. If, on the other hand, the programs are designed to be preventive in nature, then they and their evaluation procedures must be well grounded in theory.

The theory of at-riskness must be clear enough to allow for the identification of two cohorts of students (at-risk and not at-risk) and it must be focused enough to guide the design of a comprehensive set of interventions. Finally, the theory should give rise to a set of indicators/benchmarks that can be used to monitor the project. A good theory will tell us what behaviors, skills, and attitudes can mediate at-riskness and as a consequence which behaviors, attitudes, and skills need to become the focus for ongoing program monitoring.

We also must remember that the best source of data on how students are behaving is their behavior and the best source of data on how they are feeling are their own words. This data, although often uncomfortable to collect and analyze, needs to become the foundation for all our at-risk program evaluation systems. Several other corroborating indicators of program performance should also be collected and reported, such as behavioral records, transcripts, and surveys of parents and teachers.

But ultimately, the test of an at-risk prevention program's utility will be the final outcome achieved. The test of our at-risk programs must be whether we can move students all the way through the K–12 system building and maintaining the skills required to become life-long learners with the self-esteem needed to set and pursue high aspirations. The evaluation systems that we establish to assess these projects must be built on no lesser assumptions.

References

Sagor, R. D. (2000). *Guiding school improvement with action research*. Alexandria, VA: ASCD.

EPILOGUE

In this book we have discussed a potpourri of strategies that we have seen work in classrooms and schools throughout North America, in places where teachers are helping *all* students experience success.

Please keep in mind that just because a strategy worked with one group of children, in one locality, does not mean that it will work with all children in all settings. One of the marvelous things about human beings is our diversity. Different classrooms and different schools share different cultures and different chemistries. We as teachers have different styles and that is what helps us make our classrooms such special places. Not only do we think it would have been presumptuous for us to suggest that all of our readers should teach alike, but, we think such an assertion would detract from the very thing that makes education so exciting, the enthusiasm and passion each one of you brings to teaching. So our hope is that you pick and choose what you think will work for you and your children, and especially feel conformable modifying and changing of these ideas to fit you, your children, and your school.

Despite all of our wonderful diversity there are certain constants among us teachers. We all want our kids to succeed in our classrooms and schools and thrive in the world they inherit as adults. Furthermore, we think all of us agree that happy, healthy, and fulfilled adults share certain attributes:

- They feel good about themselves. They have confidence in their ability to succeed when and if they persevere. They feel **competent**.

- They are social beings who want to have friends and associations to which they want to affiliate and feel that they **belong**.

- They want to feel that they are making a difference. That the world they live in and the people they touch are better off for having crossed their path. They feel **useful**.

- They want to feel that they matter; that they possess the power to make their lives better and to positively affect the direction of their communities. In short, they want to feel **potent**.

- They want to wake up each morning confident—confident that they will have a good day and make the world a happier place for all the others who they will touch. They are **optimistic**.

What all humans want and need is to feel CBUPOs and feel it each and every day.

Having difficulty getting to sleep one evening, Dick turned on his television to see the story of a young high school English teacher, Erin Gruwell, from Long Beach, California. A young student teacher, she was getting nowhere trying to reach her class of discouraged learners. The curriculum required her to engage them in the basics of writing and an understanding of literature. Her inner city students, many of them alumni of the juvenile justice system, current gang members, and victims of street violence found little interest in the material she was attempting to impart. Here was a teacher trying to do her best to educate students who lacked the most basic of academic skills, yet, they found no meaning whatsoever in the "stuff" she was teaching.

Then as serendipity would have it an unpleasant event occurred. Upon seizing a racist characiture from a student she exclaimed, "This reminds me of the holocaust!" To her amazement the students seemed to have no knowledge of this most horrific event in modern history.

As she began to explore the evils of ethnic cleansing she found that the students could readily apply this to their own lives. She found her students were eminently capable of making connections on their own between the elements of the world they were living through and the world others had written about. The young teacher seized the moment and simultaneously had the students read about other young people who had experienced violence in their lives and write about their own experiences. They read *The Diary of Anne Frank* and *Zlata's Diary: A Child's Life in Sarajevo*. They wrote emotionally about themselves, their feelings, and the lives they were living. Now that they saw a purpose and meaning in the content Ms. Gruwell was engaging them in they eagerly engaged in her instruction in the techniques of writing and used this instruction to do the *construction* of their own stories. Four years later their stories can be found in a published volume, *The Freedom Writer's Diary* (1999), and the students are all enrolled in college, (with their tuition covered by royalties from the book). Did this occur because Erin was a gifted mastery learning teacher? After all, she succeeded in teaching her students the specific skills needed by successful writers. Was she a master of developmental constructivism? After all, she created an environment where students could construct new learning from the meaning(s) they had carried with them into the classroom.

We choose not to answer those questions or attach a label to her work. In our minds it wouldn't do justice to Erin Gruwell's excellent work to attach any label besides the one she rightfully wears with pride, she is a **teacher**. And, as a consequence of the privilege of being placed in her classroom these students have experienced and will continue to experience CBUPO!

Where will other young people gain this? Certainly from their parents, and from the Churches, Synagogues, and Mosques as well as other places where their families will gather to pass on sacred values. But, there is only one place where *all* of our children will spend 13 years interacting with a group of caring adults with no other mission but to help them become self-actualized adults. And that is in your schools and your classrooms.

That is your privilege and it embodies your calling. You, the teachers of our children, are engaged in the most important work in our society. You are the ones who can make a person's life a CBUPO-rich experience.

We stand in awe of your responsibility and every day are amazed at all that we have learned and continue to learn from you, our children's teachers!

It is our sincere hope that this book provided some inspiration for you while you continue to do God's work.

God bless you and should you have the time, please send us a note let us know how it is going!

References

Filipovic, Zlata (1995). *Zlata's diary: A child's life in Sarajevo*. New York: Penguin.

Frank, Anne (1993). *Anne Frank: The diary of a young girl*. New York: Bantam.

The Freedom Writers, Prime Time Live, ABC News (1998).

The Freedom Writers with Erin Gruwell. (1999). *The Freedom Writer's Diary*. New York: Doubleday.